About this book

Since 1996 war has raged in the Congo while the world has looked away. Waves of armed conflict and atrocities against civilians have resulted in over three million casualties, making this one of the bloodiest yet least understood conflicts of recent times.

In *The Congo Wars* Thomas Turner provides the first in-depth analysis of what happened. The book describes a resource-rich region, suffering from years of deprivation and still profoundly affected by the shockwaves of the Rwandan genocide. Turner looks at successive misguided and self-interested interventions by other African powers, including Uganda, Angola, Zimbabwe and Namibia, as well as the impotence of United Nations troops. Cutting through the historical myths so often used to understand the devastation, Turner indicates the changes required of Congolese leaders, neighbouring African states and the international community to bring about lasting peace and security.

About the author

Thomas Turner teaches at Victoria Commonwealth University. He has previously taught in universities in Congo, Kenya, Tunisia and Rwanda. He is the author of *Ethnogenèse et nationalisme en Afrique centrale: les racines de Lumumba* (2000) and co-author of *The Rise and Decline of the Zairian State* (with Crawford Young, 1985).

Thomas Turner

The Congo wars: conflict, myth and reality

Zed Books

LONDON · NEW YORK

The Congo wars: conflict, myth and reality was first published in 2007 by Zed Books Ltd, 7 Cynthia Street, London N1 9JF, UK and Room 400, 175 Fifth Avenue, New York, NY 10010, USA

<www.zedbooks.co.uk>

Copyright © Thomas Turner, 2007

The right of Thomas Turner to be identified as the author of this work has been asserted by him in accordance with the Copyright, Designs and Patents Act, 1988.

Cover designed by Andrew Corbett
Set in Monotype Sabon and Gill Sans Heavy by Ewan Smith, London
Index: <ed.emery@britishlibrary.net>
Printed and bound in Malta by Gutenberg Press Ltd

Distributed in the USA exclusively by Palgrave Macmillan, a division of St Martin's Press, LLC, 175 Fifth Avenue, New York, NY 10010.

A catalogue record for this book is available from the British Library.
US CIP data are available from the Library of Congress.

ISBN 978 1 84277 688 9 hb
ISBN 978 1 84277 689 6 pb

Contents

Preface and acknowledgements

This book is the fruit of a decades-long love affair with Africa in general and Congo-Kinshasa in particular. I have visited more than twenty African states, and have lived and worked in several of them for extended periods: Kenya, Tunisia and Rwanda, as well as Congo.

Congo is a miserable place these days, as will be discussed below. But it is a magical place as well, where some of the world's great art has been produced. The pre-colonial sculptures of the Luba people (Roberts and Roberts 1996) are marvellous. The contemporary Lingala dance music is appreciated all over Africa and beyond. 'The Congo makes Africa dance,' as the saying goes. The contemporary paintings, sold door to door in many cases, but sold from studios in the cases of the more successful artists, are extremely inventive. The cooking – meat, poultry or fish in sauce, eaten with cassava, maize, banana or rice, and a vegetable (amaranth, sorrel or cassava leaves) – is a joy.

At the centre of all this, one finds the Congolese themselves. They are lovable and infuriating, wise and foolish. As an example of wisdom, I think of Mr Kabambi, who wanted to meet my mother (and did), when my mother visited me in Kisangani. 'Where would we be without our mothers?' he asked.

I think also of John XXIII, a madman (I think) whom I met in Sankuru, while I was doing my doctoral research. He recounted to me the genealogy of the Anamongo (Tetela) people, beginning with their ancestor Mongo, passing through Membele, Onkucu and the three brothers, Ngandu, Njovu and Watambulu, and winding up (not unreasonably) with himself, John XXIII. I did not tape this performance, as I did with more conventional interviews. How I wish I had. I think it might constitute a popular version of history, comparable to the paintings of Tshibumba (see Chapter 3).

Still in the category of Anamongo (but no longer in the category of madmen), I think of Dr Michael Kasongo (Methodist pastor and professor of history), who taught me a bit of his language and a great deal about the culture of his people. The late Monsignor Paul Mambe, whom I met for the first time when he was an assistant at Lovanium University in Kinshasa, and saw for the last time at Kindu where he was bishop, was another invaluable contact. Abbé Paul, as he then was, provided an entrée in the circle of pioneers of the MNC-

Lumumba, people who were understandably suspicious of a foreign researcher. In later years, Mgr Mambe was a model of resistance to the Mobutu dictatorship, during years when many of his brother bishops were less forthright.

I did my undergraduate studies at the University of Michigan, and will always have a soft spot for the Maize and Blue. I retain a liberal orientation to domestic and international politics that crystallized during my years on the staff of the *Michigan Daily*. I learned a lot from my fellow student journalists – Richard Taub, Tom Hayden and the others – and wish to thank them here.

It was on another Big Ten campus, the University of Wisconsin-Madison, however, that I was introduced to the study of Congo. In different ways, Professors Crawford Young (political science) and Jan Vansina (history) both greatly influenced my subsequent research. My doctoral research represented a topic suggested by Vansina (the divided Tetela-Kusu community) analysed especially in terms suggested by Young (differential modernization). I owe a particular debt to the late Professor Murray Edelman, whose views of symbols and politics have guided me in this book.

We students learned from one another as well. I am particularly grateful to Georges Nzongola-Ntalaja, whose historical materialism does not blind him to value dimensions of Congolese politics. Catherine Newbury and David Newbury, friends since Madison days, have helped me to learn about Rwanda and eastern Congo. Robert Smith, historian of Congo, was also helpful as I prepared this book.

Over the years, I have learned a great deal from African colleagues and students, in Kisangani, Lubumbashi, Nairobi, Tunis, Butare and Bukavu. When they have difficulty understanding my argument, or I theirs, the initial frustration sometimes leads to illumination. I once gave a talk to professors in Kinshasa, entitled something like, 'The Tetela Lineage System, Myth or Reality'. A Congolese colleague protested (and he was right) that 'a myth can be a reality'.

Lecturing on democratization in Africa to professors in Madagascar, I presented a summary of Kenyan politics, based on newspaper accounts and conversations with Kenyans. The Malagasies were unable to understand that Kenyans speak openly about ethnicity, and somehow thought that I was introducing those categories. The Malagasies, as good Francophone intellectuals, would have been much more comfortable with categories like 'bourgeoisie' and 'peasantry'. This was a good lesson in the continuing relevance of colonial socialization. Maybe it was also an example of the chilling effect of a Marxist dictatorship on academic discourse.

Teaching in Africa has been a bit like time travel. Authors such as Gabriel Almond and David Easton, whom I thought I had left behind me in Madison, live on in the classrooms of Tunisia, Rwanda and Congo. Some of the lecture notes, by which today's African students learn about systems theory, may even be versions of notes taken when I taught about this topic, thirty years earlier. One Congolese lecturer told me recently that he still had (and presumably used) my political sociology notes from 1974. He did not accept my suggestion that he burn them. I hope I have learned a great deal about political sociology since 1974. (To be fair, not all African lecturers are peddling ideas that far out of date. Some, including Semujanga [1998] make good use of more recent approaches such as that of Foucault.)

Sitting in Tunisia, on the African side of the Mediterranean, I spent four years teaching political science and American studies to Tunisian students. The misunderstandings uncovered in classroom discussion and informal conversation were instructive. One example stands out. I summarized and criticized the main ideas of Samuel Huntington on 'The Clash of Civilizations'. The students could not accept my criticism; they, like Huntington, believe that civilizations are hermetically sealed units, rather than (as I believe) interpenetrating networks.

I owe a great debt to Professor Hamadi Redissi of the faculty of law and political science at the University of Tunis III (as it then was), on both the personal and professional levels. His insights, and those of the Tunisian intellectuals I met through him, helped me understand a bit of what was going on around me.

I also gained great insight in Tunisia into the process of rewriting history for political purposes, as well as the apparent limits to such efforts. The modernizing autocracy of Zine el Abidine Ben Ali is trying to convince Tunisians that they have a long history antedating the Muslim conquest. Many of them resist these efforts. Similar efforts to rewrite history are going on in Rwanda, and to a lesser extent in Congo. In analysing these, I am able to draw on my Tunisian experience.

The subsequent five years (2000–05), in which I taught full time in Rwanda and gave occasionally courses as a visiting professor in Congo, brought this book into focus. I don't mean simply that I learned that there are two sides to every story. What I learned is more interesting. The two sides or two stories are based on a number of shared misapprehensions, concerning the relationship between race and language, for example, or what happened at the Conference of Berlin (1884–85).

I am going to write about Congo and Rwanda in the same book,

Preface

knowing full well that neither Congolese nor Rwandans will agree
with me. Congolese believe strongly in 'the myth of the yoke', that all
their problems come from abroad. If Rwanda invades Congo, and the
Rwandan regime is backed by the UK and the USA, then Congo is a
victim of Anglo-Saxon aggression.

Rwandans, on the other hand, suffer from an extreme case of
nombrilisme (navel-gazing). My Rwandan students believe in excep-
tionalism without having heard of it. Students cannot bear to compare
their country even to its 'false twin' Burundi, let alone to Congo.

There is also a heavy dose of jealousy. Rwandan papers discuss
whether there is too much Lingala (Congolese) music on the radio in
their country, or not enough. A Kigali restaurant presents 'chicken
Congolese style' (so-called, but it bore no resemblance to Congolese
cooking). No one in Congo thought about listening to Rwandan music
or emulating Rwandan cuisine, even before this long and dirty war.

In this book, I have cast my net a bit wider than before, as to what
evidence to consider in political analysis. Thirty years ago, teaching
in Lubumbashi, I bought 'popular' paintings, as did my colleagues
Young, Fabian and Jewsiewicki. Since then, I have done less with this
'sideline' than have my colleagues. I agree, however, that this art,
enjoyable in its own right, also provides insight into Congolese ideas
regarding history and politics. I discuss it, briefly, in Chapter 3, drawing on the ideas of Edelman.

Robert Molteno of Zed Books initially accepted my proposal for
a book on the Congo wars. To him, and to the press's current staff, I
want to express my appreciation.

My courage to write this book derives in large measure from the
support of my wife, Irène Muderhwa Safi. Irène has an interdisci-
plinary background (licence in rural development from the Institut
Supérieur du Développement Rural, Bukavu). She has worked with
women's organizations and human rights organizations, both in DR
Congo and in Rwanda. She has taught me a lot about what is going
on, in this corner of the world, from a Congolese point of view. One
small example will suffice here. During the transitional government
period, Joseph Olenghankoy denounced warlord and vice president
Jean-Pierre Bemba as 'Théâtre de chez nous'. From Irène, I learned
that this is a reference to a Congolese TV soap opera ('As the World
Turns', or perhaps 'Desperate Housewives'). Since Olenghankoy now
has become campaign director for Bemba's presidential campaign,
what are we to make of his earlier characterization?

My colleagues, students, and friends – Congolese, Rwandan,
Tunisian, American and others – have taught me a great deal. May

I take this opportunity to thank them all, singling out three of my recent students, Messrs Auguste Mwilo, Yves Musoni and Geoffrey Chihasha. None of them will agree with everything I have written, in part because they do not always agree among themselves. The responsibility for what I have written is mine.

Thomas Turner
Butare (Rwanda), 2005/Harrisonburg (USA), 2006

Sources

Roberts, M. N. and A. F. Roberts (eds), *Memory, Luba Art and the Making of History*, New York: Museum for African Art, 1966.

Semujanga, J., *Récits fondateurs du drame rwandais. Discours social, idéologies et stéréotypes*, Paris: L'Harmattan, 1998; (trans. edn) *Origins of Rwandan Genocide* (Foreword Tom Rockmore), Amherst, NY: Humanity B ,oks, 2003.

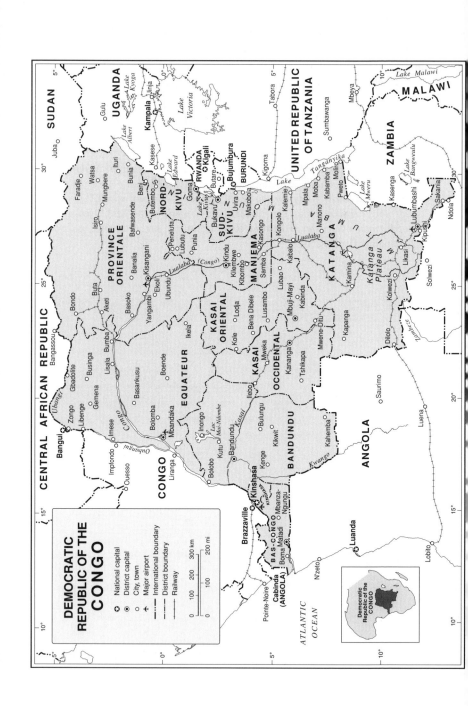

ONE
Half a holocaust

§ The bloodiest war since the Second World War unfolded in the Democratic Republic of Congo (DRC) – the former Zaire – in the mid-1990s. In 1996, Rwanda launched an invasion of DRC. This invasion was provided with double cover; that is, it was presented as the work of the Banyamulenge, a small community of Kinyarwanda-speaking Tutsi herders, living in Congo's South Kivu province, and of a coalition of anti-Mobutu elements, including the Banyamulenge. After seven months of warfare, dictator Mobutu Sese Seko had been driven out of Congo. The leader of the coalition, or front-man for the Rwandans, Laurent-Désiré Kabila, had taken Mobutu's place.

In 1998, Rwanda launched a second war, to overthrow the leader they had just installed. Again, a coalition of opponents of the Congo leader was presented as the driving force. This time, however, a stalemate ensued, and the war dragged on for four years. Millions of Congolese died. Even after a ceasefire had been signed in 2002, low-scale warfare continued in various parts of eastern Congo. Some of this warfare clearly was home-grown, but there was evidence of foreign (especially Rwandan) involvement.

From the beginning, there was disagreement as to what was going on. Some interpreted each war as international, i.e. an invasion of Congo by some of its neighbours. The war to overthrow Mobutu, in 1996–97, was hailed by Mwalimu Julius Nyerere of Tanzania, spokesman for African liberation, as the work of Africans and not outsiders.[1] For him, the implicit model was Tanzania's overthrow of the Idi Amin regime in Uganda, as contrasted to proxy wars of the Cold War era. The second war, 1998–2002, was widely characterized as 'Africa's First World War'.[2] In other words, this was the work of Africans, too. In each instance, however, there were charges of extra-continental involvement, charges that we shall have to examine.

Both in 1996 and again in 1998, some people accepted the definition of the war as a civil war against dictatorship, rather than an international war. Many Congolese supported the first war as a fight against the long-standing Mobutu dictatorship. When the second war began, a number of scholar-activists in the West took seriously the claim of Congolese colleagues that the war was a struggle against the new dictatorship of Laurent Kabila.[3] International organizations have split over this question: the World Bank continues to regard the Congo conflict as a civil war, while the United Nations has come to adopt the contrary view that emphasizes foreign involvement.[4]

The question of the type of war is linked directly to another major question, that of the responsibility for the extremely high number of deaths, especially among non-combatants, and of cases of sexual abuse. The war of 1996–97 involved few pitched battles. The number of military casualties was correspondingly small. However, many civilians were massacred, in particular Rwandan Hutu refugees.[5] The numbers are unknown, since the United Nations was prevented from completing its investigations.

During the second war and its sequels, Congo suffered millions of casualties. The International Rescue Committee estimated the total at 3.8 million deaths for the period 1998 to 2004. In contrast, the Sudan civil war produced 2 million deaths in twenty-two years. The Rwandan genocide and massacres of 1994 may have involved 1 million deaths. The Indian Ocean tsunami of 2004 killed around 300,000 people, and the terrorist attacks of '9/11' around 3,000.

Clearly, the Congolese catastrophe has not received the attention it deserves, when compared to these other horrible events. However, the message has been there, for those who want to hear it. In 2002, Refugees International had warned of a 'slow-motion holocaust' unfolding in eastern Congo. By 2003, the International Rescue Committee asserted that more people had been killed in Congo than in any war since the Second World War, and Nicholas Kristoff of the *New York Times* wrote of 'half a holocaust'. At the beginning of 2005 (at a time when the total number of dead from the tsunami was not yet known), the Belgian paper *Le Soir* referred to 'two tsunamis' in Congo every year.[6]

The wars on the ground have been accompanied by wars of words, fought to define what is or is not happening. In this chapter, I shall discuss the labelling of these wars – world war, civil war, holocaust and so on – and the realities reflected or concealed by the various labels.

The first section deals with the death toll. In subsequent sections, I will present brief outlines of the Congo wars, introducing themes to be developed in later chapters, such as pillage, disputed nationality and so on. A series of controversies regarding the nature of the Congo wars, the causes and the stakes, will be summarized. Finally, I will present the approach I shall be taking in this book.

The Congo death toll

Whether or not one accepts the terms 'holocaust' or 'tsunami' – the former term implies intentionality, the second a natural phenomenon – it must be stressed that the casualty figures in Congo are derived from serious study. The International Rescue Committee (IRC) has conducted a series of epidemiological studies. The first of its reports was published in 2000. IRC concluded that 1.7 million people had died during the previous two years as a result of war in the eastern part of the Democratic Republic of the Congo. About 200,000 of those deaths were the direct result of violence. The vast majority of deaths were caused by the destruction of the country's health infrastructure and food supplies.[7]

Two years later, the IRC estimated that at least 3.3 million Congolese died between August 1998, when the war began, and November 2002. Again, most deaths were attributable to easily treatable diseases and malnutrition, and were often linked to displacement and the collapse of the country's health services and economy. A third study, in 2004, raised the likely death total to 3.8 million. More than 31,000 civilians continued to die every month as a result of the conflict.[8]

Some may ask, how is it possible to go into the heart of a war zone and tally up the casualties? The IRC hired American Les Roberts, an epidemiologist from Johns Hopkins University, to map out an area of eastern Congo, go door-to-door, and ask families who among their relatives had died during the war and why. Roberts and his team of Congolese researchers interviewed members of 1,011 households. They primarily interviewed mothers on the assumption that mothers would have the most detailed knowledge of the health histories of their children.

Reference to a relatively small number of people killed by violence – 'only' 200,000 as of 2001 – as compared to millions dying as a result of the war, should not mislead the reader into thinking that soldiers die in fighting while civilians die in 'collateral damage'. The war has been a 'war against women', as Colette Braeckman argues. The UN has charged that various rebel groups have used rape, cannibalism and other atrocities as 'arms of war'.[9]

The first Congo war

The genocide of Rwandan Tutsi in 1994 and the seizure of power in Rwanda by the Tutsi-led Rwandan Patriotic Front led to the exodus of 2 million Rwandan Hutu to North and South Kivu provinces of the Congo. Most of them were regrouped in camps near the towns of

Goma (North Kivu) and Bukavu and Uvira (South Kivu), controlled by the authorities of the overthrown Hutu regime and its armed forces including the Interahamwe militia. From these camps, attacks were launched against Rwanda proper and against Tutsi in Congo.

In October 1996, it was reported that 'Banyamulenge' had attacked the town of Uvira. On 24 October, Uvira fell to the invaders. This could be seen as a local event. The Banyamulenge ('people of Mulenge', a small community of Tutsi pastoralists, speaking Kinyarwanda) had been in conflict with their neighbours in Uvira territory. On 7 October 1996, the governor of South Kivu had announced that all Banyamulenge would have to leave the province within a week. (For the war in South Kivu and its antecedents, see Chapter 4.) It soon became apparent, however, that this was not a local conflict. The so-called Banyamulenge quickly moved north. On the 30th, they took the provincial capital, Bukavu. On 1 November, Goma (capital of North Kivu province) fell. In each case, the refugee camps were attacked and their inhabitants dispersed.

After the offensive had begun, it was announced that it was being conducted by the Alliance of Democratic Forces for the Liberation of Congo (Alliance des Forces démocratiques pour la Libération du Congo, AFDL). The AFDL supposedly united four opposition groups to the Mobutu regime: these were the People's Revolutionary Party (Parti de la Révolution populaire, PRP), headed by Laurent Kabila; the National Resistance Council for Democracy (Conseil national de résistance pour la démocratie, CNRD), a small Lumumbist guerrilla group headed by André Kisase Ngandu; the Democratic Alliance of Peoples (Alliance démocratique des peuples, ADP), a group of Congolese Tutsi led by Déogratias Bugera; and the Revolutionary Movement for Liberation of Zaire (Mouvement révolutionnaire pour la libération du Zaire, MRLZ), a group of Shi and others from South Kivu, led by Anselme Masasu Nindaga. Of the four, the ADP and (perhaps) the MRLZ included Banyamulenge.

At its unveiling, the AFDL had two ostensible leaders: Kabila was the spokesman while Kisase Ngandu was military commander. Kisase died 'in mysterious circumstances' in January 1997, according to Georges Nzongola Ntalaja.[10] Masasu was arrested and gaoled for 'indiscipline' in November 1997, and killed by the Kabila regime in November 2000. Bugera served as secretary general of the AFDL, then (after apparently plotting against Kabila) was sidelined to a meaningless post of minister of state at the presidency. The only survivor of the original group, since the assassination of Laurent Kabila in 2001, Bugera has allegedly been living in Kigali, attempting to persuade Rwanda to back him in another rebellion once the current transition failed.[11]

By April 1997, Kabila and his backers had taken the mineral-rich provinces of Katanga and the two Kasais. Angolans poured across the border to reinforce the anti-Mobutu forces and, on 17 May, Kinshasa fell. The ailing President Mobutu Sese Seko was forced to flee.

Kabila proclaimed himself President of the Democratic Republic of Congo, as Zaire now was to be known. He formed a regime in which Rwandans and Kinyarwanda-speaking Congolese held a number of key posts. James Kabarebe, a Rwandan army officer, was chief of staff of the Congolese armed forces (Forces armées congolaises, FAC).

In July 1997, President Kagame of Rwanda admitted (Dunn and Nzongola use the term 'boasted') that Rwanda had planned and directed the so-called rebellion. In particular, Rwanda had sought out the PRP and other groups to provide a Zairian face for what was in fact an invasion.[12]

In the meantime, reports of massacres in eastern Congo began to reach the outside world. The United Nations attempted to carry out an inquiry into the alleged massacres, despite stonewalling by Kabila and his government. On 24 August 1997, a UN team began to investigate the fate of those Hutu refugees who had fled westwards when the camps were emptied, rather than returning to Rwanda. A preliminary report identified forty massacre sites. The following April, the investigators withdrew, unable to finish their work.[13]

Despite Kabila's steadfastness in resisting the UN inquiry, relations between the Congolese president and his Rwandan and Congolese Tutsi backers soon deteriorated. In May 1998, Bugera was removed from the AFDL job. In July, Kabarebe was removed as army commander and named adviser to the president. On 28 July Kabila announced that he was sending Kabarebe and the other foreign officers home. This probably was done in order to pre-empt a coup d'état against Kabila.[14] At any rate, its immediate consequences were a military 'rebellion' in Goma and an attempt to seize Kinshasa.

Africa's world war

In August 1998, Angola, Zimbabwe and Namibia foiled an attempt to overthrow Laurent Kabila. This was the opening round of the second war, which lasted until 2002, and even beyond. It began on 2 August, with a mutiny at Goma and an invasion of Rwandan troops. Ten days later, 'Congolese patriots and democrats' announced formation of the Congolese Rally for Democracy (Rassemblement Congolais pour la Démocratie, RCD), which supposedly had happened on

5

1 August, also in Goma. The RCD listed a series of grievances against Kabila, including corruption and tribalism.[15] However, as Nzongola argues, the war was 'above all a manifestation of the desire of his former allies to substitute for Kabila a new leadership team, much more competent and better able to do the dirty work of the Rwandan and Ugandan authorities vis-à-vis the armed groups fighting them from Congolese territory'.[16]

Rather than move from east to west as in 1996, the Rwandans adopted a daring strategy designed to decapitate the Kabila regime. Rwandan troops and Congolese rebels were flown to Kitona military base in Bas Congo province, west of Kinshasa. They freed and re-cruited a number of former troops of Mobutu being 're-educated' there. Others seized the nearby hydroelectric complex at Inga and the country's major port at Matadi.

By 26 August, 'rebels' and Rwandans were hiding in houses surrounding Kinshasa's Ndjili airport. Across the river at Brazzaville, 7,000 former members of Mobutu's Special Presidential Division awaited their hour of revenge. That hour did not arrive, however. Instead, Zimbabwean troops disembarked at the airport, took up position around the periphery, and began bombarding the rebel positions. Angola had already entered Congo three days earlier. Its troops moved from Angola's Cabinda enclave into Congo's coastal towns of Banana, Moanda and Boma. This was in response to occupation of Matadi and Inga by Rwandan troops.

The intervention of Angola and Zimbabwe (and a small force from Namibia) deprived Rwanda of the quick victory it had been expecting. Rwanda and Uganda jointly intervened in Congo in 1998, and jointly sponsored the RCD. However, the two allies soon fell out, and Uganda went on to sponsor its own Congolese rebel movement, the Congo Liberation Movement (Mouvement de Libération du Congo, MLC) as well as breakaway factions of the RCD.

What Nzongola calls the war of 'partition and pillage' saw Congo divided into three main sections. Kabila, from his base in Kinshasa, controlled a southern tier of territory running from the Atlantic through the southern portions of West and East Kasai, to the southern portion of his home province of Katanga. With oil from the coast, diamonds from the Kasais, and cobalt and other minerals from Katanga, this provided an adequate resource base for running his portion of the state and paying off his African partners.

A swathe of the north, including much of Mobutu's home province of Equateur, was controlled and exploited by the MLC under Jean-Pierre Bemba. As for the RCD and the Rwandans, they held a huge zone, centred on the former Kivu (the present North Kivu, South Kivu and Maniema) but including parts of Katanga, the two Kasais and Orientale.

The division was not stable. In mid-1999 the Kabila regime appeared to be on the ropes. In June, Rwandan army forces crossed the Sankuru river and seized the town of Lusambo, in Kasai Oriental province. Congolese forces fled, leaving behind their Zimbabwean and Namibian allies. By early July the Rwandans held Pania Mutombo and Dimbelenge and were only 75km from Mbuji Mayi, capital of the diamond industry. A second Rwandan force, advancing from North Katanga, had reached Kabinda, about 120km east of Mbuji Mayi. It looked as though Kabila's zone was about to be cut in half. James Kabarebe, former chief of staff of the Congo army and now deputy chief of staff of the Rwandan army, was quoted as saying: 'If Kananga, Mbuji Mayi and Kabinda are taken, then Kinshasa will fall.'[17]

Intense pressure on all the parties persuaded them to sign the Lusaka ceasefire agreement (July–August 1999), which promptly was broken by all concerned. In Equateur province, Bemba's MLC moved westwards with Ugandan support, and threatened to take the provincial capital of Mbandaka. In the east, Kabila's forces and the Zimbabweans failed to break through to Lake Tanganyika and South Kivu, while the Rwandans took the strategic border town of Pweto. From Pweto, they threatened the Katanga capital of Lubumbashi. Again, it is hard to see how Kabila could have held out without his home base of Katanga.

At the beginning of 2001, Congolese president Laurent Kabila was assassinated, apparently by one of his bodyguards. In a scenario reminiscent of the JFK assassination four decades earlier, the bodyguard was killed in turn.[18]

The Congo wars are not wars between persons – Kagame and Museveni against Laurent Kabila and his friends Mugabe, Dos Santos and Nujoma – but there is a personal dimension to these wars. There was a general recognition that the murder of Kabila and the succession of Joseph Kabila might lead to peace. Joseph Kabila was warmly received in Brussels, London and Washington and the way appeared open to a settlement. In fact, it took a year to reach a ceasefire, and another year to create a transitional government to lead the country to elections.

The logic of the transition was that each of the posts in the government of the supposedly reunified Congo, from the presidency down to seats as deputy or provincial vice governor, 'belonged' not to the individual holder but to the *composant* (component) that had nominated him. This made it impossible to create a unified government or even a unified opposition. When a minister displeased the *composant* that had put him there or, worse yet, the foreign backer of that *composant*, he would be replaced by someone more acceptable. Thus, public opinion interpreted the replacement of Foreign Minister Antoine Ghonda and of Defence Minister Jean-Pierre Ondekane as reflecting the displeasure of Uganda and Rwanda respectively.[19]

Under the ceasefire agreement signed at Lusaka in 2002, all foreign forces were to be withdrawn. However, some of the Rwandan Hutu forces (ex-Forces armées rwandaises and Interahamwe, as they were known) remained in Congo, even though they were to be disarmed and repatriated. Rwanda supposedly withdrew its forces, but the UN Mission (MONUC) reported a continued Rwandan presence. A series of incidents provoked fears of a 'third war' (see Chapters 4, 5 and 6).

Classifying and explaining the Congo wars

The wars of 1996–97 and 1998–2002 were civil wars, according to some. They were international wars designed to overthrow a dictatorship, according to others. They represent a continuation of Rwanda's Hutu–Tutsi conflict, pursued on Congo soil, for still others. They were resource wars, according to an abundant literature. The interventions of Congo's neighbours, Rwanda and Uganda in particular, were acts of self-defence. These neighbours were pawns of great powers from outside the continent. There seems to be an endless choice of descriptions and explanations. This book is meant to establish, first, what has happened in Congo, second, to sort out the explanations and, third, to offer some recommendations for the future.

At the outbreak of both wars, the theme of the battle against dictatorship was evoked. The Congolese insurgents, led or fronted by Laurent Kabila, supposedly launched the campaign to overthrow President Mobutu because of the latter's dictatorial, corrupt regime. Certainly, Kabila and the AFDL won some support on that basis.

A second theme evoked, particularly in 1996 and in scholarly circles, was the collapse of the Congolese state. Supposedly the insurgency of Kabila and his Rwandan and Ugandan backers was sucked into a vacuum, caused by the disappearance of the Mobutist state. This metaphor from Aristotelian physics – 'nature abhors a vacuum' – is ideological in that it absolves the actors of responsibility for their actions.

Some scholars argued that the time had come for Africans to solve their own problems, revising frontiers inherited from colonialism. On this point, the argument of scholars dovetailed with the declarations of the Rwandan authorities, who regularly maintain that their country had lost 30 per cent of its territory during the colonial partition of Africa. Most of that territory had been lost to what is now the DRC; so another argument for Rwandan intervention was their (tenuous) claim to territory in eastern Congo. The highly ideologized histories of Rwanda and Congo will be discussed in Chapter 3.

There is no question that many residents of eastern Congo speak the Rwandan language, Kinyarwanda, as their mother-tongue. Some of these are refugees. Others, including the Banyamulenge, have legitimate claims to Congolese citizenship. The question of their nationality and allegiance is complex, and will be discussed in Chapter 5.

The first Congo war apparently was designed to replace Mobutu. Laurent Kabila, the eternal anti-Mobutist, was supposed to defend the interests of Rwanda, Uganda, and perhaps their extra-African backers. The second war, from 1998 onwards, degenerated from a war to overthrow Kabila into a war to control and exploit one slice or other of the Congolese pie. The mutual slaughter between Hema and Lendu in and around Bunia (Ituri) has been referred to as 'ethnic' or 'tribal'. It is that, of course, but it is also fighting for control of Ituri district and its gold mines and other resources. The resources of Ituri, more than the nature of the opposing ethnic coalitions, explain the ongoing involvement of Uganda and Rwanda, backing first one group, then another.[20]

Most authors agree that the huge numbers of casualties in the east in general, and Ituri in particular, resulted from the efforts of Congolese and foreigners to control territory and resources. Braeckman, however, takes the argument further. She argues that the people of Ituri, like the Native Americans, are being driven off their land so that it can be exploited by newcomers: perhaps white farmers leaving Zimbabwe or South Africa, maybe even Israelis. Where, I wondered, was Braeckman getting this stuff about Native Americans? There was no footnote. Earlier in the chapter, however, she cited Pierre Baracyetse on mining and exploitation. Baracyetse also compares Congolese to Native Americans. Braeckman added the whites from Southern Africa and Israel. The parallel is not helpful. Native Americans lost their land due to a tidal wave of Europeans sweeping over North America but no such wave seems imminent in Ituri.[21] In contrast, the idea of a tidal wave of foreigners is a standard image in tracts concerning Kivu, where the foreigners are seen to be Rwandans, not Afrikaners or Israelis.

The waves of foreigners belong in the world of ideology and

discourse, not the world of observable reality. Both westerners and Africans have contributed to the elaboration of this world. As Dunn explains: 'The current war in the Congo has been shaped by long-term discourses on its identity – images and ideas authored not only in the West but within the Congo and Central Africa as well.'[22] One of those discourses, perhaps the most common one, presents a passive Congo, vastly rich, preyed on by outsiders. The debate about the motivation of the various actors in the first and second Congo wars becomes almost meaningless. Rwanda, Uganda and Burundi intervened to secure their respective western frontiers *and* to secure some of Congo's resources for themselves. Zimbabwe, Namibia and Angola defended Kabila, Congolese sovereignty, *and* their own material interests.[23] Clearly, Laurent Kabila did not trust his SADC allies to act on principle alone.

Pillage dates back to the days of Leopold II but a more useful starting point for understanding the present situation is the reign of Mobutu, himself a major warlord and pillager.[24] Kabila was a small-scale warlord in South Kivu in the 1970s and '80s.[25] In recent years, many Congolese have participated in the trade in diamonds, gold and coltan, as a survival strategy in an environment that offers few alternatives.[26]

Vast amounts of Congolese wealth – including minerals, timber, ivory and coffee – have been and continue to be siphoned off through neighbouring states, processes that have been documented by the United Nations. Rather than analyse how pillage occurs, most authors have contented themselves with what David Moore calls 'a new literary genre', 'a combination of political thriller, stark moral tale of right and wrong, travel-writing/journalism, and angst-ridden quest of what to do to save the world, you with the white man's burden'.[27] This literature doubtless is useful for consciousness-raising and for fund-raising. To understand what is happening on the ground, and in particular to clarify the Congolese role, it would be more useful to separate pillage (already an emotive term) from ideas about pillage, as Stephen Jackson has attempted to do, and to show how the international and local aspects of pillage are linked, as Vlassenroot and Raeymaekers do for Ituri district.[28]

Nationalism and state collapse

There is broad agreement that the Zairian state of Mobutu Sese Seko decayed, and then collapsed in the face of the invasion, and that this led to the killing and pillaging. As the eminent Congolese political scientist Nzongola puts it:

the major determinant of the present conflict and instability in the Great Lakes region is the decay of the state and its instruments of rule in the Congo. For it is this decay that has made it possible for Lilliputian states the size of Congo's smallest province, such as Uganda, or even that of a district, such as Rwanda, to take it upon themselves to impose rulers in Kinshasa and to invade, occupy, and loot the territory of their giant neighbour.[29]

Belgian-American political scientist and old 'Congo hand' Edouard Bustin offers a similar argument. The title of his chapter refers to 'The Collapse of "Congo/Zaire" and Its Regional Impact', but he explains in the text that the 'paralysis of state institutions and the collapse of Zaire's economy and public finance resulted more from the ineluctable decay of a system long rooted in pillage, than from some Machiavellian "scorched earth" policy deliberately concocted by Mobutu'. Two key state functions continued to operate under Mobutu's watchful eye, coercion and (through the national bank) the direct uncontrolled appropriation of foreign-exchange earnings by the President, or by selected warlords in his entourage.[30] Another way of saying this is that the Congo/Zaire state had been transformed into a warlord regime, as Reno argued.[31]

Braeckman of *Le Soir*, the most influential journalist writing about the Congo, discusses 'state failure' not as a reality on the ground but as a *concept qui tue* (an idea that kills) that is, an academic notion that supposedly determined America's decision to back the invasion by Rwanda and Uganda. She cites Marina Ottaway of the Carnegie Endowment for International Peace. Indeed, Ottaway argued: 'many of the states that emerged from the colonial period have ceased to exist in practice ... The problem is to create functioning states, either by re-dividing territory or by creating new institutional arrangements such as decentralized federations or even confederations.' The United States and other outsiders should be wary of assuming a 'colonial role', Ottaway advised. Instead, she advocated, 'allowing African countries to find solutions on their own', which apparently meant that the USA and Britain should continue to aid Rwanda and Uganda as they 'found solutions' by carving up Congo.[32] Braeckman presents no evidence that the Clinton administration listened to Ottaway. What she is presenting as a direct cause (an idea that kills) should be seen as an indicator of the context of understanding, within which certain policy propositions seem reasonable, others unthinkable.

As the Mobutu regime and the state itself decayed, the Congolese people paradoxically clung to the idea of their potentially rich, potentially strong state. Since the seizure of power by Laurent Kabila and his Rwandan and Ugandan backers, Congolese nationalism has not ceased to grow. The Congolese understand that these are not civil wars but foreign invasions with some Congolese participation.

Braeckman's journalistic approach occasionally crosses the line into the 'new literary genre' identified by Moore, but she is on target when she writes, '*le peuple dit non*', that is, the Congolese refuse the attempts to control their government and/or dominate part of their territory. However, I have trouble with the argument reflected in her subtitle, 'The policy of the powers in Central Africa'. She seems to suggest a direct tie between the pillaging of Congo and decisions taken by the USA, Britain and other western powers. Again, however, no proof is provided. As Kennes demonstrates, even the links between African producers, small mining companies and the major corporate actors are complex and problematic.[33]

Many, perhaps most, Congolese are convinced that the Rwandans and Ugandans invaded Congo as agents of the West and/or that the UK and USA back the Rwandans and Ugandans for economic or political reasons. There is something to this, but in that form the allegation is much too simple.

The material base of politics (control of territories and minerals, for example) is real. Representations of competition at the base (ethnicity, nationalism, state collapse, pillage and the like) exist on a different level of the same complex reality. Neither level can be reduced to the other. The task of the analyst is to understand and explain without over-simplifying, and without forgetting that millions of lives have been lost or ruined through the years of warfare and disorder in the Congo.

Levels of analysis

The Congo wars can be analysed on three levels. As John Clark has suggested, much of the behaviour of Rwanda, Uganda, Angola and other actors in the first and second Congo wars can be explained in terms of classical realism. I participated in the Clark project and in my chapter I demonstrated that Angolan behaviour can be understood in terms of the overriding foreign policy objective of the regime; that is, victory in the decades-old war against the UNITA of Jonas Savimbi. The state level of analysis is a useful place to start. However, use of state labels – Rwanda, Angola and the like – should not be allowed to obscure the role of small groups and even individuals in shaping policies and profiting from their success.

Clark sets out three fundamentally different perspectives on why the

Congo wars took place, and what this tells us about the evolution of African politics and international relations. The first sees the Congo wars 'as largely an issue of state collapse, succeeded by a scramble of unscrupulous neighbors for the lush spoils left unguarded and unclaimed'. The failed decolonization, followed by Cold War rivalries and 'the long and ruinous rule of Mobutu Sese Seko', led inexorably to the recent disasters. This view has been criticized, above.

A second, broader perspective – represented in the Clark book by the essay of Crawford Young – sees the Congo war or wars as part of a continental trend. The current varieties of internal war have a different set of motivations than early generations of warfare. Anti-imperialism and socialism have disappeared, as has secessionism (with the exception of Eritrea). World economic processes, often referred to as globalization, have made the conduct of business between the corporations of the developed world and non-state actors (including warlords) ordinary events in Sub-Saharan Africa. External state actors have withdrawn their support from client regimes in the post-Cold War era. A number of the cases of so-called 'state collapse' – Somalia as well as Congo/Zaire – can be explained in these terms. In the case of Congo, the withdrawal of support by the international financial institutions (IFIs) complemented the withdrawal of American political support. Clark adds that both the casual attitude of the major powers towards state collapse and the predatory behaviour of private business dealing with African natural resources 'may be manifestations of an emergent ideology that shuns regulation and collective management of social problems in the continent'.

A third broad perspective focuses not on state collapse but on the foreign-policy-making of the states that chose to intervene. Congo's weakness may have been a permissive condition but it was scarcely an efficient cause. Here, Clark turns to Mohammed Ayoob and his theory of 'subaltern realism'. The contemporary leaders of developing states are supposedly emulating the leaders of European states in the early modern era, building up their states through a variety of means, including war fighting. Such an approach might explain the behaviour of Museveni's Uganda and Mugabe's Zimbabwe, he suggests. Whatever the motivation, however, the outcome of Zimbabwean intervention 'has been enrichment for several of Mugabe's cronies and impoverishment for the Zimbabwean state'.

It is possible that the interventions of states sharing a border with Congo (that is, Uganda, Rwanda, Burundi and Angola, but not Zimbabwe, Namibia, Chad or Libya) might be explained in terms of their often-expressed desire to protect themselves against insurgencies operating from Congo territory. However, this explanation should not be taken at face value. Given the justified concern with cross-border attacks, might not the desired protection be attained through cooperative relations with Congo and building up an effective government there, rather than perpetuating weakness?

Clark suggests the need to take account of ideological change, in particular the delayed reaction of the West to the Rwandan genocide, but also shifts towards favouring democracy, good management and transparency. Such ideological change does seem to be happening, but its consequences are paradoxical. Uganda, for example, used its status as 'model pupil' of the World Bank support to continue exploiting a large region of northern and eastern Congo.

A final theoretical question, suggested by recent literature on the Congo in general and the essays in the Clark book in particular, is the continued use of 'the state' as the principal unit of analysis. Is this concept a western import, or a tool of universal applicability? In the ideological sphere, Congolese and Rwandans have internalized the European model of the modern state with sharp edges.

The rivalries between Rwanda-speakers and their neighbours in eastern Congo play out on a sub-state or local level. The role of the USA, UK and other extra-continental actors leads us to systemic-level analysis, since the global system constitutes the environment in which the Great Lakes wars unfold, and the role of the UN (some would say the failures of the UN) has been crucial.

Rational actor analysis inevitably fails to account for some aspects of state behaviour. As Graham Allison demonstrated, rational actor analysis of the Cuban missile crisis gives us a three-move game: (i) Soviet Union places missiles in Cuba; (ii) USA responds by a naval blockade; (iii) Soviet Union withdraws missiles. However, this game raises more questions than it answers. Why on earth would the Soviet Union challenge the USA in its backyard, rather than somewhere more favourable to its forces, such as Berlin? And why would the Soviets display a mixture of secrecy and openness in bringing the missiles to Cuba and unloading them? Why would the USA fail to react until the missiles were installed on their launch-pads? And why would the USA then choose a response that did not address the missiles themselves, already in Cuba at the time of the blockade? As Allison shows, it is necessary to deconstruct the state actors via organizational process and bureaucratic politics models, to show each state actor as a coalition of sub-state actors, each of which had its own worldview and its own modus operandi.[34]

Some authors dealing with conflict in the Great Lakes region argue for rational behaviour. Reno, for example, describes outlandish behaviour on the part of those he calls warlords, then adds: 'Rather than simply showing the failure of conventional states ... this book explain[s] how jettisoning bureaucracies, abjuring pursuit of a broad public interest, and militarizing commerce are rational responses in a setting in which very weak states have become unsustainable.'[35] Similarly, Vlassenroot and Raeymaekers argue that contributors to their book suggest that the chronic violence in eastern Congo

> cannot be understood purely with reference to the 'greed' of powerful local and international actors. Rather, the seeming intractability of the Congolese conflict can only be fully understood with reference to the ways in which conflict – together with a legacy of colonial and state policy that preceded and informed it – has created a situation in which the 'rational' pursuit of individual livelihood ends up reproducing the collectively 'irrational' phenomenon of war.[36]

I cannot disagree, and in the course of this book I will rely on the writings of Reno, Vlassenroot, Raeymaekers and others.

However (and it is a big however), I shall argue that these actors pursue their own perceived interests, and the cultural and ideological biases, shortages of information and other factors shaping their perceptions must be analysed in detail. I agree that the shortcomings of President Mobutu, for example, are not adequately described in terms of greed. But let us not forget that through his 'rational responses' Mobutu wound up burning down his own house. Why didn't he see what he was doing? In what follows I will pay attention to situations – such as the 'setting in which very weak states have become unsustainable' and the 'situation in which the "rational" pursuit of individual livelihood ends up reproducing the collectively "irrational" phenomenon of war' – but also to culture and ideology (see Chapter 3).

In my analysis of the Congo wars, I shall begin on the state level, referring to Rwanda, Uganda and so on as though they were rational actors with a coherent set of interests and perceptions. Complications will be introduced as needed, for example to explain apparent deviations from state-level rational behaviour. Timothy Longman's analysis of the 'complex reasons for Rwanda's engagement in the Congo' can serve as a model.[37] 'Humanitarian interests and ethnic solidarity' can be seen as a genuine motivation or a smokescreen. To the extent that it is genuine, it would motivate Rwanda's Tutsi leadership and not 'Rwanda' as a whole. Longman's second reason, 'security threats from the Congo', likewise applies to the leadership rather than to 'Rwanda' since other Rwandans, associated with the Hutu regime overthrown in 1994, posed the threats in question, and many Hutu apparently sympathized with those posing the threats.

Longman's third reason, 'domestic security concerns', is paradoxical in that the Hutu majority presumably resented the authorities that it saw as Tutsi. But a foreign war could serve to unite the Tutsi minority, divided into factions of ex-Ugandans, ex-Burundians, ex-Congolese and genocide survivors. And such a war could offer some opportunities to integrate Hutu into the Tutsi-led cause, notably by recruiting former Hutu fighters into the Tutsi-led Rwandan Patriotic Army.

'Economic interests' – often referred to as pillage or plunder – represent another possible motivation for Rwandan intervention. There can be little doubt that 'Rwanda' or certain Rwandans have participated in the looting of Congo, a subject I shall discuss in greater detail in Chapter 2. It will be necessary to separate plunder as a state activity from plunder carried out by individual military officers. Wamba dia Wamba, first head of the Rwanda-sponsored 'rebel' group RCD, has claimed that plunder is an activity of the Rwandan state. It might also be thought that a war begun for another reason – humanitarian concern or security threats, for example – later provided opportunities for profit. However, Braeckman quotes an RPF official as arguing that 'Congo is rich' as early as 1993, that is, before the genocide.[38]

Longman's final 'reason' is Tutsi triumphalism, which he explains as a sense of entitlement, reinforced by a series of victories, over the Obote government (as part of Museveni's NRA), over the Habyarimana government, and over the Mobutu government. This, he explains, is far from the 'Tutsi conspiracy' seen by some Rwandan Hutu and adopted by many Congolese:

> Rwandan actions in Congo have not been carefully planned out within a well-developed 'conspiracy.' Instead, the RPF leadership has been driven in a more haphazard fashion by a sense of entitlement and invincibly based more on its military might than its ethnic affiliation. This triumphalism has blinded the RPF leadership to the impact that RPF actions have on how Tutsi are perceived. Tragically, actions motivated by RPF arrogance have exacerbated anti-Tutsi sentiments, creating a difficult situation for thousands of Congolese Tutsi – as well as for other Congolese who have supported the two rebellions.[39]

I find this prophetic. Writing early in the second war, Longman has identified a dilemma that continued long after the war's formal end in 2002. I shall focus on the feedback between policies of Rwanda, Congo and other state actors, as each reacts to the perceived situation on the ground.

In this book, I am attempting to examine events that loom large in the memory of the Africans of the Great Lakes region. What I do hope to be able to do is to present and analyse those events in a way that the Congolese, Rwandans and others of the region cannot do, immersed as they are in the struggle for dominance or survival.

When one deals with events that were of great importance to the African populations, one often finds two sharply opposed versions of history, existing from the time of the event. For example, the Belgians defeated their 'Arab' rivals for control of eastern Congo, in part due to the defection to their side of Ngongo Leteta (or Gongo Lutete), a Congolese warlord. Then a young Belgian officer decided that Ngongo was a traitor, and had him shot. European accounts of the event focus on Ngongo and the accusation against him. In contrast, many Congolese accounts focus on an event that the Europeans ignore (if they know about it), Ngongo's killing of his lieutenant Mutambwe. Ngongo supposedly had Mutambwe tied up and thrown into a fire. Shocked by this, the Songye (ethnic brothers of Mutambwe) complained to the whites. The whites arrested Ngongo and tied him up. They fired bullets at him all day without injuring him. Then a Luba who had provided magical protection to Ngongo told the whites, if you want to kill him, first take his amulets, and then fire into his ear. When they did this, Ngongo died. Birds flew out of his mouth, his ears and his nose. Those were the spirits that had been protecting him until then, thanks to the Luba medicine.[40]

This problem of dual explanations continues up to now. Westerners tend to believe that President Mobutu Sese Seko died of prostate cancer. His son Niwa died a few years earlier, supposedly from AIDS. But many Congolese offer another sort of explanation. They note that Mobutu was protected by powerful magic from specialists of many nationalities. That had the effect of deflecting spells cast against Mobutu on to his son Niwa. Or perhaps Mobutu's magical protection created an imbalance; balance could only be restored by taking a victim from Mobutu's family.[41] Michael Schatzberg demonstrates the saliency of such beliefs, not only in Congo but also across Middle Africa, a belt of countries from Senegal in the west to Tanzania in the east.[42]

Are we then to look for explanations of political events, including the Congo wars, in the magico-religious sphere? Has imperialism no material basis? Of course it has, but the question is the extent to which that material basis determines cultural and political phenomena. Over a century ago, Karl Marx argued that men make their own history, but they do not make it as they wish: 'The Tradition of all dead generations weighs like a nightmare on the brain of the living.'[43]

A starting point for my analysis thus will be the political economy of Congo, during the colonial and post-colonial eras. I shall be guided, for the first period, in particular by Auguste Maurel, a.k.a. Michel Merlier, whose account remains extremely valuable, despite the decades that have passed.[44]

For the colonial period but especially for the periods of decolonization and independence, I shall be guided by another materialist account, equally valuable. I refer to Georges Nzongola Ntalaja's *The Congo from Leopold to Kabila. A People's History*. This book represents a remarkable balancing act by someone who has been a major analyst and critic, and at times a key actor. On many points, I shall refer to and defer to Professor Nzongola's account.

At the same time, I cannot completely rely on materialist accounts such as those of Maurel and Nzongola. With such a conception of history it is difficult to analyse ethno-national phenomena:

> Since Marxism became the dominant ideology of the socialist movement, one can observe a constant malaise in the analysis of national problems and cultural phenomena linked to them. This is evident very early on, starting in 1848, in the attitude of Marx and especially Engels toward the Slavs of central Europe and the Balkans, and later in their polemic against Bakunin, accused of pan Slavism.[45]

These attitudes can be explained historically, in Person's view.

> Engels never could escape entirely from the German nationalism of his youth and of his disdain, inherited from Hegel, for the peoples called 'without history' ... Marx himself changed his mind a great deal as regards Poland and Ireland, finally supporting the liberation of the latter in order to weaken the British Empire, but he welcomed the conquest of India and Algeria.[46]

Nzongola shares the Marxist difficulty in dealing with cultural phenomena. For example, under the heading 'The Construction of Ethnic Identity in Rwanda and Burundi', he reproduces the colonial account of the successive settlement of Rwanda and Burundi by Twa, Bantu (Hutu) and Tutsi.[47]

What we need to do is to take into account the material basis of politics in Central Africa without having that material basis determine all phenomena. Perhaps some of the Central African actors have motivations that do not reflect material interests. Material interest remains a useful hypothesis or starting point rather than a preordained conclusion. Central Africans, in my view, make choices among perceived alternatives. Their perception of the alternatives needs to be investigated.

In order to understand elite and mass political perceptions and resulting behaviour, I shall employ a culturalist approach to complement materialism and rational choice. 'Culture', as I understand it, refers to 'the knowledge people use to generate and interpret social behaviour'. Such knowledge is learned and, to a degree, shared. Cultural knowledge is coded in complex systems of symbols. People growing up in a society are taught 'a tacit theory of the world'. This theory is then used to organize their behaviour, to anticipate the behaviour of others, and to make sense of the world in which they live.

Such a definition of culture as knowledge shifts the focus of research from the perspective of the ethnographer (or political scientist, in this case) as an outsider, to a discovery of the insider's point of view. The insider is not a subject of research, nor a respondent, but an informant. The political scientist (me, in this case) seeks to discover the information that those being observed use to organize their behaviour.[48] Such an ethnographic approach seems particularly appropriate for this study, since it is not a question of one outsider studying one group of insiders, but of one outsider studying two groups of insiders. These people, Congolese and Rwandans, or, in some instances, members of smaller subsets (for example, Shi of South Kivu or ministers in the Rwandan government), share some aspects of their definition of the situation. Their understanding of some other aspects is sharply opposed.

Drawing on the work of ethnographers, I will be interested in certain kinds of cultural knowledge. These include categories, and taxonomies into which they are organized. Clearly, these differ from one culture to another. A Kinshasa taxi driver tells me there are two kinds of white people. Really, I ask, and what are those? Europeans and Chinese, he tells me. Another describes an accident, and enumerates several categories of victims: Europeans, Portuguese and Africans. The point is not whether such taxonomies are correct (are the Chinese or the Portuguese 'white'?) but whether one can learn anything useful about how the Congolese organize their behaviour, from the report that the Chinese are white or that the Portuguese are not European.

One

In studying politics, one attaches particular importance to a kind of cultural knowledge, known as ideology. An ideology can be seen as possessing various dimensions: cognitive, affective, evaluative, programmatic and the social base.[49] Under the cognitive dimension, one deals with the 'theory of the world', tacit or explicit. While the liberal sees the world as composed of individuals, the socialist sees classes, and the conservative, races or other 'natural' groupings. Yet they are looking at the same world.

The affective dimension is especially important when discussing ideologies of identity. The symbols attached to nations, parties and other groupings typically evoke strong emotions, even when the original meaning has been lost. (Why do leftists traditionally sit on the left?)

In the Great Lakes region, certain labels evoke strong affect: the same individual can be described as a 'mwami' (traditional ruler), a 'chef coutumier' (customary chief) or 'chef de collectivité' (administrative functionary) or even a 'sultani' (if one is speaking Kiswahili). These terms are somehow analogous but their affective weight is quite different.

The evaluative dimension refers to the fact that an ideology typically evaluates the present situation and contrasts it with some hypothetical situation that the ideology is supposed to bring about (bourgeois society v. classless society, to mention a well-known example). The programmatic dimension is virtually self-explanatory (although we shall see that Congolese political parties of the current era seem almost devoid of programme). As for the social base, it deals with the category to which the ideology appeals and whose support it seeks: the nation, the workers, the race, or whatever.

The views of many of my informants, as to phenomena I am studying, are quite different from my own views. This is particularly true as regards history, nationality and ethnicity. My Rwandan informants tend to project their idealized vision of the recent past, far into the past, so that the highly centralized Rwanda of the colonial period supposedly existed for hundreds of years. Rwanda was a 'nation-state' in the pre-colonial period, they believe. I disagree.

Regarding ethnicity, both Congolese and Rwandan informants tend to espouse an essentialist view, according to which particular cultural and even psychological orientations are inherent in one population or another (Rwandan, Shi, Tutsi, Hutu). My own view of ethnic and national identity is that it is constructed, and therefore changes over time. It can be instrumentalized – we shall see numerous examples in the pages below – but surely is not primordial or essentialist.

Interviews with informants will play a central role in this study. In addition, however, I shall have to draw on political communication very broadly defined, to complement interviews as to perceptions of politics. Young has argued for the existence of a diffuse but powerful sense of nationalism in Congo:

> this idea of a nation over the last 40 or even 50 years has been heavily promoted by all of the didactic resources of the state. Let us not forget in the creation of American Nationalism how strong a role things like the school system played in creating and instilling the idea of 'I'm an American.' Studies of how peasants became Frenchmen in the nineteenth century similarly place central stress upon the schooling. Yet, it was not just schooling; it was the media and the innumerable rituals of daily life. In multiple ways this notion of 'we are Congolese and we are not something else, we're not Angolans, we are not Ugandans; we are especially not Rwandans,' has become imbedded in the popular culture. It has roots in Lingala music, in the forms of popular art, in many sites of public expression that are more consequential than one often appreciates.[50]

Taking a cue from Young, I shall draw on popular art, music and humour.

With Edelman, I see art as 'the fountainhead from which political discourse, beliefs about politics, and consequent actions ultimately spring':

> Though only a fraction of the population may experience particular works of art and literature directly, the influence of these works is multiplied, extended, and reinforced in other ways: through variations and references in popular art and discourse; through 'two-stage flows,' in which opinion leaders disseminate their messages and meanings in books, lectures, newspapers, and other media; through networks of people who exchange ideas and information with each other; and through paraphrases that reach diverse audiences [...]
>
> [In Congo as in the United States] The construction of worlds with invented categories and invented cause–effect relationships is strongly influenced in these ways. Good and bad art provides the images and stereotypes into which we translate the news ... News reporters, editors, interest groups, and supporters of political causes help induce the public to fit current situations into these models, in which each category or image implies or presupposes a story that bolsters its political impact. Rival political groups propose conflicting models.[51]

The role of media, including songs, in preparing and implementing the Rwandan genocide has been well documented. The contrast between Hutu and Tutsi songs based on history is striking.[52] Since the RPF takeover in 1994, state-controlled and pro-regime media have played a major role in imposing a new version of Rwandan history.[53] In this book, I attempt to present similar processes at work in the more loosely coordinated Congolese political arena.

Under Mobutu, elite resistance to regime-controlled media often took the form of jokes. For example, when the regime surreptitiously subsidized large numbers of political parties, wits in Kinshasa dubbed these '*particules alimentaires*', a play on the scientific expression 'elementary particles' implying that the miniature parties served to put food on the table of their organizers. Such elite-level jokes depend upon knowledge of French.

In societies in which a minority possess the skills (French) or resources necessary for direct access to newspaper and television news, there is a multi-step flow of communication. In Kinshasa, an elderly politician's marriage to a very young woman becomes the subject of public comment. Musician Pepe Kalle releases a recording, 'Tika Mwana' (Leave the Child Alone). A restaurant owner has the title 'Tika Mwana' and a cartoon painted on his wall, making the opinion his own and passing it on to passers-by in a non-elite neighbourhood.[54]

Popular paintings often are major elements in the transactions that engender political behaviour. 'Inakale' (Impasse) is associated with the Zairian crisis of the 1980s. In this painting, a man is threatened by a crocodile, a lion and a serpent. Often, a caption directs the viewer to Romans, where Jesus is suggested as the one who will save the threatened person. In the early 1990s, a newspaper cartoonist adapts the cartoon: the three beasts are given the faces of opposition leaders and the threatened man becomes Mobutu who prays to 'George Bush who art in heaven ...'[55]

Much as 'Tika Mwana' moved from music to mural, and 'Inakale' moved from painting to political cartoon, 'Colonie Belge' and related paintings inspired wood sculptures in the 1990s. In the painting, oppression in the colonial past stood for current oppression (under Mobutu).[56] The sculptures preserved this double meaning, but a third level derived from Rwandan occupation of eastern Congo; the Rwandans were known as 'néo-Belges' (neo-Belgians) in political discourse in the Kivus.

Shula, a young Kinshasa artist, produced an extremely vivid painting entitled 'La population capture et brûle les rebelles'. The scene, which may reflect something the artist saw, depicts the infiltration of

Ndjili neighbourhood, near the airport, in 1998. Jewsiewicki situates this work in the social context of Kinshasa, where western media are omnipresent. The young Kinois (Kinshasa-dwellers) are dressed in 'modern' clothing, including red trousers, a yellow striped shirt, high-heeled boots and Adidas trainers. The captured rebels, in contrast, are wearing faded uniforms. They are put to death by the 'necklace' or burning auto tyre, borrowed from images of South Africa in the last days of apartheid. Mandela, who came to power in 1994, was believed to be the ally of Kabila.[57] Throughout this book I shall make use of songs, poems, paintings, jokes, and other cultural manifestations for the insight they offer into Congolese, Rwandan and Ugandan perceptions of their choices.

Following this opening discussion of the multiple approaches to be used, I shall devote one chapter each to the material world of the rich Congo and poor Congolese and to the culture and ideology that influence the decisions of the actors in the Congo conflicts, respectively.

Next, I take into account two additional levels of analysis. In Chapters 4 and 5, the conflicts in South Kivu and North Kivu and their antecedents will be analysed in greater detail. In particular, I shall attempt to reconstruct the history of the relations between the Kinyarwanda-speakers and their neighbours in each of the two provinces, charting the processes of ethnogenesis as they relate to changing economic and political circumstances. South Kivu and North Kivu were invaded by Rwanda (with the participation also of Burundi and Uganda) but those invasions did not take place on a tabula rasa. Pre-existing conflicts conditioned the invasions and condemned the occupation to failure.

Chapter 6 will place the Congo wars in their systemic or international context. The role of various state and inter-state actors, especially the United Nations, will be described and evaluated.

A final chapter will return to some of the themes referred to in this introductory chapter. The chances for peace and reconstruction in the Democratic Republic of Congo will be evaluated in light of what has gone before.

TWO

The political economy of pillage

§ The second Congo war was a war of 'partition and pillage' as Nzongola succinctly puts it. There were other dimensions, of course, but partition of territory and pillage of resources were central.

There has been a sustained effort to promote the idea that the Congo wars can be understood as civil wars.[1] Those who do so are minimizing a crucial aspect. During both wars, vast quantities of Congo's wealth flowed across its borders, into Rwanda, Uganda, Angola, Zimbabwe and other countries. Much of this transfer included Congo's legendary mineral wealth, including coltan (columbite-tantalite), cobalt, gold and diamonds, as suggested by Table 2.1. Agricultural produce, including coffee and palm oil, was also seized and exported during the war, as were personal belongings such as automobiles and refrigerators. Pillage of Congo's resources is not just a manner of speaking. It is a reality.

At the same time, it must be recognized that large-scale misappropriation of wealth has been practised within the country and that a few Congolese have profited from the wars. The pillagers of Congo include the Congolese.

Rich Congo and its poor neighbours

The Democratic Republic of Congo is a very large, very well endowed country that has been poorly governed, when it has been governed at all. Neighbouring states – notably the invaders Rwanda and Uganda – tend to be smaller and less rich.

The DRC is large both in area and in population. To use two time-worn expressions, it is as large as Western Europe or the United States east of the Mississippi. With an area of 2,345,410 sq. km, it is the third largest state in Africa. Only Sudan and Algeria, both of which include large swathes of uninhabited desert, are larger. In contrast, Belgium, which inherited Congo from King Leopold and exploited it for half a century, measures just 30,528 sq. km.[2]

Congo is one of the largest African states in terms of population as well. With an estimated population of 62,660,550 it trails only Nigeria, Egypt and Ethiopia. (Belgium has just over 10 million people.)

TABLE 2.1 Rwandan mineral production, 1995–2000

Year	Gold production (kg)	Cassiterite production (tons)	Coltan production (tons)	Diamond exports (US$)
1995	1	247	54	–
1996	1	330	97	–
1997	10	327	224	720,425
1998	17	330	224	16,606
1999	10	309	122	439,347
2000 (to October)	10	437	83	1,788,036

Sources: Coltan, cassiterite and gold figures derived from Rwandan Official Statistics (No. 227/01/10/MIN); diamond figures from the Diamond High Council. All figures originally appeared in the UN Panel of Inquiry Report, 2001. Table from Stephen Jackson, 'Making a Killing: Criminality and Coping in the Kivu War Economy', *Review of African Political Economy* 93/94 (2002): 525.

During the 1990s, Congo was invaded twice and pillaged by neighbours that are far smaller. Uganda is about one-tenth the size of Congo and less than half as populous (236,040 sq. km; pop. 28,195,754). Rwanda is even smaller in area (just 26,338 sq. km) and in population (8,440,820).[3]

There is a temptation to convert these differences into causal factors. Rwanda is very densely populated. That density has been seen by successive governments (starting with the colonial regime) as a handicap in their efforts to develop the country. Congo, in contrast, is rather under-populated, given its huge area. Some suggest that over-populated Rwanda has no choice but to seek '*lebensraum*' across the border. Such an analysis fails to account for a series of rather different policies since independence, despite the unchanging facts of Rwanda's population density and Congo's sparseness. Nor does it explain why densely populated Burundi has not shown expansionist tendencies to the same degree.[4]

A more rewarding approach would start from the fact that Congo and Rwanda are polar opposites in terms of natural resources. King Leopold II created the 'Congo Free State' with the idea that his colony would prove extremely rich, although little was known about Congo's riches at the time. In his efforts to extend his colony south-east into Katanga, Leopold was following a hunch; he traded petroleum along the Atlantic coast for Katanga's copper, cobalt and uranium, without knowing that was what he was doing.[5] Nevertheless, Congo soon became known as a 'geological scandal' on the basis of the vast mineral wealth discovered there, including copper, cobalt, tin, uranium, manganese, gold and diamonds. The presence of coltan and petroleum became known more recently.

The contrast with Rwanda (or Burundi for that matter) could hardly have been greater. Early accounts referred to Rwanda as a 'land of milk and honey', which it was in both a literal and a cultural sense, since these products were associated with healing.[6] However, most Rwandans did not share the prosperity of the court and the country was wracked by frequent famines. Belgium seized these German territories during the First World War, and then held on to them as a reward for its war effort, even though they offered no obvious resources to be exploited. Rwanda has small deposits of tin and coltan. There appear to be sizeable amounts of methane, potentially a fuel, in Lake Kivu, which Rwanda shares with Congo.[7] Overall, Congo is rich in resources and Rwanda is poor.

When Rwanda and Uganda organized attacks, first on the Mobutu regime then on the successor regime of Laurent Kabila, journalists and scholars evoked the earlier episode of Congolese history, in which outsiders were drawn in by reports of Congo's vast wealth, and millions of Congolese perished. In this chapter, I shall examine the appropriateness of the comparison of the Congo Free State to the Congo of Mobutu and Kabila. Rather than compare these systems of exploitation ahistorically, I will pass in review a succession of periods in Congo's history, from the Congo Free State to Belgian Congo to independence. The period of independence and neo-colonialism will be examined in stages: the Congo as Cold War battleground 1960–65, the dictatorship of Mobutu, from 1965 to the 1990s, and the period since 1996, in which a combination of internal and international war has raged. Rwanda (or Ruanda-Urundi for the colonial period) will be compared to Congo at each step along the way.

Leopold's Congo

As a young man, the future Leopold II had written, '*Il faut à la Belgique une colonie*' (Belgium needs a colony). He considered Taiwan and Guatemala before settling on Central Africa, just becoming known in Europe through the travels of the missionary David Livingstone and the journalist Henry Morton Stanley. Hiring Stanley as his agent, and proceeding through a series of innocuously named front groups, Leopold manoeuvred to gain recognition as sovereign of an vast, ill-defined territory he named the Congo Free State (in French: Etat Indépendant du Congo).[8]

This new state was Leopold's property. Because he was a constitutional monarch in Belgium, he was unable to obtain public funds to launch the colonial enterprise. Thus, the Congo had to pay for its own colonization, and produce a profit for those backers that Leopold had found, in Belgium and elsewhere. It did so, and even financed prestige projects in Brussels, including the Royal Museum of Central Africa, a veritable monument to colonialism.[9]

Most of Congo's wealth was not immediately available. Katanga copper deposits attracted the interest of investors, but it would be years before the geological surveys could be conducted, a workforce assembled and trained, and production begun.[10]

The fertility of the land seemed evident. Congo's new ruler imagined harnessing that wealth and the labour of Congo's population, to produce crops for world markets. Again, however, years would be needed to test the soil, develop appropriate plant varieties, and coerce Africans into growing those crops.

The few resources immediately available included ivory and wild rubber. The Free State established monopolies over these products and organized a system of taxes in kind. In forest areas, each village had to bring in a certain number of kilos of ivory or raw rubber, or risk punishment. As each village used up stored ivory and killed off nearby elephants, hunters had to roam farther. Similarly, as each village exhausted nearby supplies of latex-bearing plants, villagers were forced to range farther and farther into the forest. The expanding circumferences eventually overlapped, meaning that men of several villages were competing for the small amount of remaining rubber or ivory. As villages failed to meet their quotas, punishment escalated. Many Congolese lost their lives.[11]

The atrocities of 'red rubber' led to the creation of the Congo Reform Association, a predecessor of today's Amnesty International, Global Witness and other advocacy groups. The campaign of the Congo Reform Association was largely responsible for the Congo Free State being handed over to orthodox colonial rule, as the Belgian Congo. Yet this success should not be taken to indicate Belgian agreement that Leopold had failed. Arguing for acceptance of Leopold's legacy, Jules Renkin (future Minister of Colonies) told the Belgian parliament of Congo's 'inexhaustible' supplies of ivory and rubber.[12]

Belgium's model colony

The Belgian Congo rested on foundations laid by Leopold. The 'colonial trinity' that ran the colony – the state, the companies and the Church – had been put in place under the Free State. In the area of state administration, uniformity was a virtue. The entire territory was divided into nesting subdivisions – the province, the district, the territory and the native circumscription – each subdivision on each level being legally equivalent to any other. (Katanga was a marginal exception to this practice, since its head was vice governor general of the colony of Belgian Congo.) Once Belgian control of Ruanda-Urundi had been confirmed, under a League of Nations mandate, the territory was administered as part of Belgian Congo, also under a vice governor general.

In the 1920s the Belgians were intrigued by the 'indirect rule' formula they had inherited from the Germans in Ruanda-Urundi, and toyed with the idea of ruling through African kings in suitable regions of Congo, for example among the Luba of Katanga. However, they decided this would be too difficult, since various Luba chiefs had acquired a degree of autonomy that they were unwilling to surrender to their nominal sovereign.

Instead, the Belgians applied to their new territories the 'native policy' they already had developed for Congo, with suitable modifications as required. Each of the two kingdoms was divided into *chefferies* (chiefdoms) and *sous-chefferies*. As in Congo, 'schools for sons of chiefs' provided the necessary skills to the new generation of literate chiefs, who would serve as intermediaries between the colonial administration and the African masses. In Rwanda and in Burundi, in virtue of the theory that the Tutsi were born to rule, almost all the new chiefs were from the Tutsi. (On this theory and its deadly consequences, see Chapter 3.)

The company sector of Belgian Congo was unbelievably complex, and allowed Belgian private interests to control the companies despite substantial state and foreign holdings in those companies. In Katanga and in Kivu, state and private interests were fused in the form of the Comité Spécial du Katanga and the Comité du Kivu, respectively.[13]

The Belgian approach was to develop known mineral resources – the copper of Katanga, the diamonds of Kasai, the gold of Province Orientale, and so on – through monopolistic capitalism. Labour would be recruited for these enterprises on the basis of colonial stereotypes of 'suitable' populations. (On 'suitability', see Chapter 3.) For example, the Belgians considered the Luba of Kasai and Hutu of Rwanda to be hard workers, and recruited them by the thousands to work in the copper industry of Katanga. Food was raised in another region, for example maize in Kasai or rice in Maniema, and transported to Katanga to feed the workers.

In regions lacking an obvious resource, a suitable crop had to be found and imposed. In large parts of Kasai and Orientale, that crop was cotton, imposed by force. Taxation was used to generate a need for cash on the part of the peasants, cash that they could obtain only by selling cotton to the colonial companies. Congolese cotton would not have been competitive on world markets without the very low prices paid to cultivators.[14]

Ruanda-Urundi had few known minerals and so a suitable crop had to be imposed. For many Rwandans and Burundians, this meant coffee and tea.

From an early date, the Europeans (first the Germans, then the Belgians) were convinced that Burundi and Rwanda were over-populated. This statement is almost meaningless without consideration of other variables such as cattle raising v. cultivation, and confiscation of land by Europeans. Nevertheless, this conviction dovetailed with the Belgian idea that parts of Congo were under-populated, especially by 'useful' Africans. This led to programmes to transfer families from Rwanda to eastern Congo, with consequences that are still being felt.

The class structure of Belgian Congo

This political and economic organization of colonial Congo produced a complex class structure through which (as Nzongola writes) 'the interests and aspirations of the historical actors are articulated':

- The *metropolitan or imperialist bourgeoisie*, physically absent but economically and politically dominant in the country, where it was represented by the top managers of large corporations, the higher echelons of the state apparatus, and the hierarchy of the Catholic Church.
- The *middle bourgeoisie*, made up of Belgian and other European settlers who owned their own means of production and employed a large number of wage-workers in agriculture, commerce and manufacturing industry.
- The *petty bourgeoisie*, divided along racial lines, and made up of a number of fractions and strata:

  (i) the liberal professions, whose members were nearly all Europeans;
  (ii) European and American missionaries;

(iii) middle-level company managers and state officials, all European;
(iv) European shopkeepers and artisans;
(v) Asian shopkeepers;
(vi) African white-collar employees (state, company, mission); and
(vii) African traders and artisans.

- *The traditional ruling class* composed of kings, nobles, lords of the land, ancient warrior chiefs and religious authorities.
- The *peasantry*, that enormous mass of poor rural producers of food and cash crops to which the overwhelming majority of the African population belonged.
- The *working class*, consisting of the modern proletariat, and composed of two distinct fractions, one European and one African:

  (i) skilled white workers, employed in supervisory positions in the mines and large industries, and constituting a veritable labour aristocracy; and
  (ii) black workers, skilled and unskilled, constituting the largest African proletariat outside of South Africa and Egypt, who were divided into two strata: urban and industrial workers on the one hand, and rural and agricultural workers, on the other.

- The *lumpenproletariat*, or that group of proletarianized masses without stable wage employment, made up for the most part of school-leavers and rural migrants eking out a living through a variety of activities, legal and extra-legal, within the informal sector.

To exploit the colony, the imperialist bourgeoisie 'relied on the support and assistance of three classes of intermediaries: the middle bourgeoisie, the petty bourgeoisie and the traditional rulers or chiefs'.[15]

In colonial Rwanda, capitalist enterprise was less important than in Congo. This meant that the metropolitan bourgeoisie (colonial trinity) was for most purposes a duopoly of Belgian administrators and the Catholic hierarchy (many of them French or Swiss). The middle bourgeoisie was small, although Harroy notes some political participation by 'colons' or settlers during the period of decolonization.[16] The petty bourgeoisie of Rwanda likewise was small, although the same categories were present. The 'African white-collar employees', particularly those of the state sector, tended to be drawn from the 'traditional ruling class (the Tutsi nobility)', to a far greater extent than in Congo.

The European fraction of the working class in Rwanda was very small, since the territory lacked the railways and mines found in Congo. Likewise, the African working class was minuscule, except for workers in coffee and tea plantations. Bujumbura, capital of Ruanda-Urundi, was the only important town. Colonial Rwanda remained heavily rural, and the lumpenproletariat was small.

The African petty bourgeoisie provided the leadership for political parties in Belgian Africa, when at last these materialized in the late 1950s. This class initially pursued its own interests, narrowly defined. Not until it realized that it could not achieve equal status with the Belgians in the civil service did it link up with the rural masses and demand independence. Once it did so, the colonial house of cards collapsed with alarming speed. The administration attempted to promote 'moderate' (i.e. pro-Belgian) parties. This strategy largely failed, although it succeeded in mineral-rich Katanga province and in Rwanda.

Neo-colonialism in Congo, 1960 onwards

Neo-colonialism, as understood here, 'involves the uninterrupted exploitation of the country's resources, but this time in collaboration with national ruling classes. The primary mission of the latter [as Nzongola explains] is to maintain the order, stability and labour discipline required for meeting the country's obligations to the international market.'[17]

In the four decades since independence, Congolese have struggled to redefine Congo's relations with the exterior. Since colonial domination was political, economic and cultural, the struggle has had these same three dimensions. I will trace the struggle through several periods of unequal duration: (i) the victory of the radical nationalist Patrice Lumumba and his failure to retain power; (ii) the failure of Belgian and American strategies of maintaining or establishing dominance in the newly independent Congo, culminating in the Lumumbist insurgencies of 1963–66; (iii) the thirty-year dictatorship of Mobutu Sese Seko, beginning with a coup d'état in 1965 supported by Belgium and the USA and ending with his flight from Kinshasa in 1997 in the face of the invading force of Kabila and his foreign backers; and (iv) the wars that have plagued the country since 1996.

Lumumba's party did better than any other in pre-independence elections, winning 33 seats in the 137-seat lower house of parliament. He became prime minister despite Belgian attempts to find an alternative. The country attained independence on 30 June 1960, with Lumumba as prime minister and his rival Joseph Kasavubu as president. Lumumba's government was an unwieldy coalition of contradictory political forces. A number of key ministries were in the hands of politicians sharply opposed to his nationalist, pan-African ideas. Some of these ministers, notably those from the rich mining province of Katanga, would have tried to oust Lumumba. Could he have held on to power and kept the country together, had not the army mutinied, a week after independence day?

At any rate, the army did mutiny and Katanga seceded. Belgium sent troops, ostensibly to protect its nationals, and Kasavubu and Lumumba invited in the United Nations, to defend against Belgian 'aggression'. Both Belgium and the USA began plotting to eliminate Lumumba. Within a few months, Lumumba's former personal secretary, Joseph-Désiré Mobutu, whom he had named Chief of Staff after the mutiny, had ousted him from power.

The murder of Lumumba by Katanga secessionists, presumably intended to restore order, instead contributed to a downward spiral of violence. The neo-colonial Katanga regime persisted until United Nations forces suppressed it at the end of 1962. In the meantime, Katanga gendarmes and European mercenaries fought a bloody war to suppress an uprising conducted in the name of the Cartel, i.e. the alliance between the Balubakat party and the MNC-Lumumba that had very nearly won the election in Katanga province.[18] And, of course, copper and other minerals continued to flow to Belgium for refining and sale on world markets.

Belgium's neo-colonial strategy had centred on Katanga, richest of the six provinces of Congo and the one where much of its investment was centred. That was not a viable long-term strategy, since Belgian firms had major interests in the other five provinces. The Belgian government and major companies apparently intended to reconstitute a loose federal structure, within which Katanga would continue to enjoy substantial autonomy. Lumumba, seen as the principal obstacle to Belgium's neo-colonial plan, was demonized.

The Americans adopted the Belgian characterization of Lumumba as a communist and acted in terms of Cold War logic. In a telegram sent by the CIA station in Leopoldville to its headquarters in Washington, early in August 1960, the embassy and the station claimed to believe that 'Congo experiencing classic communist effort takeover government'.[19] The judgement is absurd. Lumumba was no communist and the Soviet Union lacked the capability to intervene in Congo.

Belgium's Katanga-based neo-colonial strategy failed when the UN ended the secession, and again when Katanga's Moïse Tshombe served briefly as prime minister of the Kinshasa government but was unable to consolidate power. The American policy of creating a strong, anti-Lumumbist regime in Kinshasa fared no better. One weak government succeeded another. The Americans exercised indirect rule via the so-called Binza group (named after the luxurious suburb where they lived) that controlled the ministries of foreign affairs, finance, and other key posts.

The exclusion of Lumumbists and other radical nationalists from power led to insurgencies that swept over much of the country. Pierre Mulele, Lumumba's education minister, went to China for training and then returned to his home area in Kwilu (Bandundu). As Nzongola explains, Mulele attempted to systematize the ideas of the masses into a coherent analysis of the situation, through a Marxist–Leninist framework of class analysis. He combined this with a Maoist strategy of political education and guerrilla warfare. Mulele's slogan, 'the second independence', appears to have emerged from the masses. Mulele's men captured much of Kwilu province but were unable to occupy either Gungu or Idiofa, the main towns in the zone they controlled. Nor were they able to break out of their ethnic base.[20]

The rebellion in the east, in contrast, quickly came to control almost half the country. It began in Uvira-Fizi, South Kivu, and then spread southward into North Katanga, the home of Laurent Kabila, and Maniema, the home of Gaston Soumialot. The 'Simba' (Lions) of the People's Liberation Army (APL) were less disciplined than the men of Mulele, and relied heavily on magical protection, 'Mai Mulele' (later, 'Mai Lumumba'). Rather than working in the countryside in a Maoist manner, they moved from town to town, in trucks. Their strategy nearly worked. Towards the end they fell victim to the same sort of ethnic closure as Mulele, in their case an over-identification with the Tetela-Kusu, the ethnic group of Lumumba and of Soumialot.

The decolonization of Rwanda followed a very different trajectory. Tutsi associated with the monarchy demanded immediate independence, which the Hutu counter-elite feared. The Catholic missionaries, the colonial administration and the settlers helped the Hutu counter-elite seize power. The resultant regime was very moderate, except on the 'racial' question, i.e. its opposition to Tutsi domination. The first republic in Rwanda (1962–73) remained very close to the former colonial power. This neo-colonial relationship, however, was as much political or ideological as economic.

The (brief) rise and (long) decline of the Zairian state

General Mobutu seized power in Congo in November 1965, in the name of the army high command. The immediate motivation of the putschists probably was military. The central government had just decapitated its rival, the People's Republic of the Congo. More accurately, Belgian paratroopers had dropped on the rebel capital Kisangani from American planes. The parachutist operation was necessitated by the threat of Christophe Gbenye, head of the People's Republic, to massacre the western hostages being held at Kisangani. The city would have fallen even without the parachute drop. A ground force led by white mercenaries and incorporating many former gendarmes of the secessionist regime in Katanga, was a few days away from the rebel capital. The Katangans had been reassembled by the former Katanga prime minister, Moïse Tshombe, now (incredibly) rehabilitated to serve as prime minister of the country from which he had tried to secede.

Tshombe was a likely candidate for the presidency, in elections to be held in 1966. His probable opponent, the incumbent president Joseph Kasavubu, tried to move to the left in order to better oppose Tshombe. He promised, during a meeting of African heads of state and government, to send away the mercenaries, a symbol of neo-colonialism. Mobutu and his fellow officers, knowing only too well how dependent the Congolese army was on these foreign fighters, struck first, dismissing Kasavubu and the government.

At first, Mobutu served as president while a popular military man, General Léonard Mulamba, was prime minister. Then the constitution was amended, eliminating the duality that had led to so many rivalries: Kasavubu v. Lumumba, Kasavubu v. Tshombe, and so on.

The regime gradually embraced the formula of the party-state, then so prevalent in Africa. Reaction to the new structures, as I witnessed it, was one of bemusement. People could not understand what it meant to say that the ministries or the universities were being incorporated into Mobutu's political party, the Mouvement Populaire de la Révolution (MPR).

In the economic sphere, Mobutu attacked the Belgian-dominated corporations that had constituted one of the persons of the 'colonial trinity' (state, companies, Church) and attempted to form a new Zairian capitalist class centring on him. His efforts were somewhat successful in the short term, but catastrophic in the long term, leaving Congo/Zaire more dependent than ever before.

Tshombe supposedly had settled the '*contentieux belgo-congolais*' (a bundle of disputes concerning assets and debts of the colonial state) during his brief tenure at the head of the central government. Mobutu, anxious to gain popular support for his new regime, accused Tshombe of treason for accepting a settlement too favourable to Belgium. He reopened the '*contentieux*' but was unable to do much better. As regards the Union Minière du Haut-Katanga (UMHK), the most important single Belgian holding, Mobutu attempted to nationalize it, first by obliging the company (and others in similar situations) to relocate its corporate headquarters. When the company refused, Mobutu created a Congolese corporation, the Générale des Carrières et de Mines (General Company of Quarries and Mines) or Gécamines. This company managed the holdings of the former UMHK within Congo, but was unable to find an alternative to the 'downstream' refining and marketing arrangements in Belgium. Subsequently, a second state enterprise SOZACOM (Société de Commercialisation des Minerais) was entrusted with marketing the production of Gécamines and other Zairian producers. The company did not greatly improve Zaire's leverage in the sale of copper and other minerals. Instead, SOZACOM became a new source of embezzlement and kickbacks; it was wound up, under pressure from the IMF and the World Bank, in 1986.

Given the extreme unpopularity of Mobutu in the last years of his rule, it is worth stressing that his government initially was quite popular. His moves against the politicians ('liars' according to public opinion) were supported. Nationalization of the universities was popular with professors and students, two important constituencies. Congolese, like most people, make political choices in terms of their perceived economic conditions and interests. From 1968 to around 1974, economic conditions were good, thanks to the restoration of order and the high price of copper on international markets.

Starting in 1974, there was a series of disasters, some of them self-inflicted. 'Zairianization' of the economy damaged the system of distribution of consumer goods, and made the term *acquéreur* (acquirer, one who had acquired a foreign-owned business) into a term of opprobrium like *politicien* a few years earlier.

In the early 1970s, the Mobutu regime launched a 'rash of poorly conceived industrial development projects ... that were launched without sensible and comprehensive economic planning and institutional support. A substantial percentage of projects for which loans were being sought were unviable and only ended up raising the nation's debt profile.'[21] These projects included the hydroelectric plant at Inga, the Voice of Zaire radio-television centre and the World Trade Center at Kinshasa. The whole approach was characterized by the steel mill at Maluku, designed to substitute steel made from Zairian/Congolese iron for imported steel. Since no iron ore was available, the plant made steel reinforcing rods from imported scrap, at a cost greatly exceeding the cost of importing rods from East Asia.[22]

Mobutu's army underwent a series of humiliations. He intervened in the Angolan civil war only to see his men routed, and earned the enmity of the victorious MPLA. In 1977 and 1978, small forces of 'Tigers' of the Congolese National Liberation Front (FLNC) invaded Katanga from Angola, and Mobutu had to call on foreign allies for help. Repeated efforts to rebuild the army or to add new security forces (for example the Civil Guard) were undermined by nepotistic appointments at the top and by generalized corruption. The inability of Mobutu's men to repel Kabila's forces in 1997 should have surprised no one.

Non-governmental or civil society organizations opposed the Mobutu dictatorship and pushed for democratization. Students offered determined resistance to the Mobutu regime, especially in the early years. Some of their demands concerned their study and living conditions, whereas others challenged the ideological monopoly being established by Mobutu. When the General Union of Congolese Students (UGEC) called for 'scientific socialism', and Mobutu responded by denouncing foreign ideologies, it marked the end of the brief honeymoon between Mobutu and the students. Student unrest was a major factor leading to nationalization of the universities and creation of the National University of Zaire (UNAZA). Subsequently, they played only a minor role. As Nzongola observes, the student movement produced some trenchant criticisms of Congolese government and society, but the conflict between their corporate interest and broader social interest left them unable to provide leadership for the mass democratic movement.[23]

Trade unions offered little resistance. Congolese trade unions supposedly represented both petty bourgeois (African white-collar employees) as well as proletarians (the African fraction of the proletariat). They were divided into Catholic and socialist federations, under Belgian influence. Mobutu merged the rival federations into a single movement, the National Union of Zairian Workers (UNTZa), which functioned as a wing of the MPR (single party). Kithima bin Ramazani, formerly a trade unionist, was co-opted as secretary general of the MPR. Not until 1990, when Mobutu's monolith was beginning to crumble, did the UNTZa reject the leader imposed by the MPR.

Over the years, more consistent opposition came from the Catholic

Church. The Protestants and the Kimbanguists, who had been granted formal equality with the majority Catholics, tended to align themselves with the regime.

Despite the contradiction between conservative bishops and more radical young priests and lay members of Catholic organizations, the Church went beyond criticism to offer an alternative vision of Congolese society. When the political system opened up in the 1990s, the student movement was nowhere to be seen. In contrast, Catholics became a major element in the constituency for change. This could be seen in particular in 1992, when thousands of Catholics and other Christians marched for a reopening of the Sovereign National Conference (CNS), closed by Mobutu. Security forces fired on the marchers and over thirty were killed.

The broadly-based but ultimately unsuccessful democracy movement of the early 1990s showed how greatly Congolese wanted change. The skilful manoeuvring of Mobutu and key allies such as Kengo, and the ineptitude of opposition leaders, notably Etienne Tshisekedi, both contributed to the failure.

In the meantime, Rwanda was beginning its own descent to the depths. Its second republic dated from 1973, when General Juvénal Habyarimana overthrew the first president, Kayibanda. The new president promised to reunite the Rwandans but soon reverted to scapegoating of the Tutsi minority. Habyarimana's vehicle for uniting and dominating Rwandans was a party-state modelled on that of Mobutu. The country remained very dependent on foreign aid, as Uvin has shown.[24] A decline in world prices for coffee and tea had a grave impact on Rwanda. About the same time, international pressure led an unwilling Habyarimana to adopt multi-party politics. From 1990 onwards, the regime faced a challenge from a Tutsi-dominated invasion force, the Rwandese Patriotic Front (RPF). In 1994, the combined impact of these economic, political and military pressures led to the genocide of nearly one million Tutsi and the seizure of power by the RPF.[25]

When Rwanda and Uganda recruited Laurent-Désiré Kabila as a front-man and invaded Congo in 1996, this was an unnecessary war in the eyes of many Congolese, since Mobutu was dying. According to an unrealistic plan, Kabila was supposed to be weak enough to obey his backers yet strong enough to secure their common borders. To survive as president, in the face of strong Congolese hostility to the Rwandans and Ugandans, Kabila broke with them and turned to people from his home province of Katanga.

The Rwanda-supported Congolese Democratic Rally (RCD) proved spectacularly unpopular. Throughout the RCD zone – North Kivu, South Kivu, Maniema, northern Katanga and so on – local resistance groups sprang up, often under the name 'Maï-Maï' (Mayi-Mayi). These used the same sort of magical protection (water that repelled bullets) as the rebels of 1964 with their 'Maï-Mulele'. Some Maï-Maï, for example those in Katanga, appear to have been bands of killers with no clear objective. In South Kivu and Maniema on the other hand, the Maï-Maï were thorns in the side of the occupiers and RDC, and enjoyed broad popular support despite their abuse of civilians. Their accomplishments earned them a place in the transitional government, along with the other belligerents.

Laurent Kabila inherited an economy in disastrous shape after years of corruption and mismanagement under Mobutu. Production and living standards were far lower than at independence, and half of all transactions, services and merchandise were in the informal sector.

The ouster of Mobutu created expectations of improvement but Kabila soon revealed himself to be a second Mobutu. As the UN Panel of Experts on the Illegal Exploitation of Natural Resources and Other Forms of Wealth of the Democratic Republic of Congo later put it, Kabila 'wielded a highly personalized control over state resources, avoiding any semblance of transparency and accountability. Management control over public enterprises was virtually non-existent and deals granting concessions were made indiscriminately in order to generate quickly needed revenues and to satisfy the most pressing political or financial exigencies. Familiar patterns of unaccountability, corruption and patronage re-emerged rapidly.'[26]

Early in the Kabila presidency, there were efforts to improve the economy. A Colloquium on National Development Priorities met, but came up with little more than a catalogue of good intentions. Foreign investors showed little enthusiasm for the triennial development programme, aiming to plan the total amount of investment needed – estimated by the Congolese government at \$3 billion, of which 40 per cent was to come from abroad. The meeting of Friends of the Congo held in Brussels in December 1997 to put in place a trust fund to receive foreign contributions led nowhere. The fund received few contributions and withdrawals were subject to strict conditions and controls, all of which left President Kabila bitter.

Kabila's most successful initiative was the monetary reform of 1998 in which the old and new Zaire currency was replaced by the Congolese franc, in order to reunify the country and reduce the use of the US dollar. This reform was partially successful, according to

Lanotte, in that prices and the franc–dollar exchange rate were stabilized to a degree. However, this reform was wiped out by the second war, which divided the country once again and led the government to demand sacrifice in the name of the war effort.

The mining sector, central to the Congolese economy since the early decades of the twentieth century, could have acted as the locomotive for economic recovery. Instead, it suffered from 'juridical insecurities and the approximations and postponements' of the government, according to Lanotte. The Congolese state was not a unified bloc in its dealings with companies, but rather a collection of factions and of clientelist networks.[27]

Gécamines was only a shadow of the Union Minière du Haut-Katanga, central element of the colonial economy. Its collapse dated back to 1990. In 1995, the government of Prime Minister Kengo had accepted a World Bank/IMF proposal to privatize the company. Several western companies invested in Gécamines at this point, and a number of small companies (especially Canadian) began joint ventures with Gécamines or signed agreements on exclusive prospecting zones.

The AFDL military campaign, started in 1996, drew the interest of foreign investors, especially 'mining speculators or Australian, Canadian, Ugandan or British "Juniors" trying their chances', according to Willame.[28] Braeckman claims that these relatively small players were acting as 'pilot fish' for the major mining companies. There is some evidence to support each position. The Union Minière, inheritor of the refining operations of colonial Congo, invested in American Mineral Fields' Congo operations. Anglo American, a major if ever there was one, formed a joint venture with American Mineral Fields (AMF) to exploit the cobalt-rich mine tailings at Kolwezi but the partnership soon soured.

What is clear is that AMF, American Diamond Buyers, Banro Resource Corporation and other investors bankrolled Kabila. The AFDL's Economic and Financial Commission demanded a non-reimbursable deposit corresponding to 15 per cent of the total investment envisaged. The war effort of Kabila and his backers was financed to a large extent by these deposits or 'war taxes' paid by AMF and the others. AMF even lent an aircraft to Kabila during the war.

It is also clear that once Kabila became self-proclaimed President of the Democratic Republic, the junior companies were 'benched' (Lanotte's term) because of their inexperience and especially their inability to come up with the very large sums needed to restart Congo's mining industry.[29]

The Kabila regime initially proclaimed its intention to stamp out corruption, and for some months an improvement was seen, but as a Lubumbashi resident explained: 'The chiefs are generally newcomers, but since they don't know the inner workings of the state, the "old timers" retain real power. And little by little corruption came back, slowly at first, to test the terrain, but afterwards more openly.'[30]

Not only the formal economy but also even the informal sector that had kept ordinary people afloat now collapsed. The result was an 'economy of luck', according to anthropologist René Devisch, in which people abandoned family structures and turned instead to churches and sects.[31] The disastrous economic situation, and the return of the corruption associated with Mobutu, was eating away at the popularity accorded to Kabila as liberator, when the second war gave him a new lease on life.

Partition and pillage

The first 'war of liberation' in 1996 ushered in a new wave of illegal exploitation of Congo's resources by foreigners, aided by Congolese. By 1997, a first wave of 'new businessmen' speaking only English, Kinyarwanda and Kiswahili had begun operations in eastern Congo. Theft of livestock, coffee beans and other resources was frequently reported.

The UN panel suggests that the first war was important also in giving the Rwandan and Ugandan military officers an idea of how easy it was to obtain riches in Congo. Several informants told the panel that Uganda's decision to take part in the second war, in August 1998, was defended by high-ranking officers who had had a taste of the business potential of Congo. Sources associated with the RCD spoke of the eagerness of Ugandan officers to occupy areas where gold and diamond mines were located. Both President Museveni and his brother, General Salim Saleh, were reportedly involved in discussions on setting up a firm to import merchandise into Congo and to export natural resources. General Salim and his nephew, a son of Museveni, apparently had visited eastern Congo a few months before the second war began.

Starting in 1998, aircraft began flying to Congo from the military airports at Entebbe (Uganda) and Kigali (Rwanda), transporting arms, military equipment, soldiers and merchandise, according to the panel. On the return trip they carried coffee, gold, diamond traders and business representatives, and occasionally soldiers.

Between September 1998 and August 1999 (still according to the UN panel) occupied zones of DRC were drained of minerals, agricultural and forest products, livestock and cash. Regardless of the looter, the pattern was the same: Burundian, Rwandan, Ugandan and/or RCD soldiers, commanded by an officer, visited farms, storage facilities, factories and banks, and demanded that the managers open the coffers or doors. Soldiers then removed the relevant wealth and loaded it into vehicles.

The panel cites the example of SOMINKI (Société minière et industriel du Kivu), which allegedly had seven years' worth of coltan in stock in various areas, along with sizeable quantities of cassiterite (tin ore). Between 2,000 and 3,000 tons of cassiterite and between 1,000 and 1,500 tons of coltan were removed from the region between November 1998 and April 1999. The RCD presented the panel with an 'official' document acknowledging it had removed 6 tons out of a total of 200 tons of cassiterite from SOMINKI, for a value of US$722,482. Much of the rest apparently was removed by Rwanda.

Meanwhile, in the northern zone occupied by Uganda, soldiers of General James Kazini reportedly made off with stockpiles of timber belonging to the logging companies Amex-Bois and La Forestière. In January 1999, in Equateur Province, Jean-Pierre Bemba and General Kazini launched an operation for the confiscation of coffee beans. Bemba allegedly initiated, encouraged and perpetuated such practices in Equateur. In a letter, he urged one of his commanders to release a large vehicle because it was urgently needed. It took two months to remove the enormous quantities of coffee. The Société congolaise de café, the largest owner of coffee stocks in the area, went bankrupt. In one instance, Bemba even seized 200 tons of coffee beans from SCIBE, a company owned by his father, Bemba Saolona. Similar looting reportedly occurred at banks throughout eastern Congo, both in the Rwandan and Ugandan zones.

The scale of the looting can be guessed at from official figures, which show a huge increase in the amount of gold exported from Uganda, and in the amount of coltan exported from Rwanda (see Table 2.1). The UN panel points out that the governments of Uganda and Rwanda could scarcely have been unaware of the pillage carried out by their forces, given its scale. However, it seems that there is an important difference between the two countries. Much of the pillage carried out by Ugandans seems to have benefited high-ranking officers, such as Generals Salim (brother of Museveni) and Kazini. In the case of Rwanda, there allegedly was a 'Congo office' close to the presidency, through which proceeds of pillage were processed. Some of this money was used to finance the war in Congo, which thus became self-financing.

The land

Stress on gold and copper, uranium and coltan, skews the discussion of Congo's riches and the struggle to control them. In some areas the struggle to control land has been equally important. Vlassenroot interprets the Congo wars in terms of linkage between local land disputes and 'the larger, regional struggle for economic control and politico-military power'.[32] A class of 'businessmen, politicians, traditional authorities and land owners' worked out strategies to increase their control over tracts of land.

King Leopold began building his colony by declaring all vacant land to be the property of the state. What that was supposed to mean is not clear: was land really vacant in a country where so many people practised shifting cultivation, or grazed their cattle over broad areas of grassland, or hunted across vast forests? At any rate, a large percentage of Congolese land was taken from the Congolese, then granted in concessions to development companies or to religious missions, or used by the colonial state for its own purposes, including huge national parks.

Conflicts over the rest of the land, supposedly left in Congolese hands, were exacerbated during the colonial period. The Belgians restructured 'traditional' political institutions and mechanisms of allocation of land. Local collectivities were the lowest level of the state administrative structures and many collectivities were ethnically defined. 'Chiefs' tended to build up their collectivities by allocating land both to locals (members of their group) and to 'strangers' as well. During decolonization and the first years of independence, clashes between locals and strangers were frequent, based in part on the question of control of land.

Under Mobutu, linkages between 'land access, ethnic citizenship and economic development' were further consolidated and instrumentalized. The so-called Bakajika Law made all land, including land held under 'custom', into state property. In reality, this did not eliminate the role of the chiefs. Instead, as Vlassenroot explains, it meant that new networks emerged, based on alliances of 'new rural capitalists', politicians, administrators and chiefs or their representatives.[33]

Class structure of contemporary Congo

The Congo of Joseph Kabila remains capitalist, but its class structure is different from the colonial structure described by Nzongola. In the place of the *metropolitan or imperialist bourgeoisie* of colonial days, there is a more diverse high bourgeoisie, located in South Africa, Europe, North America and elsewhere. Its dominance can be seen in the language adopted by the younger Kabila, compliant with the wishes of Belgium, the European Union, the United States and the Bretton Woods institutions. The hierarchy of the Catholic Church, once the ideological and social service arm of the tripartite colonial system, now constitutes an influential counter-elite.

The '*middle bourgeoisie*, made up of Belgian and other European settlers who owned their own means of production', has almost entirely disappeared, and, with it, many of the jobs for wage-workers in agriculture, commerce and manufacturing industry. Many Congolese politicians or people with political connections have become plantation owners, traders or (rarely) manufacturers. Vlassenroot's 'new rural capitalists' could be assigned also to the middle bourgeoisie. The middle bourgeoisie has been stunted by the wars and by the degradation of the transportation network, but can be expected to grow if a durable peace takes root. Foreigners, including Africans, Asians and Europeans, are well represented in the commercial sector of the middle bourgeoisie.

The *petty bourgeoisie*, once divided along racial lines, now is largely Congolese. Increased access to higher education has meant that most of the members of the liberal professions – doctors, lawyers, architects and the like – are Congolese. Many of these people are in exile. Small numbers of European and American missionaries remain, but the vast majority of clergy are Congolese. Middle-level company managers and white-collar employees are mostly Congolese as well, although total numbers are down due to the shrinking of the companies inherited from the colonial state. Both civilian and military rosters are greatly inflated; 'ghost workers' and 'ghost soldiers' have plagued the system since the Mobutu days. Most shopkeepers and artisans are Congolese, although a small number of Asians (Arab, Indo-Pakistani and others) are present as well.

The *traditional ruling class*, composed of kings, nobles, lords of the land, ancient warrior chiefs and religious authorities, has undergone substantial transformation. Nowadays, many 'chiefs' have completed secondary or even post-secondary education. Even during the colonial era, access to land was a main source of chiefly power. In the post-colonial era, it 'became one of the central elements of the political economy of the DRC', as Vlassenroot and Raeymaekers point out. Chiefs derive revenue from their ability to allocate and reallocate land, especially as the market penetrates rural economies.

The *peasantry*, 'that enormous mass of poor rural producers and food and cash crops to which the overwhelming majority of the African population belonged', still constitutes the majority of Congo's population. The situation of these people has become far more precarious, due to the decay of the transportation network and the continuing insecurity in many regions of the country.

The *working class* or modern proletariat continues and (as in colonial times) is composed of two distinct fractions, one European and one African. Skilled white workers are found in a few sectors, for example petroleum and construction. Black workers, skilled and unskilled, urban and industrial workers on the one hand, and rural and agricultural workers, on the other, continue to constitute an important category although growth has stagnated.

Finally, the *lumpenproletariat* or 'that group of proletarianized masses without stable wage employment, made up for the most part of school-leavers and rural migrants eking out a living through a variety of activities, legal and extra-legal, within the informal sector', has greatly increased. The various militias, especially in eastern Congo, recruit heavily from this category. The violence of these people, directed against peasants and especially women and girls, accounts for much of the mortality since 1996. Disarmament will be unsuccessful so long as it is not accompanied by effective reintegration, including education and jobs.

Conclusion: from Leopold II to Kabila II

Pillage is an area of apparent continuity, from the Congo Free State to the era of the Kabilas. However, it is not helpful to present the matter in that way, without making important distinctions. The pillage of Leopold's day was what Marxists call 'primitive accumulation', designed to make the colony pay for itself (including the construction of railroads) and also generate short-term profits. The mining of copper, diamonds and other riches under Belgian colonial rule also generated profits for shareholders in Belgium and elsewhere, but an important amount of the profit was ploughed back into the enterprise, modernizing the equipment, for example. The workers in the mines and refineries of Katanga and South Kasai were well paid compared to other Congolese. The schools, clinics and roads of the so-called model colony were financed from the state share of the proceeds of this mining.

Under Mobutu, however, reinvestment in mines and refineries nearly stopped. Much of Mobutu's share of the pillage of his own country went overseas, but some of it remained in the country in the form of luxurious buildings, white elephant industrial projects, and payments to presidential associates.[34]

In the post-Mobutu era, the shares given to Zimbabwe and Angola, in the mineral and petroleum sectors respectively, represent a trade-off in return for defence of Congolese territory and the Kabila regime. Resource extraction from eastern Congo, occupied by Uganda and Rwanda until recently, would seem to constitute 'pure' pillage. Table 2.1 and an equivalent table for Uganda cannot be explained away. Much as in Free State days, the Congo was financing the occupation of a portion of its own territory. Unlike Free State days, none of the proceeds of this pillage was being reinvested. In some cases it has fuelled ongoing fighting.

However, the plundering is not always conducted at gunpoint. A case in point is the abandoned mine at Shinkolobwe, Katanga, which produced the uranium for the atomic bombs dropped on Japan in 1945. When the Belgians left, they flooded the mine. Today, it functions again, after a fashion, having been revived in 1997. Each day, 6,000 miners enter, armed with shovels. They have dug a huge quarry, alongside the 'historic' mine. They worm their way into pits, from which they extract cobalt. Somewhere, perhaps at Shinkolobwe, perhaps elsewhere in Katanga, uranium is being extracted, and apparently sold on the international black market.[35]

Many Congolese are in the position of the poorly remunerated miners of Shinkolobwe. They are taking advantage of one of the few avenues to obtaining cash, in a country whose formal economy has collapsed. As so many Congolese have done since independence, they are obeying the fictional 'Article 15' of the South Kasai constitution, 'débrouillez-vous' (cope). Their resourcefulness constitutes one of the few bright spots in a country that seems always to have more potential than accomplishments.[36]

As the country moves away from total chaos, different kinds of economic operators are attracted to Congo. Some were tempted to jump the gun, and as a result have become embroiled in the aftermath of the second war. In October 2004, there was a small-scale uprising in the town of Kilwa, near Anvil Mining's Dikulishi mine, in eastern Katanga. Kilwa is crucial to Anvil's copper and silver mining operation, as it is a port on Lake Mweru from which the ore is shipped across to Zambia.

Anvil told the UN that its vehicles were used to bring in Congolese army troops from the town of Pweto and that it made available space on the planes it leases to fly in reinforcements from Lubumbashi (capital of Katanga). Anvil vehicles, some driven by Anvil employees, were used by soldiers. About 100 people, the majority of them innocent civilians, were killed during the operation. Some allegedly were summarily executed.[37]

The episode raises two questions. First, was Anvil's assistance given willingly or unwillingly and, second, 'whether Anvil fully and promptly disclosed what it knew about alleged human rights and security problems at Dikulushi in its reports to the Canadian and Australian stock exchanges and to the World Bank's Multilateral Investment Guarantee Agency (MIGA)'.[38]

The World Bank has come under criticism, not for ignoring the Anvil problem but for withholding a report concerning its assessment of Anvil's role. The insurrection took place just one month after MIGA had approved a guarantee for the Dikulushi project. Some people pointed out the contradiction between the World Bank's apparent indulgence of Anvil, and its suspension of the Chad pipeline loan guarantee.[39]

Phelps Dodge, one of the world's leading producers of copper and copper products, appears to be taking a long-term view of its activities in Congo. The company announced that despite regional violence and other challenges, it was determined to develop the largest, highest-grade undeveloped copper/cobalt project in the world at Tenke Fungurume (Katanga). It hopes to begin producing copper from this site in 2008.[40]

After the virtual destruction of the mining sector under Mobutu, Congo is being reintegrated into the world economy. So far, however, there are few signs that the proceeds will be spread around. Rather, international companies and local elites are pocketing revenues from copper and cobalt production instead of sharing it with local communities or spending it to reduce poverty.

The London-based Global Witness says that despite being one of the richest copper- and cobalt-producing areas in the world, Katanga remains severely poor and the population has little or no infrastructure or public services. 'The profits are serving to line the pockets of a small but powerful elite – politicians and businessmen who are exploiting the local population and subverting natural riches for their own private ends,' says the report, whose authors based their findings on field research in November and December 2005. Global Witness also reported that government officials are actively colluding with mining companies to skirt regulations and the payment of taxes.[41]

The report, 'Digging in Corruption', explains that a significant share of the copper and cobalt is mined informally and exported illicitly, representing a major revenue loss for the Congolese economy and a lost chance to reduce poverty. A local source quoted in the report estimated that, at the end of 2005, at least three-quarters of the minerals exported from Katanga were leaving illicitly. Since the

DRC's recorded copper and cobalt exports were estimated at $390 million last year, that means the illicit trade could amount to as much as $1.1 billion. And since most of the products mined by hand are exported in raw form, even when these exports are declared, the DRC is losing out on the higher prices it could obtain if it processed the minerals before export.

Patrick Alley, director of Global Witness, stressed the link between economics and politics in the current era: 'In the run-up to elections, politicians and companies have been scrambling to get their hands on ever-greater shares of the lucrative mineral trade, with little or no regard for the welfare of the Congolese population ... The plunder of the DRC's natural resources continues to undermine the country's opportunities for peace, stability and development.' As in 1960, control of Katanga will be crucial to post-election Congo. That being so, it is not surprising that money from the mining sector should be channelled into the election process, particularly by people associated with President Kabila.[42]

Congo and neighbouring Zambia are drawing increased interest as the world's appetite for minerals increases. Copper is sought after for use in power transmission and generation, building wiring, telecommunications, and electrical and electronic products. Cobalt is used in super-alloys to make parts for gas turbine aircraft engines and demand is continuing to soar as it is used for rechargeable batteries in globally popular mobile phones and devices.

The price of copper quadrupled between 2001 and 2006. This rapid rise was largely fuelled by the needs of rising industrial powers, especially India and China. World production of copper is expected to increase by 6 per cent and total use by 5 per cent in 2006, with the DRC–Zambia copperbelt playing a major role. The copperbelt contains 34 per cent of the world's cobalt and 10 per cent of the world's copper. Since 2004, there has been a massive influx of foreign companies pouring into Katanga on the DRC–Zambia border. Those companies and banks include the Canadian mining firm First Quantum Minerals Ltd, the Rand Merchant Bank in Johannesburg, and Adastra, a Canadian company with its head office in Britain.

Global Witness says operations have been marred by price fixing in contract negotiations in the capital Kinshasa, where politicians have quickly approved several large contracts with multinational companies, leaving only a small share for the state mining company, Gécamines. The Kamoto copper mine, the Dima-Kamoto Concentrator and the Luilu hydro-metallurgical plant are one example, with Kinross-Forrest inking a deal with Gécamines that gave the former a

75 per cent share and Gécamines 25 per cent. The main shareholders of Kinross-Forrest are George Forrest International in Britain and the Canadian company, Kinross Gold Corporation.

Global Witness also says the World Bank is involved in copper and cobalt mining in DRC and in promoting foreign investment despite classifying the country in one of its publications as the worst country in the world in which to do business. The International Finance Corporation (IFC), the World Bank's private investment arm, has provided financing for a feasibility study carried out by Adastra, which is hoping to establish a copper and cobalt project in Kolwezi. The IFC now has a 7.5 per cent stake in Adastra's project that was taken over by First Quantum, another Canadian mining company.

The report called on private companies to help reform the sector and declare all mineral exports, pay the appropriate taxes and ensure that the working conditions of the estimated 150,000 miners who supply them meet minimum health and safety standards – or refuse to buy products originating from those mines.

The average miner in Katanga earns about two or three dollars a day. Most work without protective clothing, equipment or training, and scores die every year in preventable accidents, the report says.

'We know that the Congo is rich. But despite this, we don't even have enough to eat. Only one category of people profits,' one miner told Global Witness.

THREE

'Congo must be sweet' – image and ideology in the Congo wars

If I had means, I would surely relocate to the Democratic Republic of Congo, where I would also get something to be proud about.

The first to confess the beauty of DRC was Lt. Gen. Yoweri Kaguta Museveni who said he had got two good sticks from Congo.

After a fierce fight with their brothers RPA [Rwandan Patriotic Army], the UPDF [Ugandan People's Defence Force] returned home with columns of beautiful Kabila daughters following them.

Other people are rumoured to have got precious stones which have fetched them dollars, while others cannot make up their minds on which number plates to put on their sleek cars, allegedly got from Congo. Seriously, someone help me. I want to go to Congo so that I can also get something to show my grand children in future.

(Letter to the Editor, *The Monitor*, Kampala)[1]

§ In the Ugandan's view, all the varied treasures of Congo – its timber, its precious stones and its sleek cars – are there for the taking. One might need to fight one's erstwhile allies the Rwandans, but the Congolese themselves have nothing to say about it. (The 'daughters' are an apparent exception, following their soldier husbands willingly.) Also striking is the openness with which the plundering of Congo is discussed in Uganda. In neighbouring Rwanda, the official line – there has been no pillage – is not contradicted so openly.

The Ugandan letter writer presents a contemporary, African version of the European cliché of Congo as a 'geological scandal'. In the mouth of a Belgian, the cliché expressed a naïve satisfaction that 'his' part of Africa was so well endowed, scandalously so, in relation to other parts of the continent. The Congolese adopted the phrase, so that Mobutu could proclaim that he was going to create an 'agricultural scandal' in Congo/Zaire. And indeed he did so, disorganizing the production and distribution of food and cash crops in this predominantly agricultural country.

The term 'geological scandal' was revived in the 1990s. Nzongola uses it to refer to the pillaging of Congo during the recent wars, as does Braeckman.

The expressions 'geographical scandal' and 'Congo must be sweet' reflect similar attitudes. In Dunn's terms, however, they correspond to two different moments in 'imagining the Congo'. The stakes in these struggles, including the recent wars, are not limited to obtaining resources. They also include definition of Congo's identity.[2]

Dunn's first moment is the creation of Congo, beginning with the arrival of the Portuguese on the shores of the Kongo kingdom in 1482, and culminating late in the nineteenth century when Leopold II organized 'his' colony.

The second moment is decolonization, when the Belgians reluctantly handed over what had become 'their Congo' to their former subjects. In so doing they created what became known as the 'Congo Crisis'. Unwilling to lose control through this ill-prepared transfer of power, they demonized the nationalist Patrice Lumumba.[3]

Dunn's third moment is Mobutu's reimagining of Congo as Zaire. Mobutu tried to invent a new country, giving the former Belgian colony the name of a neighbouring province in Portuguese Angola.

Cancer symbolizes Dunn's fourth moment, of state collapse and the replacement of Mobutu by Kabila. Mobutu's disease – prostate cancer – comes to stand for the cancer of the state: 'two hollow, diseased bodies in the final stages of life'. At that point, after three decades of Mobutu's rule, it seemed clear that he had failed to re-imagine Congo. A decade after Laurent Kabila renamed the country Congo, Mobutu's failure is not so evident. Some people tell me that they were proud to be Zairois. Being Congolese again is shameful.

The Ugandan letter writer's theme of Congo's wealth, there for the taking, runs right through the four moments distinguished by Dunn. The Portuguese tried but failed to locate gold mines in Kongo and had to content themselves with exporting manpower. Millions of Central Africans were sent to North and South America, over a period of four centuries. 'America' entered into the collective imagination of the Kongo community as the place where people went after they died.[4]

Leopold's Congo built on this earlier heritage. Congo became for Europeans 'the heart of darkness'. For Africans, the state became 'Bula Matari', the crusher of rocks.[5] The post-colonial state still refers to itself as Bula Matari, in radio broadcasts in national languages. Leopold had been drawn to Congo by stories of vast mineral wealth, but most of the wealth extracted from the colony during the period of the Free State came in the form of ivory and wild rubber, torn from the Congo forests. It was not until Congo became a Belgian colony

– 'King Leopold's Legacy' – that copper, cotton, coffee and other products of industry and agro-industry began to flow to Europe in large quantities.[6]

Colonial economic relations were supposed to continue after independence, while a number of 'moderate' Congolese participated in management of the former colony, alongside the Belgians. The fiery Lumumba came to symbolize a radical break with the colonizer, for which he was killed by the 'moderate' Congolese of mineral-rich Katanga, who were all too ready to play Belgium's neo-colonial game.[7]

Mobutu was quite willing to play the game of the West and especially the United States, in terms of Cold War politics. In terms of management of the Congolese economy, however, his policies were far from neo-colonial. First through the attempted nationalization of the mining sector, then through 'Zairianization' and 'radicalization of the revolution' and various prestige projects, he restructured the country's economy. The main winners were the president himself and his close associates; the losers were everybody else.[8]

Since the 1990s, the period of 'cancer' and 'state collapse', Congo's wealth has again attracted the interest of outsiders. Foreign invaders seek to make their efforts self-financing (much as Leopold did, a century earlier). Congolese warlords set themselves up as managers of one or more mineral deposits, and build business relationships with foreign armies and companies on that basis.

In this chapter, I shall borrow from Dunn's small but outstanding book. However, given the central role of Rwanda in the Congo wars, I shall compare Congo more systematically to Rwanda than he does. Several themes will be developed that Dunn neglects, beginning with race.

The fevers of race

Did Belgium export the fevers of race into its African colonies, as the journalist Colette Braeckman has written?[9] The idea is superficially appealing. The former Belgian Africa continues to be the theatre of genocidal violence. After generations of lower-intensity conflict, Belgium itself has been transformed into a loose federation of ethno-national states.

However appealing, this argument is unacceptable. The fever metaphor 'explains' by a little story: race fever passes from the Belgians, to whom it was serious but not fatal, to the Africans, who die victims of this imported pestilence. Several questions are unanswered. Did the Belgians consciously infect the Africans? Were some people 'resistant' to the imported diseases? Ultimately one must ask whether the disease metaphor is helpful or (as I think) does it conceal more complex and interesting linkages between Belgian colonialism and conflict in Central Africa?

In my view, the Belgians and other Europeans exported a salad of ideas to Central Africa, including Congo and its neighbours. Among these ideas, in addition to geological scandals and racial hierarchy, one finds older ideas concerning the Mountains of the Moon and the source of the Nile. Centuries of holy war between Christendom and Islam led to the ideas of conversion or reconversion of Africa to Christianity, and of the fight against the Arab slave trade. These were powerful motivations for certain Europeans, for example the anti-slavery struggle for Cardinal Lavigerie, the source of the Nile and the anti-slavery struggle for David Livingstone. Most Africans seem not to have absorbed these ideas, although nowadays there are hotels and restaurants called The Source of the Nile in Uganda, Rwanda and Burundi.

Missionary evangelization and education led to new ideas concerning power. Christianity in Great Lakes Africa may have been superficial (as some have argued in the aftermath of the Rwandan genocide), but the belief in schools as a way out of manual labour and into new forms of employment continues to be strong.

The Europeans exported a new concept of the state, with clear boundaries and equal subdivisions, and a particularly lethal subtype, the 'nation-state', where nation (cultural community) and state (political structure) coincide or should coincide. This concept of the state led to irredentism in eastern Congo.

The Europeans also exported several systems of representation of the state. These included national history. They exported maps, including some showing the boundaries of states and others showing the boundaries of ethnic domains. These imported ideas shaped the cognitions of local people, served to organize them and justified their choices. The extremely violent politics of recent years is best regarded as a consequence of all of these, and of the economic changes discussed in Chapter 2, rather than the direct result of one idea, even one as 'infectious' as race.

'Race' in the Great Lakes region

Classification of conquered peoples by 'race' and their supposed racial characteristics has long been a common practice. In exporting racialist ideas into Central Africa, Germany and Belgium were following a path traced two generations earlier by France in Algeria. Alexis de Tocqueville established an 'intimate connection between ethnological production and colonial conquest'.[10] He described Algeria's Arabs and Kabyles in stereotypical terms that were adopted by many French and some Algerians. Arabs were nomadic and fanatical. Rather than being completely savage, Islam represented a 'half-civilization' caught in a 'feudal' or 'aristocratic' past. France needed to bring 'Africa' into the historical path of 'the movement of the civilized world'.

Unlike the nomadic Arabs, Tocqueville's Berbers of Kabylia were anchored in their mountain refuges and held land through individualized tenure closely resembling European systems of private property. The French administration followed Tocqueville in seeking an ally 'to aid them in their colonial venture and to justify their civilizing mission'. The Kabyles were seen as 'puritan businessmen' whose political structure somehow brought them close to Liberty, Equality and Fraternity. Basically, the Kabyles were useful allies because Kabyles and Arabs were two 'races' divided by primordial hatred: 'The same primordial struggle between the French coloniser and the Arab, between Christian and Muslim civilisations, between the Mediterranean sedentary and the Saharan nomad, then, was mapped directly onto the Kabyle/Arab ethnic dichotomy.'[11] This tells us more about France than about Algeria.

Similar racialist ideas came to the Great Lakes through the activities and writings of a British explorer, John Hanning Speke. He was the first European to reach Lake Victoria in East Africa, which he correctly identified as a source of the Nile. In *The Discovery of the Source of the Nile* (1868) he wrote: 'It appears impossible to believe, judging from the physical appearance of the Wahuma (i.e. Hima), that they can be of any other race than the semi-Shem-Hamitic of Ethiopia.' Later he speculated that the Hima descended from the Galla (Oromo), the cattle-raising nomadic branch of the Abyssinians, and that both branches were 'ancient Christians'. The Tutsi were a branch of the Hima, he asserted. There it was, thirty years before a European set foot in Rwanda, a complete theory about the Ethiopian and Christian origins of the ruling group. The key elements were preconceived ('ancient Christians') or speculative, based on the alleged resemblance of Galla-Oromo and Hima-Tutsi.[12]

By the time the Germans arrived in Rwanda to take possession of this far corner of German East Africa, other books had been published that added another important ingredient to the salad of imported ideas. These included the writings of Tocqueville's student Gobineau (1854) as well as a radical formulation of Social Darwinism, *Der Rassenkampf* (*The Racial Struggle*, 1883), by the Austrian sociologist Ludwig Gumplowicz.[13] It is probable that the first

German-speaking visitors, Oscar Baumann, the Count von Götzen, Captain Bethe and Dr Richard Kandt, were familiar with the ideas of Gobineau, Speke and Gumplowicz on race.

Götzen, the first European to visit the Rwandan court, wrote of having seen a large population, divided into three categories. These were hundreds of thousands of Bantu Negroes, the Bahutu, in 'servile dependence' on the 'Watussi', a 'foreign caste'. The country was administered and exploited by these 'Watussi'. Finally, there was a 'tribe of dwarves', the Batwa. (One wonders what the count could have observed that led him to conclude that the Tutsi constituted a caste, or that they were foreigners.)[14] In 1898, Captain Bethe identified the three categories as 'races'.[15]

When Dr Kandt (later, German resident at the mwami's court) arrived at court in 1898, everything he saw seemed to confirm what he had read in Götzen: tall, high-ranking Tutsi, numerous Hutu who tried to swap provisions for gifts from the European but were driven off with sticks, etc. To the Hutu who complained about their situation, Kandt asked as a joke how they could accept domination by the Tutsi. The Hutu were one hundred times more numerous, yet they lamented like women.[16]

In these descriptions, one sees a double error, which would be endlessly repeated. First, the social situation in and around the court is taken to represent the situation throughout Rwanda. Second (like Tocqueville's Arab and Kabyle), each category is personified and assigned singular characteristics. There is no place in this model for Hutu chiefs or for so-called 'small Tutsi', that is, those without high rank or many cattle. The Germans describe the Twa of the court but ignore those of the forest.[17]

There is no reason to think that the Tutsi rulers of Rwanda be-lieved, at that point, that their ancestors came from Ethiopia. Perhaps they accepted this imported idea because it was isomorphic with their belief that their ancestors had 'fallen from heaven'.[18] Probably they came to see this argument as useful, in the new situation created by European colonialism. At any rate, the theory of racial superiority was internalized. Speaking to a French parliamentary hearing on the genocide, Chrétien cites *Servir* (To serve), the newsletter of the graduates of the Groupe scolaire d'Astrida (then Rwanda's only secondary school), which wrote in 1948:

Of Caucasian race as much as the Semites and the Indo-Europeans, the Hamitic peoples have nothing in common with the Negroes, as to their origins. The Caucasian physical type has remained clearly marked among the Batutsi ... Their great height – rarely less than 1m 80 – ... the fineness of their features impregnated with an intelligent expression, all this contributed to the deserved description given by the explorer: aristocratic Negroes.[19]

The problem with this as an explanation of the genocide of the Rwandan Tutsi (as Chrétien presumably realizes) is that most of the old boys of Astrida were Tutsi.

The myth of Tutsi superiority was propagated in the primary schools as well, but until the end of the colonial period only a small percentage of school-age children went to school. For most Rwandans, the main vehicle of racialist ideology was the colonial administrative system itself. Rwandans were made to carry identity cards mentioning ethnic group (*ubwoko*). The kingdom was divided into chiefdoms and sub-chiefdoms, most of them in the hands of Tutsi chiefs. As Prunier explains:

> The Tutsi 'superior race' may have been shorn of all power at the centre, but made up for this by monopolising local administration and contractual means of economic control (*ubuhake*) ... these forms of authority and exploitation, which were real and had physical substance, were legitimised through a traditionalisation process which purported to show that Tutsi dominance had always existed under such forms.[20]

'The racialisation of consciousness affected everybody,' Prunier writes. Even the 'small Tutsi' who did not benefit from the system 'started to believe that they were indeed a superior race and that under the same rags as their Hutu neighbours wore, a finer heart was beating'. The Hutu neighbours were exploited by the whites and by the Tutsi rulers, and 'were told by everyone that they were inferiors who deserved their fate and also came to believe it'. They came to hate all Tutsi, even the 'small' ones.[21] I believe that Prunier is correct in linking racialization and traditionalization, but I wonder how he knows what 'small Tutsi' were thinking.

The racialization of history on both sides of the Rwanda–Congo border has contributed to recent crises, and in turn has been reinforced by them. In Congo (as in Rwanda), schools taught that the first peoples in Central Africa were the so-called Pygmies or Twa. Later, Bantu-speakers came from the north or north-west (present Chad, Cameroon, Nigeria). Still later, 'Hamitic' or 'Nilotic' pastoralists came to the Great Lakes region and established kingdoms where they ruled over the Bantu majority.

Congolese learned that they were Bantu, i.e. speakers of a cluster of closely related languages, in a zone running from Cameroon to South Africa. This was extended into the past: Congo as a natural community of Bantu-speakers. To believe that, one must overlook the fact that most neighbours to the south and east also spoke Bantu languages, while many peoples of northern Congo did not.[22] More dangerously, the racialized ideology gave a new meaning to the term Bantu, which had begun as a category of languages rather than peoples. Authors began discussing Bantu philosophy[23] and eventually Bantu physical characteristics.[24] As Vansina remarks, this takes us back to 1933 and Germany's Nazis.[25]

Propagation of racist ideas in the Great Lakes, since the terminal colonial period, often takes the form of circulation of fake documents.[26] Lately, one of these has played a major role in mobilizing anti-Tutsi sentiment. It is a supposed plan for the establishment of a 'Tutsi–Hima Empire' in the Great Lakes region. To an outsider, this plan looks like a clone of the Protocols of the Elders of Zion, exposed as a fake many years ago. Of course, the Protocols are alive and well, and seem to explain to some people (Arabs especially) the supposed strength of the Zionists.

Looking for 'useful' natives

Throughout Africa, the Europeans searched for suitable subordinates among the 'natives', in order to rule their new dominions. In Algeria, a settler colony under direct rule, the Kabyles were unable to derive much benefit from their favoured status. In Rwanda, under indirect rule, the traditional elites were favoured, especially once they had undergone appropriate training.

In Congo, similar logic led the Belgians to search for appropriate subordinates, but the vast area and the many political and ethnic groups inhabiting it rendered the task more complex. The favourites of Stanley and other early state officials included the 'Bangala' of the middle section of the Congo river and the 'Batetela', both peoples considered to be fierce and courageous. Their alleged cannibalism was in no way seen as an obstacle to military recruitment.[27]

Recruitment to more skilled jobs was based on supposed 'openness to European ideas'. The case of the so-called 'Baluba' is revealing. The first Baluba to be considered open to European ideas were the people later known as Lulua. Under their leader Kalamba, they had won the favour of the German von Wissmann, and the town of Luluabourg was built in their area because of the favourable assessment. Later, the Belgians concluded that the Lulua were not in fact such good candidates for recruitment and the stereotype of the intelligent, open Baluba was transferred to the people now known as Luba-Kasai. They began to be labelled 'Jews of Africa' (like the Tutsi in Rwanda, or the Igbo in Nigeria). There is a strong element of self-fulfilling prophecy in all this, since not only state posts but also mission schools were built in places where the people were considered most suitable.[28]

After their involvement in an abortive revolt in 1945, the Luba lost favour, and the Belgians turned again to their rivals, the Lulua. During decolonization, the administration was at least neutral and perhaps actively involved in Lulua violence against Luba living on 'their land'. Many were killed, and hundreds of thousands fled to south-east Kasai, where they created the city of Mbuji-Mayi. The parallel to administrative encouragement of Hutu violence against Tutsi is evident.

Recently, the image of the Luba-Kasai was further racialized as the Luba came to be seen as 'white'.[29] Many Central Africans concluded that the 'black Europeans' or 'African Jews' of Congo and Rwanda were related.

Looking for Constantine or Clovis

In Algeria and in Tunisia, the ideological link to Christian and classical Africa was promoted especially by the Missionnaires d'Afrique or White Fathers (so-called because they had adopted Muslim dress in a vain attempt to gain acceptance in Muslim Africa). Monsignor Lavigerie, founder of the order, had been drawn into overseas work by the massacre of Maronite Christians in Lebanon. As Archbishop of Algiers, he won the support of Emperor Napoleon III and was able to establish villages for orphans despite the colonial government's disapproval of missionary work among Algerian Muslims.

Lavigerie founded the Société des Missionnaires d'Afrique in 1868 and devoted his life to converting Africa to Christianity. By 1878 he had sent missionaries into Uganda. In 1884 the pope named him primate of Africa and archbishop of the restored See of Carthage (near Tunis), with the hope of reviving the church of St Augustine.

First in Uganda, then in Rwanda and in Congo, the White Fathers searched for another Constantine or Clovis, who could lead his people to Christianity.[30] In Uganda, the White Fathers lost out in a three-way struggle with Protestants and Muslims for control of the Buganda monarchy, although they were quite successful at the mass level. Rwanda, where the Protestants were few, seemed more promising. However, they faced a resolutely 'pagan' Mwami and nobility. Many of their early recruits were Hutu. The solution was to pursue evangelization and teaching, and bide their time. In the 1920s, chiefs and other Tutsi began to convert to Catholicism. The Church was able to persuade the administration to send the mwami and the queen mother into internal exile. The Belgians installed Rudahigwa, a Catholic son of the former mwami, as the new king. The Church had won. In 1946, Rudahigwa consecrated his country to Christ the King, and Rwanda indeed became overwhelmingly Catholic.

In what became DR Congo and Angola, Christian evangelization began in Dunn's first moment, soon after Portuguese contact with the Kongo kingdom in 1482. The Portuguese also employed a 'Constantine' strategy, targeting the king and his family. An early success came when the army of the first Christian king, Affonso, reportedly was victorious over a 'pagan' contender due to the aid of Saint James.[31] By the early eighteenth century, Christianity had penetrated Kongo society to the point that a young woman Kimpa Vita, alias Dona Beatrice, proclaimed herself an incarnation of Saint Anthony and a prophet to the Kongo people.[32] Subsequent Kongo prophetic movements, notably the Church of Jesus Christ on Earth by the Prophet Simon Kimbangu (Kimbanguist Church), owe a great deal to this tradition of Kongo syncretism.

In the second half of the nineteenth century, both Protestants and Catholics began renewed evangelization campaigns, in the context of campaigns against the Arab slave trade followed by the partition of Africa. David Livingstone visited the Congo river town of Nyangwe (Maniema) in 1871. His report on a massacre of Congolese by 'Arabs' had a great influence on western opinion, justifying Leopold's subsequent conquest.

By the beginning of the twentieth century, the whole of the vast colony was divided into a double grid of missionary territories, one for the Catholics and the other for the Protestants. The Catholic Church was a partner with the administration and the big companies in what some have called, irreverently, the 'colonial trinity'. The Protestants worked at a disadvantage, receiving no state subsidies for their schools until after the Second World War.

TABLE 3.1 Religious belief in Congo (%)

Roman Catholic	50
Protestant	20
Kimbanguist	10
Muslim	10
Other syncretic sects and indigenous beliefs	10

The Kimbanguist Church was only one of many independent churches, representing Congolese efforts to break the white man's monopoly. Its success is reflected in recent estimates of the country's religious breakdown (see Table 3.1).[33]

Reorganizing the state

In Congo, as in Rwanda, the Europeans imposed a model of the state based on their own recent experience. The distinction between pre-colonial and 'artificial' states, a commonplace of African political science, is misleading in that all of these states were remodelled if not created from scratch.

In Rwanda, the Europeans found a state with a core under tight control of the monarchy and a periphery where central control was episodic. This is clear from Kandt's account of his travel after the visit to the mwami. Several days' march to the north (perhaps 60km) everything changes: 'no more giant warriors, no more cohorts of people bringing offerings, no more chiefs with whom to argue'. Plundering hordes of locals have to be driven off by rifle-fire. Whereas at the court, pastures predominated, here pastures and cultivated fields followed one another. In this new landscape, Kandt spots a few Tutsi 'chiefs' who behave more cordially than their counterparts in Nduga (near the capital) and warn that this or that hill is inhabited by thieves.

Still further north, there are almost no Tutsi to be seen. Hutu attack Kandt's column continuously. One day, an elderly Tutsi tells Kandt to watch out for the locals 'who are in principle under the domination of the king, but they are eternally rebellious and recalcitrant', especially since the recent death of the Mwami Rwabugiri.[34]

In other words, the monarch's political control was real on a daily basis in Nduga, near the centre. Elsewhere it was rather theoretical and episodic, such as when an army was in the immediate area. Yet as Vidal points out, the model of the strongly centralized kingdom of Rwabugiri, especially as manifested in Nduga, was adopted by the Europeans, first the administrators and then the anthropologists. It is still strongly held by many Rwandan academics.[35]

In Rwanda, first the Germans and then the Belgians opted for indirect rule, using the Tutsi monarchy for their own purposes, but reshaping it as needed. When Belgian administrators arrived in 1916, they requested the help of the Catholic missionaries. Father Léon Classe presented them with a document entitled, 'L'organisation politique du Ruanda au début de l'occupation belge'. This served as a guide to the administrators as they took charge of Belgium's new possession.[36]

Classe's major theme was that Rwanda's political regime 'can be assimilated rather exactly to the feudal regime of the Middle Ages' in Europe. Theoretically, all power was concentrated in the hands of King Musinga, but in reality the Queen Mother and her brothers monopolized it. The king's maternal uncles were the great chiefs of the peripheral provinces. In Nduga, centre of the kingdom, power was fragmented because each major chief wanted at least a small domain close to the sovereign.

Such a regime was too personalistic and patrimonial for Belgian needs. The multiple networks of chiefs – chief of the land, chief of the cattle and chief of the army – had permitted the mwami to manipulate the system to suit his purposes. For the Belgians, this was counter-productive.

The administrative reform carried out in the late 1920s and early 1930s (after the Belgians had helped the mwami to impose full control over the Hutu chiefdoms of the south-west and north-west) gave Rwanda a French-style prefectoral system, with each chiefdom and most sub-chiefdoms in the hands of Tutsi representatives of the mwami.

History and ideology in Rwanda

A central element of Rwandan ideology, to this day, is the colonial synthesis of pre-colonial history. White Fathers Albert Pagès and Louis de Lacger, Rwandan priest Alexis Kagame, and Belgian anthropologist Jacques Maquet made key contributions.

Father Pagès legitimated the concept of Rwanda as 'Hamitic kingdom'. Echoing Speke, he saw the Tutsi as carriers of a Monophysite Christian tradition.[37] Canon de Lacger confirmed the identification of the Tutsi ruling group as foreigners and 'Hamites', describing Rwanda as occupying the northern half of the 'Abyssinia of the Great Lakes'. He took his native France as an example of the 'natural' development of a state. Although Rwanda did not have an 'inevitable' shape – such as the French hexagon – the growth process formed a 'rising curve, continuous and regular'.[38]

The Abbé Kagame identified a 'code' of monarchical institutions, crystallizing a static vision of pre-colonial institutions.[39] As regards chronology, Kagame was a 'trick cyclist',[40] manipulating the average length of reigns and cycles of royal names to push the founding of the kingdom far into the past. During the 1930s, when Belgium was supervising the transfer of large numbers of Rwandans to the present North Kivu province of the Democratic Republic of Congo, Kagame moved nineteenth-century Rwandan incursions into the sixteenth century. This provided ideological justification for population movements of the time, and later would justify post-independence irredentism.[41]

Late in the colonial era, Maquet produced a functionalist interpretation of the Rwandan social system, in which all the elements interacted harmoniously, in the ethnographic present. Pre-colonial Rwanda 'enjoyed harmony, so the story went, because its chief social institution – ubuhake cattle clientship – had facilitated social mobility across fluid occupational categories'.[42]

This vision of pre-colonial harmony was the fruit of research collaboration between Maquet and the Abbé Kagame so one should not be surprised that Maquet confirms Kagame's static view. Maquet's interpretation, oriented towards the Tutsi aristocracy, was derived from aristocrats. He had declined to work with Hutu informants because 'the more competent people on political organisation were the Tutsi' and his 'aim was not to assess the opinions and knowledge of the Rwandan population on their past political organisation but to discover as accurately as possible what that organisation was'.[43]

Maquet's use of the ethnographic present seems to have blinded him to changes in Rwandan society, including the centralization carried out under Mwami Rwabugiri in the nineteenth century. Pottier points out that while the categories Tutsi, Hutu and Twa had existed earlier, 'Rwabugiri's administration not only rigidified social distinctions in ethnic terms, but also engendered a process of ethnic self-consciousness among groups of Tutsi in Nduga, central Rwanda'.[44]

Thus, the Europeans did not so much divide the Rwandans as add ideological themes (race, migration) to a well-defined system of stratification. They simplified Rwandan stratification by eliminating Hutu chiefs, and crystallized it by distributing identity cards bearing the label 'Tutsi', 'Hutu' or 'Twa'. Opportunities for post-primary education were largely restricted to Tutsi males. Hutu attended Catholic seminaries, then found they were unable to compete for jobs in the colonial state, virtually the only major employer in Rwanda.

Since the 1950s, Rwandans have put forth diametrically opposed versions of Rwandan history and society, both rooted in colonial simplifications. Hutu intellectuals adopted the racialist version, according to which the Twa (Pygmies) were the original inhabitants, followed by Bantu (ancestors of the Hutu), and then (much more recently) by Hamites or Nilotes (ancestors of the Tutsi). Tutsi intellectuals have followed Maquet's vision of pre-colonial harmony, destroyed by the colonizers.

Maps are territories[45]

In 1998, in a press conference at Kigali's Meridian Hotel, Rwandan president Pasteur Bizimungu unfolded a map that showed pre-colonial Rwanda's boundaries. In particular, large portions of Congo's North Kivu province were shown as former Rwandan territory. In the context, when Rwanda had just launched its second major invasion of its larger neighbour, this seemed a clear claim to revise the boundary inherited from colonial rule. The map was reproduced from the Abbé Kagame's *Abrégé de l'ethno-histoire du Rwanda* (1972). It showed as parts of pre-colonial Rwanda not only the undoubtedly Kinyarwanda-speaking areas of Bwisha (in Congo) and Bufumbira (in Uganda) but vast spaces the Rwandan armies had supposedly conquered in the centuries when Rwanda in fact was centred far to the east, if indeed Rwanda existed at all.[46]

A few decades earlier another African president, Mobutu Sese Seko, unfolded a map. On this map, apparently a reproduction of a Portuguese map from the sixteenth century, Congo bore the label 'Zaire'. This was Mobutu's response to those critics who queried his changing the country's name from Congo to Zaire. The latter name somehow was authentic, much as Mobutu Sese Seko was authentic while Joseph-Désiré Mobutu was not. Mobutu ignored the fact that 'Zaire' was only a Portuguese mishearing of the Kikongo word *nzadi* (river). One imagines the scene. A Portuguese asks, using gestures, 'What is that called?' A Kongo answers, 'The river'.

To find the name 'Zaire' Mobutu did not have to delve into the fifteenth or sixteenth century. The Portuguese and Belgians had done that for him. To this day, the Portuguese name 'Zaire' designates the Kongo-speaking province of northern Angola, adjacent to DRC's Bas-Congo. As for the Belgians, rather than restarting their academic journal *Congo*, publication of which had been interrupted by the Second World War, they started a new one called *Zaïre*. So, the name Zaire, far from being authentic, was thoroughly colonial.

Maps are a powerful form of representation. Indeed, their ubiquity in post-colonial African discourse suggests that they are understood as a form of white man's magic. Maps are tools, not just to tell how to get from here to there, but to 'prove' that something or other is true, on the ground.

Much of the story of this book could be told through maps and accompanying text. One could begin with a map of the Catholic Church in Africa, as it might have hung on the wall in the office of the pope or of Monsignor Lavigerie. The 'Zaire' map of Mobutu, if I could locate it, would be important.

Once the explorers began criss-crossing Africa in the nineteenth century, there would be plenty of candidates for maps to be included. Stanley took many measurements on his trips, and each of his self-promoting books contains a map too. Some of these were extremely inaccurate. Nzongola tells a nice story about the Berlin Conference:

> The Congo case illustrates both the lack of effective occupation at the time of partition and the arbitrariness of territorial boundaries. Stanley's expedition, on which King Leopold's claims were based, had covered the territory along the Congo River from Boma to Kisangani. But when the two men sat down to draw up the original map of the Congo on 7 August 1884 at Ostend, it covered a vast territory in Central Africa, stretching 'from the coast to Lake Tanganyika from four degrees north of the Equator to six degrees south'. This is the map that Germany had reluctantly accepted in its bilateral treaty with the AIC [Association International du Congo, predecessor to and screen for the Congo Free State] on 8 November 1884. Anticipating French objections to the inclusion in this map of the Kouilou-Niari or Pointe Noire region, Leopold went into his study on Christmas Eve, 1884, to ponder over changes in the design. By the stroke of a pencil he modified the map, giving up the said territory in the southwest and adding in compensation new lands in the southeast. He extended the map beyond six degrees south of the Equator and annexed the Katanga region. Although the adjustments made ultimately resulted in the loss of areas whose rich oil reserves were not yet known, such as Pointe Noire and the Cabinda enclave, they represented a masterful stroke with respect to Katanga, which was to prove extremely rich in minerals, particularly in its 'pedicle'.[47]

As Nzongola explains, these boundaries were accepted by other powers, the British approval resulting from a bureaucratic blunder.[48] The present Rwanda and Burundi were both included in the 'Conventional Basis of the Congo' (approved at Berlin) within which free trade would be guaranteed.[49]

Another shaky Stanley map played a major role in determining the boundaries between Uganda, Congo and Rwanda. He thought he had seen and claimed a mountain called Mfumbira, and on that basis the British insisted on including Kinyarwanda-speaking Bufumbira in their new colony of Uganda.

Once Africa had been divided among the outsiders, the question of international boundaries largely disappeared, except for during wartime and the period leading up to wars. The British, who seem to specialize in giving away other people's property, reportedly were willing to appease Hitler by giving him control of Belgian Congo, in order to satisfy Germany's demand for restoration of its colonies.[50] Ceding Congo certainly would have been less costly to Britain than restoring German East Africa (Tanganyika, Rwanda, Burundi), Southwest Africa (the present Namibia), Cameroon, and Togo to German control.

The 'science' of ethnographic maps

The human sciences – ethnography and linguistics in particular – were used in Belgian Congo as tools of administration. The Belgians needed to know the people whom they were attempting to administer. Two related operations had to be carried out: (i) to classify the various peoples under colonial domination, and (ii) to describe these peoples and especially their political institutions. To recognize a 'chief' (supposed native ruler and in any case the authorized intermediary between the European administrations and the population), an inquiry (*enquête*) had to be carried out and written up. The *rapport d'enquête* had to be accompanied by a map showing the area inhabited by the people in question and ruled by their chief. Since there were more than 200 'tribes' or peoples inhabiting the Belgian Congo, and each of these had a number of recognized subdivisions, the administration was obliged to draft literally thousands of *rapports d'enquête*.

To deal with a problem in a particular circumscription, an administrator needed to consult the particular report. For other purposes, however, the administration needed synthesized versions of this mass of material. These were produced by the ethnographers of the time, missionaries or administrators, and often published by the Royal Academy of Colonial Sciences back in Brussels. Such syntheses include Verhulpen's *Baluba et Balubaïsés du Katanga*, Moeller's *Les Grandes lignes des migrations des Bantous de la province orientale du Congo Belge*, and *L'Ethnie mongo* of van der Kerken. (Between them, these works covered most of central and eastern Congo, since the Province orientale of Moeller's synthesis included Kivu-Maniema.)[51]

The three vast syntheses are based on two dominant tropes, namely migration and cultural change (being 'ized'). The assumptions are that (i) many people came from far away (like the Tutsi who supposedly came from Ethiopia), and (ii) that many people have lost their 'real' culture (again like the Tutsi, who supposedly lost their Cushitic language and adopted the Bantu tongue of the Hutu).

Each of the three books was accompanied by a map, which proved to be influential in its own right. For example, when Benoît Verhaegen was looking for historical background for his admirable study of the 'rebellion' of 1964 in Maniema, he republished Moeller's map of migrations. In so doing, he gave new life to a colonial mishmash that should have been allowed to rest in peace. Hundreds of students, who have never seen the Moeller book, reproduce or cite in their thesis the map that they have found in Verhaegen's book.[52]

Even more influential than the works of Verhulpen, Moeller and van der Kerken is a series of 'ethnographic maps' (in reality, a map accompanied by a lengthy book, with material on each of the groups covered) compiled and edited by Olga Boone of the Royal Museum of Central Africa, at Tervuren, near Brussels.[53] In the 1961 volume, Boone distinguished no fewer than fifty-five groups in Katanga alone, 'presented as durable if not permanent realities ... ' Her categories 'coincide perfectly' with the preoccupations and the administrative practices of the colonial state, as M'Bokolo points out.[54] That is, Boone took as her framework for the groups she distinguished, the *chefferies* and *secteurs* (fusion of several small *chefferies*) as they existed in 1948–49. This helps to explain the 'conceptual uncertainties' of the Congolese groupings she discusses: *la peuplade* (small people) and sometimes *la grande peuplade* (large small people?), *la tribu* (tribe) and sometimes *la petite tribu* (small tribe) or *sous-tribu* (sub-tribe), and finally *l'ethnie* (ethnic group). The criteria apparently were both objective (size, organization) and subjective (cohesion, historic consciousness). Despite the 'lack of seriousness' (M'Bokolo's expression) of these classifications, they have enjoyed 'a remarkably lively posterity' in independent Congo/Zaire, and 'are taken up, as such, propped up, and given a sort of seal of authenticity by numerous local intellectuals, whether they be simple ideologues, amateur historians, or part-time ethnologists'.[55]

Given the origins of such works in colonial administration, it is perhaps surprising to find that they are still being published. A recent contribution to the genre is Father de Saint Moulin's 'Conscience nationale et identités ethniques. Contribution à une culture de paix'.[56] Despite the optimistic subtitle, the article and the accompanying maps seem more likely to inflame relations among neighbours than to calm them. Map 6 presents 'Kivu-Maniema'. Some of the ethnic blocs displayed are very large (Lega, for example) but Saint Moulin manages also to show tiny territories inhabited by the Wagenia at Kisangani and Kasongo. Yet the Rwandophone (Kinyarwanda-speaking) Banyamulenge of South Kivu are omitted. This may be due to their administrative status at the time. They were divided between three zones (territories), Uvira, Fizi and Mwenga. In these zones, they formed minorities, facing majorities of Fulero/Vira, Bembe and Lega respectively. Saint Moulin refers briefly to Rwandophones having arrived 'at various moments' and living among the Fulero among other peoples.

In North Kivu, Saint Moulin's map shows only one bloc of territory inhabited by Rwandophones, discreetly identified as Banya Bwisha. In the text, he explains that this unit was recognized in 1920 as an autonomous *chefferie* (chiefdom) under the Mwami Ndezi, who reigned until his death in 1980. There is no indication that Banyarwanda had inhabited Bwisha prior to colonial rule. Saint Moulin goes on to discuss the colonial policy of labour recruitment, under which many thousands of Rwandans were brought to Masisi territory. He mentions that they live among the Hunde, without observing that they outnumber Hunde in the homeland of the latter.

The Banyamulenge language is not indicated on linguistic maps. Consulting such maps, or texts such as that of Saint Moulin, other Congolese argue that the Banyamulenge are not a Congolese ethnic group, and that they do not speak a Congolese language. This circular argument fails to take into account the peculiar conventions of ethnographic and linguistic maps, which indicate the supposed homelands of indigenous peoples and languages, in the ethnographic present. Towns and immigrants are excluded, as are second languages.

The Congolese, trying to take their destiny in their own hands, have attempted to find a 'scientific' basis for politics and administration. To answer such questions as which languages are Congolese languages, or what 'tribes' (ethnic communities) have a right to Congolese citizenship, they have turned to the syntheses produced by the Belgians, either during or after the colonial era. These maps and syntheses – by Moeller, Verhulpen, Boone, de Saint Moulin and others – are the equivalents for the Congo of the Rwandan histories produced by de Lacger, Kagame and Maquet. Like those histories, they are not 'science', standing outside politics; instead, they are fatally flawed by their colonial, political origins.

Ideologies of resistance to colonial rule

Movements devoted to the ideological goal of self-rule in Congo passed through five 'partially overlapping stages' according to Young.[57] These reflected both the processes of material change sketched in Chapter 2, and a series of syntheses of imported and indigenous ideas.

Primary resistance – 'armed opposition to the establishment of colonial occupation and usually led by traditional rulers' – was widespread. It was most frequent when the Free State 'met well-structured traditional states in areas remote from the colonizer's initial operating bases'. Examples include the Zande, Yaka, Shi and Luba of Kasongo Nyembo.[58]

The uprisings of the Boa (Babua) and the Mbuja (Budja), both segmentary systems of the forest, typify a second type of primary resistance. Both peoples 'felt the impact of harshly enforced rubber and ivory deliveries of the "red rubber" era. These were peasant uprisings of a sort, a reaction of the entire society to the severities of the Free State.' But most of the small communities of the forest zone found their best defence was to retreat further into the forest.[59]

The 'Batetela mutinies' constitute a 'third and particularly interesting variant of the primary resistance theme', according to Young. This example highlights a problem with the concepts of 'conquest' and 'resistance'. The Free State fought the Afro-Arabs for control of Maniema with the help of Ngongo Leteta, and then fought against the so-called Batetela mutineers, that is, former men of Ngongo, of various ethnic backgrounds. Auxiliaries recruited from among the men of Ngongo, including ex-mutineers, carried out much of the conquest of Sankuru on behalf of the Free State.[60]

As the Belgian period began (1908 on paper, around 1912 in practice), many Congolese peoples were still resisting colonial rule. In northern Kasai, the Ndengese took part in a large-scale revolt in the 1930s, as did the Nande in northern Kivu.

Most armed risings seem to have been preceded by adoption of a 'medicine' believed to provide immunity. For example, a medicine called Lowambo appeared among the Ndengese in 1917 or 1918. It was believed to protect against witchcraft and to have 'the power to create darkness before the eyes of any European who penetrated into the country beyond the spot where it had been placed, and also to render their guns powerless'. Members of an organization called Inkunia passed this medicine from village to village. At the same time, an influenza epidemic caused many deaths. It was said that the Europeans had propagated this disease by means of currency and identity cards. To oppose the disease Africans would have to join Inkunia and obey its rules, including an oath not to pay taxes, to burn identity cards, and to refuse European currency. In December 1919, an insurrection broke out among the Ndengese and spread to the other peoples who had adopted Lowambo. The chief of the western Kulumbi of Lodja showed his disdain for the state by hanging his chief's medal around the neck of a goat. The Lowambo revolt was not suppressed until 1921.[61]

Although its own reports cited political and economic grievances, the colonial administration drew the conclusion from revolts such as those of 1920–21 and 1931 in Kasai, and from the unrest associated with the Kongo prophet Simon Kimbangu, that revolts were made possible by the medicine or charm employed, and that the medicine or charm was spread by a 'sect'. Revolts could be prevented by stamping out medicines and sects as well as by improving communications and ties to the market economy.

Messianic movements such as Kimbanguism are better understood as a second stage in the evolution of anti-colonial nationalism, characterized by a 'synthesis of ideas and symbols assimilated from the colonizer and traditional religious elements'. In Young's view, these occurred 'when no secular remedy to the frustrations engendered by the colonial situation seemed available. The disequilibria introduced in traditional communities by colonial contact found temporary remedy through the millennial dream.'

The most important Congolese messianic movements were Kimbanguism in the west and Kitawala in the east. The Kimbanguist movement began in 1921 when 'Simon Kimbangu, a Kongo villager, began to heal the sick and to raise the dead', according to the beliefs of most Kongo, whether Kimbanguist or not. He was 'hailed as a prophet, a man chosen by God to bring to Africans, and especially to the BaKongo, the kind of salvation that the Catholic and Protestant missionaries had preached but as it seemed, had failed to provide'. Protestant missionaries were inclined at first to be sympathetic to the new movement, according to MacGaffey, 'but Catholic missionaries and the industrial employers whose labourers had downed tools to go to Nkamba prodded the government to take action against it on the ground that it was "xenophobic," that is, anti-colonial and a threat to the peace'.[62] Nzongola argues that Kimbangu indeed had been influenced by followers of Marcus Garvey, as the administration charged at the time.[63]

Kimbangu died behind bars in Lubumbashi in 1951. Kimbanguists were sent into internal exile, on the assumption that they could do no harm in areas where they did not speak the language. Some exiled Kimbanguists died at Kole (Kasai) for example, but not before passing on their ideas to some of the local people.

The other major millenarian sect, Kitawala, was an Africanized offshoot of the Jehovah's Witnesses. In the Belgian Congo, where Kitawala was rigorously suppressed, it became far more radical. Among the Komo (Bakumu) of Kivu and Orientale provinces, Kitawala was 'at the root' of a major revolt in 1944. The message of Kitawala gave the Komo 'a means of expressing in a radical and modern manner the pent-up frustrations of the colonial experience'. Kitawala preachers replaced Komo circumcisers who had been banned by the Belgians. The movement strengthened Komo unity. Although the unity was ethnic, Kitawala and other messianic movements may have 'created a pre-disposition toward subsequent diffusion of explicitly nationalist ideas'.[64]

Stages three and four of Young's typology – urban riots and pre-political modern associations – could not develop until large cities had emerged, after 1940. His 'third phase in the evolution of a nationalist response' was marked by a series of large-scale urban disorders. These did not reject modernization but were 'attributable to frustration and hostility toward the colonial situation of the town wage-earners'.

They were leaderless, mass movements, whose participants had partially entered the modern sector. There were no explicit objectives. They were ephemeral outbursts rather than sustained revolts. The two main examples grew out of demonstrations by African workers (Elisabethville 1941, Matadi 1945). Young squeezes into this category 'a somewhat different manifestation of this phenomenon', the Force Publique mutiny of 1944. He does so because (i) the 'experience and frustrations [of the troops] were not unlike those of the newly urbanized unskilled worker'; and (ii) because the mutiny was followed by 'a night of rioting and looting in the city, in which a part of the population participated'. The mutiny in fact was part of a much larger scheme that failed to materialize, due both to the gap between *évolués* and less educated Congolese, and that between Luba and Congolese of other ethnic backgrounds.[65]

These events of the 1940s were 'all overshadowed by the massive Leopoldville riots of January 4–6, 1959', Young writes. The riots broke out when a scheduled rally of the Kongo party ABAKO had to be postponed because administrative authorization was refused.

For a brief period, the explosion mobilized virtually the entire African population of the city. Police and troops could only seal off the European residential quarters; for one night all control over the African quarters was relinquished to a leaderless mob, which vented its fury on Portuguese shops within its zone, and such visible symbols of the colonial system as the social centres and Catholic missions.[66]

Hundreds of Africans were killed.

The first three stages, from primary resistance to urban riot, 'had in common an essentially mass character and a diffuseness of goals. All

69

were clearly movements in reaction to the colonial situation,' Young writes. In contrast, the 'pre-political modern associations' reflect the class that comprised them, the so-called *évolués*. By the post-war years, there had emerged a substantial Congolese elite. The Belgians classified most members of the African elite as *évolués*, that is, people who had 'evolved' upwards from African cultural standards. This class would lead the anti-colonial nationalist movement when it emerged. Until the late 1950s no political parties were permitted to exist but the 'pre-political modern associations' contributed to the emergence of political parties. A few of them made the transition from association to party – the Kongo ethnic association ABAKO is an example – but even where the linkage was less direct, such associations provided leadership personnel to the parties which followed.

African associations included trade unions, *cercles des évolués*, alumni associations and tribal associations. They were pre-political in that they defended the interests of the *évolués* rather than calling for a change in the political relationship between Congo and Belgium. However, as the *évolués* became frustrated with their efforts to improve their individual status and as news trickled in of African progress toward emancipation elsewhere in the continent, the *évolués* turned to anti-colonialism. This process began in the cities although, as Weiss suggests, the radicalism of the movement derives from the linkage of city-based activity to the grievances of the countryside.[67]

Young's five-stage account of the development of Congolese nationalism is confirmed by the 'history' painted by Tshibumba. The painter's account of Congo history begins with the arrival of the Portuguese navigator Diogo Cão, portrayed side by side with the King of Kongo. Lest anyone miss the connection, Tshibumba portrays the Portuguese in colonial uniform, complete with pith helmet.[68]

Another painting represents the slave trade. Blacks are shown beating their captives. Here again the artist links one period to another, as the whip or lash will figure prominently in representations of European colonial rule.

Young's primary resistance period is seen in King Msiri of Garenganze (in the present Katanga) killing the representative of the Free State, Bodson, followed by Free State soldiers carrying the severed head of Msiri. The 'Batetela revolt' is shown taking place at the state post of Lodja, apparently because Lodja is the 'Batetela place' par excellence. (This anachronism probably is unintentional. Tshibumba may not have known that Lodja had not been founded at the time of the revolt.)

Tshibumba shows Kimbangu preaching and being arrested. Young's urban violence stage is represented by the strike of Union Minière workers and the Kinshasa uprising of 1959.

For stage five, parties and elections, there is a series of paintings in which Tshibumba recounts the victory and the downfall of his hero, Patrice Lumumba. He shows Lumumba's speech on Independence Day in the presence of King Baudouin, conflict with President Kasavubu, his arrest, and his murder in Katanga. Lumumba, for Tshibumba as for many Congolese, was a Christ figure who died for Congo.

Many of the events and representations in Tshibumba's history reflect a school-curriculum version, as Young has pointed out. Yet some paintings reflect a parallel version of history that exists in popular consciousness. A clear example is 'Simba Bulaya' (Lions of Europe), described by the artist as follows:

> This is how it worked. If you, a black person, left your property at night because you wanted to go to the toilet, you might meet two or three of them. Among them were our brothers whom they had hired; black people were in it, they began to work for the whites. One white man would be in command, and once he got there they grabbed the person. They took his clothes, his papers, all he had on him, and left them right there. Then they carried him away and killed him.[69]

Tshibumba inserted into his history series, as presented to Fabian, the famous painting 'Colonie Belge', not an event but a symbolic condensation of the entire colonial period. Flogging is seen as the essence of Belgian rule, all claims of the 'civilizing mission' to the contrary. This painting epitomizes the parallel version of history in popular consciousness.[70]

Resistance in Rwanda

If memories of resistance contribute to nationalist ideology, as in Congo, then surely it is relevant that there was much less overt resistance to colonial conquest in Rwanda. Mwami Rwabugiri knew of the presence of Europeans in neighbouring states and knew that some of his fellow rulers had obtained firearms from them. He seems to have been awaiting his chance to do likewise. When Count von Götzen arrived at his court, there was almost no resistance, apart from an incident in which the German struck one of the mwami's relatives. The Germans took the lack of resistance as acquiescence to German overrule.

One could perhaps cite as 'resistance' the 1896 clash between

Rwandan forces and the forces of the Congo Free State, ensconced at Shangi, east of Lake Kivu. The death of a Rwandan general, killed by a bullet to the head, must have reinforced the idea that Rwanda needed white allies.[71]

Rwabugiri died shortly thereafter (returning from a campaign against the Shi or Havu of Congo). Then his son and successor Rutalindwa was murdered. An infant mwami, Musinga, was installed in his place. The new authorities – the queen mother and two of her brothers – needed support to stabilize Musinga's rule, and the Germans were there to provide it.

There followed a series of campaigns in which German officers led Rwandan troops against Kinyarwanda-speakers who were resisting direct rule from the centre. These included two expeditions against Bugoyi (Gisenyi province) and one against a pretender to the throne, Ndungutse, in 1912.[72]

In 1912, a man claiming to be Ndungutse, a son of Rwabugiri and thus a more legitimate mwami than Musinga, gained considerable support in the north. A Rwandan army led by the German Lieutenant Gudovius defeated him and his allies. Nahimana, historian-ideologue, claims that Ndungutse and his allies – 'brigands' in the eyes of the court, the German administration and the White Fathers – were heroes in the eyes of the populations of the north and north-west.

After the Belgians drove out the Germans in 1916, they adopted the German policy of reinforcing Musinga's authority and imposing a network of Tutsi chiefs, on areas that hitherto had their own bami (pl. of mwami). This process was not completed until around 1930.

The efforts of Musinga to safeguard his status as a sacred monarch probably also should be cited as resistance. As Vidal points out, the territory of Rwanda was a 'mystic zone' that the mwami and the royal drum Kalinga 'protected against the influx of adverse magic'.[73] If he abandoned the traditional religion, condemned as superstition by the Catholic missionaries, the ideological underpinning of his rule would vanish. In the event, he did not take this step, and instead was dethroned in favour of his son Rudahigwa, a Catholic. Doubtless there were parallels in the case of some Congolese monarchies, but none of these corresponded to an entire province, let alone the whole colony.

There are no real equivalents of syncretic religious movements such as Kimbanguism, nor could there be urban riots in a country without cities. Pre-political modern associations appeared on the scene very late. The main Hutu party Parmehutu (Parti d'Emancipation du Peuple Hutu) was founded in 1957 as the Mouvement Social Muhutu

(Hutu Social Movement). The main Tutsi party, the monarchist Union National Rwandaise (UNAR, Rwandan National Union) emerged from an organization called the Association des Éleveurs du Ruanda-Urundi (Association of Cattle Raisers of Ruanda-Urundi), which had been created in 1957 with the support of the mwami and the Tutsi abbés (priests) of Nyundo.[74] UNAR's programme consisted largely of a call for immediate independence.

The contrast between Rwanda and Congo, in ideological terms, could hardly have been greater, as the two territories moved towards independence. The Belgian administration and the Catholic Church having changed horses, a 'moderate' Hutu party that favoured continued close ties with Belgium was able to win a sweeping victory. In Congo, the Belgians attempted to back so-called moderates but with the notable exception of Katanga province, they were unable to help these allies win power. Elsewhere, the pro-Belgian Parti National du Progrès (National Progress Party, PNP) did very badly.

Rwanda's struggle between two nationalisms can be seen in political songs of the early 1990s. The Hutu-controlled radio broadcast a song called 'The Sons of the Father of the Cultivators' (i.e. the Hutu). This anti-Tutsi song, not traditional but drawing on the writings of the Abbé Kagame, claimed, for example: 'I carried out divination for Ndungutse and for Basebya ... I told them they had been betrayed, that they would be killed and that Rukara would be hanged.'[75]

The Tutsi-dominated RPF arrived in Rwanda, singing songs that presented its own radically different version of history. They sang that the whites had divided the Rwandans. Rwandan resistants Musinga and Basebya (the same Basebya!) were associated with Mandela and Machel, heroes of the liberation struggle in southern Africa.[76]

Conclusion

The Europeans imported many ideas to Central Africa. These included race, with its linked concepts of essential difference and of hierarchy. The idea of race was applied by the colonial administration, by assigning various colonial subjects to various categories, which would receive appropriate training and carry out appropriate tasks. At the top of the racial hierarchy sat the 'Europeans'. They were the philosopher-kings of Belgium's 'Platonist' regime,[77] the only ones capable of seeing far enough ahead to direct the society.

Congo and Rwanda represent two variations of this general theme. Leopold's Congo Free State had declared sovereignty over a patchwork of African systems, some of them monarchical, others segmentary. In the early years of Belgian rule (the 1910s and 1920s) the colonial minister Louis Franck toyed with adopting indirect rule. In the end, however, they retained a more direct, interventionist approach. Externally, of course, Belgium's dependencies like other colonies had clear-cut borders. Internally, a uniform grid of provinces, districts, territories and native circumscriptions was imposed on the variegated Congolese political systems. Concessions to African realities were made only at the lowest level, where several sorts of 'native circumscriptions' were recognized. In principle the *chefferie* (chiefdom) corresponded to a pre-existing collectivity, whereas the *secteur* (sector) resulted from the fusion of several *chefferies* too small to be useful to the Belgians. However, distinctive regional administrative traditions developed. In Kivu province, to be discussed in Chapters 4 and 5, there was a marked preference for the *chefferie* formula, even where the legislation would seem to call for a *secteur*.

Colonial administrative theory and practice was internalized by the Africans, and in particular by the '*évolués*'. When the '*évolués*' of the Songye ethnic community wanted to create a separate province for their group, in 1962, they called it 'Lomami' after 'their district' that had existed for a number of years before being divided between Katanga and Kasai provinces.

Rwanda often is considered to be a 'traditional' state. In fact, however, the Rwandan 'nation-state' to which contemporary Rwandan intellectuals are attached is not the nineteenth-century Rwanda but the Rwandan state as modified by the colonial administration. Under the influence of the imported model of the state, many Rwandan intellectuals confuse Rwandan culture with the Rwandan state.

Congo often is considered to be an 'artificial' state, that is, created out of whole cloth by the Europeans. In fact, Leopold imposed a state framework on peoples that shared membership in a cultural network covering the Congo river basin. The present Congolese state, like Rwanda, is the work of Europeans. Yet the Congolese have internalized this alien creation.

Rwandan nationalism is neo-traditional. The Rwandan Patriotic Army, attacking from Uganda, called itself 'Inkotanyi' (the battlers) after one of Rwabugiri's armies. The RPF as hegemonic party keeps this label, RPF-Inkotanyi. As an example of 'Rwandan political thought', a leading political scientist suggests, 'Rwanda attacks, Rwanda is not attacked'. A general turned popular historian proposes that a new Rwandan patriotism be developed around the supposed pre-colonial practice of martyrdom on enemy soil. And although the official policy is to respect state borders, many intellectuals and students are attached to the idea that large areas of present Congo and Uganda were formerly parts of the Rwandan state.[78] Rwanda did not invade Congo because of this belief; but there can be little doubt that such a belief shaped the choice to invade and legitimates the invasions.

I turn next to two provincial case studies of the Congo wars, in South Kivu and North Kivu. In each, the global, regional, national, provincial and local levels of the political economy and of the world of symbols are linked in ways that we shall explore.

FOUR
War in South Kivu

The Banyamulenge were the first to denounce the invasion of Congo and are resistants to the occupation of the RDC.

(Manassé [Müller] Ruhimbika, Banyamulenge community activist)[1]

§ On 7 October 1996, the vice-governor of South Kivu province announced that all 'Banyamulenge' would have to leave the province within a week. On 25 October, so-called 'Banyamulenge' seized the town of Uvira, in the southern portion of South Kivu, near the border with Burundi. The Banyamulenge ('people of Mulenge', a small community of Tutsi pastoralists, speaking Kinyarwanda) had been in conflict with their neighbours in Uvira territory for several years, and the uprising seemed a direct consequence. In reporting the fall of Uvira, the United Nations referred to 'Banyamulenge-dominated forces'. The BBC carried an interview with a spokesman for the 'Alliance of Forces for Democracy and Liberation of Congo–Zaire' who claimed to be in Bukavu. He said that his group had taken the town with a force of 400 men.[2]

On 30 October, the AFDL or Banyamulenge-dominated forces took the provincial capital, Bukavu. On 1 November, Goma – capital of North Kivu province – fell. At each of these stops, the 'Banyamulenge' or AFDL fighters attacked the nearby refugee camps, killing some people and scattering the majority. Some of the refugees returned to nearby Rwanda whereas others fled westwards, deeper into Congo. Some of those who fled to the west were later massacred, supposedly by Banyamulenge or forces of Laurent Kabila, but in reality by Rwandan troops hiding behind the labels of 'Banyamulenge' and of Kabila's AFDL.[3]

One can see the 'Banyamulenge' question as a smokescreen. Rwanda used the pre-existing conflict between Banyamulenge and their neighbours, in South Kivu, as a pretext in order to attack the refugee camps. In these camps, civilian and military officials of the Hutu regime that had carried out the genocide of 1994 'held hostage' a vast number of civilian Hutu refugees. When the camps were attacked, the innocent returned home while the guilty fled westwards with their leaders. This is the version I was given in an interview with an adviser to the RPF, ruling party in Rwanda.[4] There was no broader objective, such as installing a friendly regime in Kinshasa or pillaging the Congo or (heaven forbid) annexing eastern Congo. James Kabarebe – the Rwandan general who served for a time as Congo army commander under President Laurent Kabila – described the attacks on the camps in the film *L'Afrique en morceaux*.[5] Clearly, he was proud of his role.

This Rwandan argument cannot be accepted at face value, even though it appears candid. The Rwandans are saying in effect, we hid our role at first but now we are admitting it. In my view, the link between (i) the conflicts within eastern Congo (North and South Kivu) and (ii) between Congo and Rwanda is more complex than a simple dichotomy between 'pretext' and 'real motive'. Without understanding each conflict in its own right, and the links between them, we shall be unable to follow the shifts over time. In particular, we shall be unable to evaluate more recent disagreements, including the question of whether Rwanda withdrew from eastern Congo, as it undertook to do in 2002, and whether it continued to intervene in eastern Congo, as it denies doing but frequently threatens to do.

The question, or cluster of questions, as to the origin and ethnic identity of the Banyamulenge and their relationship to Rwanda connects international, regional, national, provincial and local politics. The outbreak and subsequent course of war in South Kivu are incomprehensible without taking into account the interests and images of the Banyamulenge and their neighbours.

Thus, this chapter and the next two present three interrelated themes: the war in South Kivu, its antecedents, and its development; the war in North Kivu, its antecedents, and its development; and the efforts of the United Nations and the 'international community' to put an end to the war. The separation is somewhat artificial, and it will be necessary from time to time to refer the reader to matters developed in another chapter.

Recent conflict in South Kivu is much more than a conflict between the Banyamulenge and their neighbours. To understand the multi-faceted conflict within the province, I shall look first at the Banyamulenge situation, then at two other areas where Congo–Rwanda relations have a local dimension, namely Ijwi Island and Kalehe Territory. Recent events in the capital, Bukavu, will reveal linkages between the multiple levels of conflict in South Kivu: local, provincial, national, and on the level of the Great Lakes region.

The Banyamulenge in South Kivu

South Kivu is one of eleven Congolese provinces. It shares boundaries with North Kivu to the north, Maniema to the west, and Katanga
to the south. To the east, there are international borders with Tanzania (across Lake Tanganyika), Burundi and Rwanda.

South Kivu, North Kivu and Maniema were united under the name
Kivu, from 1933 to 1962, and from 1966 to 1988. Many residents of
South Kivu display a strong attachment to their province, especially
since it has been (in their view) under attack since 1996. At the same
time, there is some sentiment in favour of reunification of 'le Grand
Kivu', likewise reinforced by the wars since 1996. Either way, the
others tend to view the Banyamulenge as outsiders.

Three linguistic–cultural zones meet in South Kivu. Along the eastern border, many peoples of South Kivu belong to the interlacustrine
or Great Lakes civilization, along with the Ganda, Nkole, Rwanda,
Rundi and other peoples of Uganda, Tanzania, Rwanda and Burundi.
According to Schoenbrun's map, 'Linguistic Geography of the Great
Lakes Region Today', South Kivu apparently includes the following
interlacustrine language communities (from south to north): Bwari,
Vira, Furiiru, Shi, Havu and Tembo. I write 'apparently', because the
small map covers the entire Great Lakes region and on that scale it
apparently is not possible to represent minorities such as the Rundi
and Rwanda speakers of South Kivu.[6] There is another possibility,
however. Perhaps the Rwanda-speaking Banyamulenge are not represented because they are considered to be recent arrivals, i.e. more
recent than the ethnographic present of Schoenbrun's map. Father
van Bulck indicated no presence of Kinyarwanda-speakers in South
Kivu in his *Carte linguistique du Congo belge* of 1954.[7]

To the west and south, the main neighbours of the Great Lakes
Bantu of South Kivu are so-called Bantu of Maniema, including the
Bembe to the south and the Lega to the west.[8] Further south and west,
finally, there are peoples classified as belonging to the Kasai-Katanga
and Tanganika–Haut–Katanga cultural zones, speaking Luba-type
languages.

The Banyamulenge live along the meeting point of zones. Their
immediate neighbours are the Vira and Furiiru, also interlacustrine
Bantu, and the Bembe, from the Maniema zone. Perhaps more important than being classified in the interlacustrine zone, however, is
the fact that the Banyamulenge are Tutsi and identify themselves as
such.

The Banyamulenge arrived in what is now DR Congo in the nineteenth century, before Congo itself became a colonial state. In terms

of Congolese law, it can be important to have been on Congolese soil prior to the proclamation of the Congo Free State in 1885. Weis writes that Banyamulenge began coming to South Kivu towards the end of the nineteenth century. They established themselves first around Lemera, in the Chefferie des Bafulero, before moving west on to higher ground. A few arrived at Galye, in the Chefferie des Bavira, in 1881 and 1884.[9] This is crucial for the Banyamulenge cause, because it puts them (that is, some of their ancestors) in Congo before 1885, the point of reference for Congolese laws on nationality.

Some versions of their history relate that the Banyamulenge left Rwanda to escape from the abuses of Mwami Rwabugiri, during the second half of the nineteenth century, while other versions cite an earlier mwami. However, if one asks a different question, namely the origins of the families making up the Banyamulenge community, a different and incompatible answer tends to be offered. The majority of the 'clans' supposedly are of Rwanda origin, but others trace their origins to Burundi. Some descend from Shi (Bashi) or from slaves obtained from the 'Batetela mutineers' of Congo Free State years. The best answer as to where the Banyamulenge came from may be that their community formed in South Kivu, uniting persons of various origins around a nucleus of Tutsi from Rwanda.[10]

Colonial documents and oral accounts agree that the Banyamulenge were under the domination of the Mwami of the Fulero or Furiiru (cattle-herding speakers of an interlacustrine language), living in the present Uvira Territory.[11] Then, because of the cruelty of this ruler (a common cliché in Central Africa), they fled westwards into the highlands. Some moved southwards from the Fulero Collectivity into that of the Vira, or further south, into Fizi Territory (South Kivu province) and even Moba Territory (Katanga province).

Contacts with outsiders, first the Arab-Swahili traders from East Africa and later the Europeans, had a lasting impact on local peoples. These contacts usually provided advantages to those groups who had the first contacts, advantages that they sometimes were able to consolidate under colonial rule. Groups that were considered intelligent and adaptable benefited from having state posts, missions and schools on their territory. Groups that resisted longer often found themselves a generation or more behind in terms of access to markets and to schooling, with lasting consequences. I shall refer to these advantages and disadvantages as 'differential modernization'. In what became South Kivu, the Vira of the Lake Tanganyika shore were among the earliest to profit from contact with the Arab-Swahili and then the Belgians. However, the head-start of the Vira was short-circuited in the 1930s, when the administrative centre was displaced north to Bukavu.[12]

The Banyamulenge and the Belgians

The Belgians pursued an incoherent policy towards the Kinyar-wanda-speaking Tutsi pastoralists of Uvira and Fizi, the people who later would call themselves Banyamulenge. For decades, they ignored their presence, or considered them to be foreigners. Some time after the Second World War, they recognized a *groupement* of 'Ruanda' within the Chefferie des Bavira, even placing people of other ethnic origins under the authority of the chief of this *groupement*; in 1952, they dissolved it. The subsequent conflicts between the Banyamulenge and their neighbours were due in large measure to this incoherent, self-serving Belgian policy.

In 1906, the administration of the Congo Free State in what was then 'Tanganika Sector' awarded chief's medals to several supposed leaders of Congolese communities in what is now South Kivu. These medals went to communities living along the lakeshore. The Banyamulenge, living in the hills, were ignored.

In those days, 'native policy' (*politique indigène*) hardly existed. The Europeans had a vague idea that all Africans had 'chiefs' (natural rulers) and that under colonial rule such chiefs could serve as intermediaries in dealings with the population. They distributed medals to supposed rulers. According to later criticism by Belgium's minister of colonies, some medals were given to 'straw men' put forward by rulers who preferred to remain distant from the Europeans. In other cases, the Free State practised divide and rule, giving medals to men who were subordinates of another legitimate ruler.

The Charte coloniale (a constitutional document adopted in 1908, as Belgium took over the former Free State) recognized 'customary law' as the law governing relations among Congolese. Criticism of the existing *chefferies* by Renkin led to the decree of 2 May 1910, which reaffirmed the 'traditional' responsibilities of the chiefs in the political and judicial fields. The colonial administration should intervene only when custom 'contravened public order, legislation, or rules' or when there was either a power vacuum or, in contrast, abuse of power by chiefs. Renkin criticized the policy of 'divide and rule' but noted that prudence would be needed in restoring the prior situation, if one wished to avoid 'grave perturbations'.

About the same time, the colonial administration began to realize that it would have to study in greater detail the political history and practices of the Congolese peoples. The *Recueil à l'usage des fonctionnaires et des agents du Service territorial,* first published in 1918,[13] provided a model of the report on the inquiry to be undertaken before any new *chefferie* was recognized. One required point was 'links connecting the *chefferie* to other native groups'.

Despite Renkin's announced intention of restoring the unity of Congolese groups, Congo continued to harbour many small *chefferies* through the 1920s. It was not until 1933 that the institutions of South Kivu were remodelled so as to 'restore' the unity of the various groups and to create larger, supposedly more viable circumscriptions. At that point, the Belgians recognized one Chefferie des Bafulero and one Chefferie des Bavira. The various clusters of Banyamulenge were incorporated into these circumscriptions. In terms of Belgian 'native policy', a unit including populations of various origins probably should have become a *secteur* rather than a *chefferie*, but the administration of Kivu province preferred the *chefferie* formula and applied it almost everywhere.[14]

The Belgians used ethnicity as an organizational variable in creating and remodelling administrative units. For a time, this was reflected in the names of territories such as Territoire de l'Ubembe (Bembe Country) in South Kivu, or Territoire des Bahutu in North Kivu. It was never possible to achieve substantial ethnic homogeneity at the level of the territories, and such names were dropped. There was, however, a general 'territorialization of ethnicity' in that the administrative subdivisions were supposed to assemble people according to their natural characteristics. Congolese adopted these labels, so that (for example) Bembe tend to think of Fizi Territory as belonging to them, even though it is no longer called Ubembe, and some of the inhabitants are not Bembe.

In organizing South Kivu, the Belgians paid considerable attention to the larger and more self-conscious communities, notably the Lega, Bembe and Shi. In so doing, they reinforced the sense of ethnic identity on the part of these communities.

The Belgians ignored some other communities, perhaps because their populations were smaller or they lived farther from the towns and the communication routes. One of these communities, ignored by the Belgians, was what became known as the Banyamulenge. They remained divided between the territories of Fizi, Uvira and Mwenga. At Fizi, they were dominated by the Bembe majority, at Uvira by the Vira and the Furiiru or Fulero, and at Mwenga by the Lega.

Ethnicity was one of several organizing principles. Politics was another. In some cases (for example the Pende of the present Bandundu and West Kasai) troublesome groups were deliberately kept divided. The Banyamulenge acquired a reputation as uncooperative. Towards the end of the colonial period, the geographer Weis wrote, 'these pastoralists showed the administration more reticence than the Vira'. They resisted taxes and the census and destroyed high-altitude forests. They threatened 'to dominate the Congolese people' and to reduce European influence over the Congolese. Because of all these factors, they faced 'severe discrimination'.[15] Weis does not say whether this discrimination included Belgian refusal to give the Banyamulenge their collectivity. He does imply that the Belgians thought the (future) Banyamulenge might not be Congolese.[16]

Perhaps the most basic organizing principle was convenience. The Belgians were attempting to supervise a very large territory and a substantial population, with a small European staff. The Banyamulenge were too few, and too far away from population centres, for their grievances to be taken into consideration. In 1944, for example, the Belgians rejected a request that all the Banyamulenge groups within the Bavira *chefferie* be united in a separate Banyamulenge *chefferie*.[17]

The colonial era ended with the Banyamulenge under the rule of others. In 1961, soon after independence, Banyamulenge reopened the question of their autonomy. During a meeting of the territorial council of Uvira Territory, the former capita (village head) Mushishi, a Munyamulenge from Bijombo, asked that a *groupement* of Bijombo be recognized, within the Bavira *chefferie*. This proposal was rejected, and the Banyamulenge area of the Bavira *chefferie* retained the status of *sous-groupement* or *localité*.

In 1969, after the disruptions of the 'rebellion' or 'Second Independence' movement, Banyamulenge returned to their homes on the high plateaux, and a Munyamulenge named Kabarure was installed as chief of Bijombo *sous-groupement*. The Vira chief soon dismissed him, but the commissioner of the sub-region (district) reversed the decision.[18] The question of chieftaincy and administrative autonomy has continued to trouble relations between the Banyamulenge and their neighbours up to the present day.

The material and ideological basis of relations with neighbours

In the 1970s, Depelchin reported that the immigrants from Rwanda 'have always sought to isolate themselves from the surrounding ethnic groups. They did achieve some measure of cultural and social isolation, but not so economically.'[19] He attributes this cultural isolation in part to 'the aloof and patriarchal attitude typical of members of the ruling class which will not mix with the commoners' and partly to 'self-preservation'.

Depelchin confirms the frequent complaint of other inhabitants of South Kivu that the Banyamulenge discouraged intermarriage:

> Even though intermarriages have taken place, they were not encouraged. Intermarriages between Furiiru and Rwanda remained a rarity for several reasons. First, the Rwanda tend to isolate themselves geographically. Second, and probably more importantly, the kind of wealth that is exchanged on marriage occasions among the Rwanda would allow only the wealthiest Furiiru men to marry Tutsi women. The less fortunate Tutsi, even if they do not possess wealth, would rather marry one of their ethnic group than someone from the Furiiru or from any other group which is not Tutsi. There are exceptions to this rule. For example, if a Tutsi wishes to expand his household, he is likely to bring in a second or third wife who will not be Tutsi. But the offspring from these unions will not have the same status as children from pure [sic] Tutsi parents.[20]

Many of Depelchin's Rwanda (Banyamulenge) informants gave the impression that their distrust of the Furiiru grew out of the 1964–65 rebellion because it was led by Furiiru, but in his opinion the lack of confidence and communication date back to 1924–27 when Mokogabwe, mwami of the Furiiru, seized cattle from many Rwanda. In 1964–65, Rwanda lost many cattle 'to raiding bands which were – almost invariably – made up of Furiiru'. As a result of these events, resentment between the two groups was so deep that, as recently as 1970, the Furiiru refrained from travelling on the high plateaux, or did so only in groups. Depelchin adds that if the Rwanda or Banyamulenge were the targets of raiders, they were 'a natural target because, on the average, they possessed more cattle than any of the other ethnic groups'.[21] At any rate, the rebellion of 1964–65 reinforced Banyamulenge isolationism, and 'in areas where other ethnic groups are represented, the Rwanda will ensure that no stranger lives on the same hill'.[22]

In the beginning, relations between the Furiiru and the Rwanda were less antagonistic. Almost all of Depelchin's Tutsi informants attributed their migration from Rwanda to Rwabugiri's abuse of power, especially his forcible appropriation of cattle from the wealthiest members of his entourage. When the Rwanda arrived, the mwami of the Furiiru gave them grazing land. In exchange, they were to pay tribute in animals to him. They moved from the valley to the slopes, until they reached a placed called Mulenge at about 1,800m. For many years, 'Mulenge was to be the quasi-capital of the Rwanda', so much so that their companions who stayed behind in the lowlands referred to them as 'Banyamulenge' or Mulenge people.[23]

Around 1924, the Tutsi who had fled their homeland in order to escape kingly abuse were confronted with similar excesses on the part of the mwami of the Furiiru. In response, the Tutsi asked the Belgian administrator for permission to move to Itombwe, further away from the Furiiru capital of Lemera. 'Paradoxically, however, the movement away from the Furiiru capital increased the Tutsi's reliance on the Furiiru for food.'

The Tutsi arrived in South Kivu not as conquerors but as 'fugitives seeking a safe place for their property', that is, their herds. Initially, they did not treat the Furiiru as 'Hutu' (clients) but as time went on they attempted to do so. Depelchin explains that this should not be surprising, since 'the Tutsi did come from the ranks of the ruling class. They believed in and upheld the class divisions that existed in Rwanda. While they easily rid themselves of an abusive ruler by moving away from him, they did not reject the material basis and the ideology upon which Rwandan society was founded.'

At first, the Tutsi (future Banyamulenge) produced their food, according to Depelchin's informants. Over time, they came to use their cattle as 'a means of economic domination over those Furiiru who had nothing else to offer but their labor'. In exchange for food brought by the Furiiru, the Tutsi would offer banana beer, a goat or milk, or sometimes a cow if the exchange were made on a regular basis. They were prevented from transforming the Furiiru into Hutu-like dependants by the fact that they did not own the land. A Furiiru could either take surplus food to the market or take it to the Tutsi 'with the hope that he would eventually receive a cow. The latter course was the safest, even if economically exploitative, for beyond the material exchange, a friendship bond could develop which could be very helpful in times of hardship.'[24]

The Furiiru were pushed into relationships with the Tutsi by the cultural requirement that cows be given as bride wealth. By 1972, however, Furiiru were no longer eager to carry food to the Tutsi. They had realized that the same quantity of food sold on the market could buy two or more cows. Both the Tutsi (Banyamulenge) and the Furiiru were being squeezed, as Depelchin points out. The Tutsi had lost many cattle in the 1964 rebellion and were trying to rebuild their herds. The Furiiru found that cultivable land was growing scarcer.

The Itombwe plateau was well suited to production of potatoes, maize and beans, but, according to Depelchin, the Rwandan Tutsi culture discouraged farming: 'the Tutsi would not touch the hoe, their dignity requiring an upright position: no load in one's hands – save a pipe – or on one's head – save a hat. To this accoutrement one must add the eternal herding stick which also acts as a third leg for those long and arduous journeys up and down the plateaux.' On the plateau, the Tutsi encountered small bands of Nyindu. 'As with the Hutu and the Furiiru, the Tutsi treated the Nyindu with social disdain while relying on them as their food producers.'

Even though some Furiiru earned cows by trading with or working for the Tutsi, they were not real cattle raisers in Tutsi eyes. A Tutsi elder told Depelchin: 'The Furiiru cannot raise cattle mostly because they cannot stand the physical proximity of the cows. They don't drink milk, they don't know what to do with cow dung.' Depelchin finds this 'overly stereotypical and partly untrue'. In any case, it reveals the attitude of some Tutsi towards their neighbours.

The Tutsi had regarded their cattle almost as family members, but this was changing at the time Depelchin was doing his research. In the aftermath of the rebellion, they realized that a more mercantilist attitude towards cattle would be the only way of preserving their superiority over the Furiiru.

Indeed, after the rebellion, some Tutsi had been forced to till the soil or to hire themselves out as labourers to wealthy Furiiru. Depelchin explains:

> Generally speaking, when a Furiiru asks a Tutsi to look after his cattle, there is no salary to speak of. Instead, the keeper is entitled to all the milk he wishes. This could amount to a substantial quantity, since the keeper often tends cattle belonging to several Furiiru (which may total between 20 and 40 head). In the long run, however, the keeper may find himself the owner of a sizeable herd because of a well-established custom that requires the depositor to give his trustee the third or fourth calf born from each cow. The Tutsi have complained bitterly that this custom is no longer followed as rigidly as in the past.

The Tutsi expressed bitterness against those they blamed for the 1964 rebellion, that is, the Furiiru. Depelchin reported a personal impression that Tutsi resentment was directed against themselves, for 'having fallen so low'.[25]

Decolonization led the Furiiru to tell the Rwanda (Banyamulenge) and Rundi (of the Ruzizi valley) that they ought to go home like the Europeans. This reaction was similar to that of Lulua and Lunda against Luba-Kasai. Depelchin maintains that the Furiiru 'were in fact venting frustrations that had been caused by the colonizers' administration rather than by social and historical forces produced by the colonized society'.[26]

Neither independence nor the creation of a new province of South Kivu evoked much response from the Banyamulenge. However, their social and political situation changed drastically, beginning in 1964, when South Kivu became the launching pad of the eastern front of the Lumumbist revolt.[27] Only a few young Banyamulenge felt drawn to the Lumumbist ideology of the Simba (lions). For many, the egalitarianism of the rebels came down to *kugabana inka n'ababembe* (free distribution of their cattle to the Bembe).[28] Those who eventually joined the rebels did so mainly to protect their families.

Once they had been defeated in the Ruzizi Plain and at Uvira, many rebels of Furiiru, Bembe and Vira origin retreated to the Haut Plateau in 1966. The rebels imposed taxes on the Banyamulenge, or simply raided their cattle. In response, the Banyamulenge aligned themselves with the Congolese army (ANC). Some of the young Banyamulenge who had joined the rebellion now turned against it and helped the ANC to create a humanitarian corridor to enable the Banyamulenge civilians to escape to the Ruzizi Plain and Baraka. This transformed the rebellion against the Kinshasa government and for a second independence into an ethnic war between Bembe (and Vira-Furiiru to the north) and Banyamulenge. Young Banyamulenge, armed and trained by the ANC, pushed back the Simba, enabling the civilians to return to the Haut Plateau.

Following the rebellion, the Banyamulenge were rewarded by Kinshasa:

> For many young Banyamulenge, their enrolment in the ANC
> meant the start of a military career. As compensation for their war
> efforts on the Haut Plateau, the central government also offered
> them full access to education, social services and employment
> opportunities. The result was the formation of a new politico-
> military Banyamulenge elite and a socio-political emancipation of
> the entire Banyamulenge society that became well aware of its own
> identity and its delicate position within Congolese society.[29]

In consequence, the Banyamulenge were resented by the Bembe and other neighbours, who regarded them as traitors for having aligned themselves with Kinshasa. In this new context, and in order to differentiate themselves from those Banyarwanda (Tutsi refugees of 1959) who had supported the rebellion, the Kinyarwanda-speakers of the Haut Plateau adopted the name Banyamulenge.[30]

From the late 1960s onward, the Banyamulenge struggled on two levels. Locally, they continued to seek recognition of their own territory and collectivity. They also attempted, at first successfully, to represent the Uvira area in the national legislature. Gisaro Muhoza, a university administrator, was elected deputy in 1977, with support especially from Protestants. (Resentment of Banyamulenge was not yet so great as to prevent this.) He is credited with having popularized the label 'Banyamulenge' for the people hitherto known as Banyarwanda of South Kivu. Gisaro tried but failed to win the re-establishment of an autonomous Banyamulenge collectivity. As a compromise solution, the Banyamulenge of the Bavira collectivity were given their own Locality of Bijombo, which was, however, headed by a Muvira, Tete, from the family of the Mwami of the Bavira.[31]

Gisaro died in the early 1980s. He was the last Munyamulenge legislator until the occupation of South Kivu by Rwanda and the RCD. Joseph Mutambo, a Munyamulenge, presented his candidature in 1982 but was struck from the list by the authorities of the party-state in Kinshasa, on the grounds of 'doubtful nationality'. Two further Banyamulenge candidates were disallowed in 1987.

The success of Gisaro and the failure of Mutambo and the others do not reflect the individual characteristics of the candidates. Rather, they reflect the changing fortunes of the Kinyarwanda-speakers of Zaire/Congo during these years. The law of 5 January 1972 granted Zairian identity to 'all persons of whom one of the ascendants is or was a member of one of the tribes established on the territory of the Republic of Zaire in its limits of 15 November 1908'. It further stipulated that people from Ruanda-Urundi living in the Province of Kivu before 1 January 1960, and having continued to live in Zaire, acquired Zairian nationality on the date of 30 June 1960.[32] The first clause would appear to recognize as Congolese all the 'true Banyamulenge', whereas the second would recognize later immigrants to South Kivu, including some of the Tutsi refugees fleeing the 'Social Revolution' in Rwanda. Gisaro was elected during the time when this quite liberal law was in effect.

By 1981, the law of 1972 had been replaced by a more restrictive law of 29 June 1981. Congolese nationality was withdrawn, retroactively, from many thousands of Rwandophones. Now one had to demonstrate majority descent from a member of one of the tribes living in Congo before August 1885 (creation of the Congo Free State). Apart from the problem of the validity of a retroactive law,[33] it was difficult if not impossible to discover who in fact was excluded.

The effects of the 1981 law were political more than legal. The law was not enforced, and the identity cards of Kinyarwanda-speakers were not revoked. However, politicians who feared the number of votes represented by Kinyarwanda-speakers in proposed elections stirred up feelings against them among members of neighbouring ethnic groups. At the time of the National Conference in 1991, Anzuluni Bembe, a member of the Bembe ethnic community of South Kivu, moved to exclude the Banyamulenge, claiming they were not Zairians but Rwandan immigrants.[34] Banyarwanda from North Kivu were similarly to be excluded. After this, leaders of other ethnic groups increasingly challenged the right of Banyamulenge and other Kinyarwanda-speakers to Zairian citizenship.

In 1989, a special census or survey was conducted to identify Congolese and non-Congolese. It clearly was aimed at 'Rwandans' since it was conducted only in North and South Kivu and in two territories of north-east Katanga, Kalemie and Moba, home of the so-called Banyavyura. In some sites, the survey was completed without difficulty, but there were accusations of bribery by persons wishing to be certified as Congolese. In several locations, the survey personnel were chased away by stone-throwing youths.

Banyamulenge delegates were refused entry to the Sovereign National Conference in Kinshasa in 1992, as were Banyarwanda from North Kivu. Given the frustrations faced by the Banyamulenge community, it is not surprising that some of them responded favourably to recruitment drives by the Rwandan Patriotic Front, which invaded Rwanda from Uganda in 1990.

However, South Kivu remained relatively calm during the early 1990s at a time when North Kivu was already experiencing civil war between ethnically defined armed groups. Tension mounted when President Ndadaye of Burundi was assassinated in 1993, ethnic murders followed, and many Burundian refugees fled to South Kivu. In this new situation, Banyamulenge were stoned in the streets of Uvira where (as Ruhimbika explains) thousands of Burundians had sought refuge.[35] This violence apparently was in part the work of the Burundian Hutu. It would be interesting to know whether other youths – Zairian Kirundi-speakers from the plain of the Ruzizi, Furiiru and Bembe – joined in.

In 1994, the genocide and the RPF seizure of power in Rwanda led hundreds of thousands of Rwandan Hutu to flee to North and South Kivu. The transitional parliament of Zaire responded by creating the so-called Vangu Commission to investigate the situation of 'foreigners' in the east. The commission was stacked with 'anti-Banyarwanda' elements, according to Mamdani, and its conclusions reflect a spirit of ethnic cleansing according to UN rapporteur Roberto Garretón. The Vangu Commission alleged that Rwanda had been attempting to acquire Zairian territory and to supplant its indigenous inhabitants for years and that the Tutsi were now preparing to create a 'Hamitic Kingdom' to be known as the United States of Central Africa or the Republic of the Volcanoes. All Zaire's problems were blamed on the United Nations, westerners in general, Tanzania (for organizing the Arusha Conference), Burundi and Rwanda. These allegations culminated (according to Garretón) in a call for the 'liberation' of Kivu.[36]

Feeling increasingly threatened by harassment and arrests and talk of expulsion,[37] many young Banyamulenge went to Rwanda to join or be trained by the RPA, which also supplied them with weapons. Others organized their own militia in South Kivu; one witness told Human Rights Watch that the Banyamulenge (Tutsi) bought weapons from Interahamwe (Hutu) in the refugee camps.[38]

In August 1996, Zairian authorities banned Milima, a human rights and development NGO working among the Banyamulenge, and arrested several prominent Banyamulenge leaders. On 9 September local people in Uvira town mounted a demonstration against Banyamulenge, declaring Uvira a '*ville morte*', calling on the 'foreigners' to leave the country and attacking their homes and property. The demonstration followed a weekend in which Zaire soldiers had broken into several religious establishments in the town, arresting local church members and missionaries and seizing vehicles, documents and communications equipment. Reports soon emerged that, during the weekend of 6–8 September, Zaire soldiers had killed five Banyamulenge. One man, Bolingo Karema, was allegedly beaten and stoned to death in Uvira town, while four others were killed in surrounding villages. Soldiers allegedly had looted the offices of a local Banyamulenge NGO, Groupe Milima, while its director, Müller Ruhimbika, was in hiding after a warrant had been issued for his arrest. Ruhimbika had played a prominent role in drawing attention to the situation in Uvira during 1995 and the first half of 1996.

Over subsequent days the army sought out Banyamulenge, arresting men while allowing women and children to go free. The arrests were reportedly carried out at the instruction of the zone commissioner (or territorial administrator) of Uvira, Shweka Mutabazi. Amnesty International singled out Shweka for criticism, citing reports that he had encouraged the takeover of Tutsi property and authorized the enrolment of youths into the armed forces to fight the 'Tutsi armed group'. Amnesty also undertook to investigate reports that more than thirty-five Banyamulenge had been 'extrajudicially executed' by Zairian authorities and more than 50 others 'disappeared' at the start of the month.[39]

Reports of fighting between Banyamulenge militiamen and Zairian soldiers also began to emerge, with three soldiers reported killed during the week beginning 9 September. The Zaire army declared the Uvira area a 'military zone' and was reported to be reinforcing its presence with troops from Goma, Bukavu, Shaba and Kinshasa. On 13 September the Zaire government accused Rwanda of having enrolled 3,000 Banyamulenge in its army and of training and infiltrating them to destabilize eastern Zaire, with Burundi providing them with rear bases. Both governments categorically rejected the charges, at the time.

At the same time, Banyamulenge, some of whom had been held in detention, were expelled or fled the country and began entering Rwanda and Burundi. Several hundred refugees were reported as having reached Cyangugu in Rwanda and others as having gone to Cibitoke and Bubanza provinces in Burundi. At the end of the month, UNHCR estimates put the number of recent Banyamulenge arrivals at over 500 in Rwanda and over 400 in Burundi. Zairian authorities had expelled 535 of these people and the rest had left Zaire spontaneously.

During the weekend of 14 and 15 September, Zairian television reported accusations by the authorities that the UNHCR and IOM (International Organization of Migration) had been assisting armed groups to infiltrate Zaire from Rwanda and Burundi with the aim of destabilizing Kivu. Following these accusations two UNHCR staff were beaten up by Zairian soldiers. On 17 September, UN Secretary-General Kurt Waldheim dismissed the claims as being 'completely unfounded'. He subsequently sent Ibrahim Fall as a UN Special Envoy to Zaire to seek clarification on the allegations. The Zairian authorities, meanwhile, confirmed that the activities of IOM throughout Zaire had been suspended.

On Sunday 22 September, an exchange of mortar fire underlined the growing tension between Rwanda and Zaire. This was repeated during the following two days, killing one Zairian and injuring five others. It also prompted the United Nations to relocate twenty-three 'non-essential' expatriate aid agency personnel to Nairobi and the International Federation of the Red Cross to evacuate three of its delegates, after two shells landed in the garden of a hotel where IFRCS staff had been staying.

Rwanda and Zaire accused each other of having started the exchanges of fire. On 23 September, the government of Rwanda released a statement detailing its version of events. It accused the government of Zaire of targeting Kamembe town in Cyangugu prefecture with automatic weapons fire and artillery shelling between 6 p.m. and 11 p.m. on 22 September. These attacks were said to have caused neither injuries nor material damage.

The Rwandan government linked this alleged 'act of aggression' with an attack in mid-September on the prison in the neighbouring commune of Gishoma (on the Burundi border), in which a group of infiltrators had sought to free prisoners. According to the statement, the RPA 'repulsed the attackers, who fled under cover of automatic weapons fire from the Panzi camp in Zairean territory'.[40] The dispute over who had started the attacks continued, however, although a ceasefire was agreed on 25 September. Zaire alleged that Rwanda broke the ceasefire on 26 and 29 September, a claim denied by Rwanda.

At the same time, a Banyamulenge spokesman in exile reported that on 22 September the Zaire authorities had executed forty Banyamulenge being held in detention. The authorities had arrested them the previous week at Baraka in Fizi zone. The summary executions were said to have been in retaliation for the killings of Zairian soldiers by Banyamulenge militia.

On 22 September Zaire also repeated allegations that soldiers were infiltrating into Kivu from Rwanda and Burundi in order to support the Banyamulenge militia. Government spokesman Oscar Lugendo was quoted in the press as saying that Zaire troops killed three 'Rwandan' soldiers and captured five others at Kiringye (near Uvira) on 31 August. He claimed that Banyamulenge who had been officers in the Zaire army but had gone to Rwanda after the RPF victory in July 1994 were commanding the infiltrators.[41]

Violent combat was reported at Uvira (South Kivu) on 18–20 October. So-called Banyamulenge attacked the Uvira refugee camp. It seems likely that many of the attackers were in fact regular troops from the armies of neighbouring Burundi and Rwanda. Several hundred thousand refugees were displaced, mainly Rwandan and Burundian Hutu. Some fled south into Tanzania, others north to Bukavu. According to some reports, Banyamulenge or other 'rebels' mixed in with the fleeing Hutu so as to arrive in Bukavu without attracting attention.

On 25 October, a week after the first attack on the Uvira camp, the 'rebels' announced the creation of the Alliance des forces démocratiques pour la libération du Zaïre (AFDL). As already mentioned, this supposedly was an alliance of four Congolese resistance groups, including one of Banyamulenge and others from South Kivu, and another of Banyarwanda (mainly Tutsi) of North Kivu. Clearly, the AFDL did not launch the first attacks at Uvira, since it had not existed at the time. Some of the violent incidents seem to have been carried out by foreigners. The Burundian army may have carried out the massacre at Lemera hospital (Uvira Territory), to eliminate Burundian Hutu rebels being treated there.

Msgr Munzihrwa, Archbishop of Bukavu, had been calling for resistance to the Rwandan invasion, even arguing that if a snake comes into your house you don't flee, but instead take a stick and kill it. Many Bukavu residents believe he was killed by Rwandan troops.[42]

By 31 October, violent battles were reported from North Kivu, leading to the flight of hundreds of thousands of refugees, mainly Rwandan Hutu. (Subsequent developments in North Kivu are discussed in Chapter 5.)

The seizure of power first in South Kivu, then in Kinshasa, left the Banyamulenge in a paradoxical position. The war had been waged first in their name, then in that of the AFDL. Even before Kabila's forces reached Kinshasa, however, the rebel movement was disintegrating. Kabila and other Congolese 'rebels' were showing signs of asserting their independence vis-à-vis Angola, Rwanda and Uganda. 'Tutsi' and 'Katangans' exchanged gunfire at Goma and at Lubumbashi.[43]

Rwandophone Tutsi surrounded the new president, Laurent Kabila. The army commander, James Kabarebe, was an English-speaking Tutsi, raised in Uganda and having no prior connection to Congo. Déogratias Bugera, a Tutsi from North Kivu and leader of the Alliance Démocratique des Peuples, became secretary-general of the AFDL, then minister to the presidency under Kabila. Bizima Karaha, who served as foreign minister in the Kabila government, was the most prominent Munyamulenge. He was widely seen as Rwanda's man in Congo, however, rather than a spokesman for the Banyamulenge community.

The second war, beginning in 1998, clearly represented an attempt by Rwanda and Uganda to replace Kabila with a more malleable agent. Kabila himself referred to 'another Bizimungu',[44] meaning that he was supposed to be a figurehead like Pasteur Bizimungu, President of Rwanda to Kagame's vice president. A heterogeneous collection of Congolese associated themselves with the effort to overthrow Kabila, including Congolese Tutsi with close ties to the RPF. As Nzongola suggests: 'The authentic leaders of the Banyamulenge understood [the danger for their community] from the very beginning of the war, and this is the reason why they refused to join the Rwandan- and Ugandan-based Congolese rebels.'[45]

The RCD endured a series of splits and leadership changes, apparently reflecting the impossible reconciliation of Rwanda's desire to maintain its control over the movement, and its desire to see the movement gain substantial support from the Congolese. Eventually, the Munyamulenge Azarias Ruberwa wound up as president of the RCD-Goma and vice president of Congo under the infamous 'one plus four' formula (one president plus four vice presidents). There seemed little likelihood that the Banyamulenge could continue to enjoy this level of prominence, once their Rwandan backers had withdrawn and a new Congolese government had been elected.

The Banyamulenge were supposed to constitute a major component of the RCD without, however, threatening Kigali's control. The difficulties implicit in such a policy soon became evident, as Banyamulenge troops under Commandant Patrick Masunzu revolted against the RCD in 1999. Eventually, this led to large-scale fighting in 2002. Rwandan army units with air support and a considerable numerical advantage were able to disperse Masunzu's force but not to destroy it.[46]

From the beginning of the second war, the RCD behaved as an occupation force. Banyamulenge relations with their neighbours suffered as a consequence. Among abuses too numerous to recount, perhaps the most egregious concerned the Nyindu of Mwenga.

What Human Rights Watch described as 'possibly the largest massacre of civilians' in 1998 took place on 24 August in villages near Kasika in the Lwindi collectivity of Mwenga territory. RCD forces apparently retaliated for casualties suffered in an ambush by Maï-Maï in the Lwindi collectivity on 23 August. Reportedly angered by the deaths of several officers during the ambush, the RCD forces, described by witnesses as 'Rwandan and Ugandan' or 'Banyamulenge', attacked the Catholic church at Kasika the following day where they killed thirty-seven civilians, including the parish priest (Abbé Stanislas), three nuns and parishioners. Many witnesses and residents of Bukavu considered the killings as 'a punishment' for the Maï-Maï ambush the day before. Others were killed in the surrounding communities; estimates of the total number of dead, probably at least several hundred, and the extent of destruction of houses and other infrastructure were impossible to verify due to poor security conditions and, in particular, uncertainty regarding the protection of witnesses.[47]

The RCD forces also killed the Mwami Mubeza, chief of Lwindi collectivity, and members of his family. Many victims were executed by machete or other sharp objects; a smaller number were shot. One church official stated that a nun had been cut entirely in two from the head through the entire body. Many bodies of children and babies were found in latrines. One witness interviewed by Human Rights Watch had identified many of the church officials before their burial in Kasika and assisted with the extrication of corpses and surviving children from latrines.[48]

The murder of the mwami had repercussions well beyond his own small Nyindu ethnic community. The Shi of Walungu, Katana and Kabare territories, as well as the Vira and Furiiru of Uvira territory, consider that they are Nyindu or come from Nyindu country, and their chiefs derive their authority from the mwami of Lwindi collectivity.[49]

On 24 August 1998, the RCD forces carried out a scorched earth campaign along the main road through the Lwindi collectivity, killing civilians and burning houses. Among the villages attacked in this fashion were Kilongutwe, Kalama and Kalambi. Several Congolese investigators who had participated in burials and/or investigations in the days following the massacres claimed that the RCD forces destroyed many houses, at times burning civilians alive inside them. Most of the killings took place in Kilongutwe, where it was market day. The destruction of civilian infrastructure, displacement of much of the local population, and widespread fear resulting from the killings continued to make it difficult for residents in the Kasika-Mwenga area to find food, water or access to healthcare.

Again in 1999, many people were killed and several houses looted at Kiombu-Kalambi in the Lwindi *chefferie*, Mwenga territory. These killings allegedly were the work of Rwandan soldiers serving the RCD, assigned to accompany truckers on the road between the mining town of Kamituga and Bukavu. Many of the victims reportedly were killed with knives. They included a fish seller, a Free Methodist pastor, a schoolteacher, and numerous women. The attackers allegedly also carried out violence against numerous women, ranging from forcing them to walk nude in public to raping them with sticks and even burying them alive.

Héritiers de la Justice, a Protestant human rights NGO, commented that such mass killings generally represent reprisals for exchanges of gunfire between RCD troops and Maï-Maï guerrillas. In this case, according to Héritiers' informants, such exchange of fire did not happen. However, the attack seems to have been a reprisal of sorts, since the Rwandan troops pillaged the residence of the new chief of the collectivity, Mwami Bugoma Mubeza IV, who had succeeded his brother, assassinated the previous year.

At the provincial level, first the AFDL and then the RCD-Goma chose governors from among the local people, attempting with limited success to give themselves a popular base. In 1996, the AFDL named a respected historian of Shi background, Professor Anatole Bishikwabo Chubaka, as governor of South Kivu. He had enjoyed good relations with Mobutu's party, the MPR, and allegedly had been named director general of the Higher Pedagogical Institute of Bukavu (ISP) due to his good relations with the minister Mushobekwa, his co-ethnic. Bishikwabo allegedly was also close to some of the Tutsi professors at the ISP. However, this appointment was unpopular with many community leaders. When Bishikwabo was named a minister in Kinshasa, Professor Magabe of the Catholic University of Bukavu (a Muhavu from Ijwi) replaced him as governor.

When the RCD took over in 1998, it installed Kantitima Bashengezi (from Kaziba) as governor. He was succeeded by Patient Mwandanga, a Mushi from Ngweshe, head of an ethnic militia known as Mudundu 40 (after a medicinal plant that can supposedly fight many diseases).

The Shi (Bashi) and their ethnic militia Mudundu 40 adopted a position between outright collaboration and resistance to the AFDL, the RCD and the Rwandans. The Shi reportedly felt that they should have been included in the planning of the overthrow of Mobutu in 1996; instead, they felt that they were seen as one of the biggest threats against the AFDL rebellion. This was one of the reasons why they created their own militia, Mudundu 40, early in 1997. Another reason (according to interviews conducted by Hans Romkema of Life and Peace) was the desecration of royal tombs and the killing of the Mwami of Lwindi.[50]

The leaders of Mudundu 40 and its political arm, the Forces de Résistance et de la Défense du Kivu (FRDK), went to see the Rwandan authorities around 2000 and offered to collaborate in the fight against the Interahamwe, in return for being allowed to manage Bushi. Other Congolese, both within the Shi community and outside, for example the Maï-Maï of Padiri, regarded the Mudundu 40/FRDK position as treasonous.

In 2003, when Rwanda officially withdrew its forces from South Kivu, its client the RCD installed Xavier Chiribanya as governor of the province. Chiribanya, a Shi from the Bukavu area, was known on the street as 'Number Nineteen', for his presumed place on the list of assassins of Laurent Kabila. He allegedly maintained a militia outside the military command structure.

In the aftermath of the peace agreements of Sun City and Pretoria, Congo was supposed to create a unified national army and civil–territorial administration. Some Rwandophone officers of North and South Kivu led the resistance to *brassage* (intermingling) of officers and troops from the various composants. The two most prominent of these were Colonel Jules Mutebutsi (a Munyamulenge from South Kivu) and General Laurent Nkunda (Rwandophone Tutsi allegedly from Rutshuru in Kivu). These officers led a mutiny against their superiors, and briefly took over the city of Bukavu (capital of South Kivu).

Lengthy negotiations in Kinshasa had led to a formula for redistributing military and civilian posts. The large blocs of territory occupied by the two major rebels factions – the MLC in the north, and the RCD in the east – or held by the central government were to be broken up. Two principles were to govern this redistribution. First, each composant – including not only the central government and the major rebel movements, but also the unarmed opposition and the civil society – would receive posts of governor and vice governor in numbers roughly corresponding to their political weight, and, second, no composant was to control both a province and the corresponding military region.

For South Kivu, this meant that the former RCD military officers were to be placed under a commander loyal to Kinshasa. This meant also that the province was to be headed by a governor and two vice governors, each named by a different composant. The governor of South Kivu was to come from the former unarmed opposition, seconded by vice governors from the RCD and the civil society.

Throughout 2004, public opinion in the east of Congo in general and in the city of Bukavu in particular, feared the 'third war' after those of 1996–97 and 1998–2002. A series of incidents, some rather minor in retrospect, kept this fear alive. Colette Braeckman of *Le Soir* (Brussels) evoked the possible 'third war' for the first time late in February, after a night of shooting at Bukavu. The following day, a large demonstration was held, denouncing the passivity of the United Nations mission (MONUC).

Early in 2004, Kinshasa sent General Prosper Nabyolwa, a veteran of Mobutu's army, to Bukavu as commander of the 10th Military Region. He attempted to take effective control, notably by seizing arms caches in the residences of various civilian and military authorities, including Chiribanya. In response, Nabyolwa's second in command, the Munyamulenge Colonel Mutebutsi, ordered an attack on Nabyolwa's residence. Two guards were killed. The general was unhurt but was forced to go into hiding.[51]

Braeckman explains these clashes by the presence at Bukavu of a group of officers called 'Friends of Masasu', after the former partner of Laurent-Désiré Kabila, later executed for treason. These men were implacable opponents of Kinshasa. Some were implicated in massacres of civilians; others had been sentenced in absentia by a Kinshasa military court for their alleged roles in the assassination of Kabila. These 'Friends of Masasu' had supposedly hidden arms in the city, in preparation for launching a 'third rebellion'. General Nabyolwa had attempted to seize these arms.

Nabyolwa returned to Kinshasa in March and was replaced by Brigadier General Félix Mbuza Mabe. Mutebutsi was suspended but continued to circulate freely at Bukavu with a contingent of men under his orders.

As Braeckman reports, the population of Bukavu was convinced that the soldiers who occupied strategic points in the city were in reality Rwandan soldiers who had crossed the frontier during the night and put on RCD uniforms. (This may belong in the realm of myth, but Bukavu people would have been able to recognize 'new faces' among Mutebutsi's men.)

From 26 May to 9 June, there was sustained fighting for the control of Bukavu. On one side were soldiers under the command of Colonel Mutebutsi and General Nkunda. On the other side were men of the 10th Military Region, under General Mbuza Mabe. On the face of it, this was a clash between units loyal to Kinshasa and Kinyarwanda-speaking mutineers, but some interpreted the struggle as the beginning of a third Congo war, launched by Rwanda.

General Nkunda had been named by the central government to command a military region. However, he had refused to go to Kinshasa to be sworn in, in the framework of reunification of the national army, as had his colleague Erik Ruhorimbere. At Bukavu, rumours circulated regarding alleged clandestine meetings between Nkunda, Ruhorimbere, and Mutebutsi (suspended as commander of the 9th brigade at Uvira) and on the recruitment of militias and their training in the territories of Kabare, Kalehe and Uvira.

Late in May, Colonel Mutebutsi attempted to cross from Bukavu to the neighbouring city of Cyangugu (Rwanda), with a group of armed men. Troops at the border prevented him from doing so. Human Rights Watch identifies this clash between soldiers loyal to Mutebutsi and others loyal to Mbuza as the catalyst for the subsequent violence.

At least one soldier from Mbuza's forces was killed in the fighting. Over the following two days other soldiers from Mbuza's forces killed Banyamulenge civilians in apparent reprisal for the killing of their comrade.[52] This set off battles in Bukavu, between Mutebutsi's men and those of Mbuza. MONUC (the UN mission) attempted to resolve the conflict by negotiation. It persuaded Mutebutsi to return to camp and lay down his weapons.

In the meantime, General Nkunda was advancing on Bukavu from the north, at the head of a column of several thousand men. They reportedly overran several military positions, killing a UN observer and soldiers from a 'Katangan' unit loyal to Kinshasa. Nkunda took control of Bukavu on 2 June. Nkunda claimed he wanted 'to protect his people'. There had been some killings of Banyamulenge as well as of other civilians, but the claim that the military operation was motivated solely by this concern seems unlikely, according to Human Rights Watch.

Public news reports in Rwanda exaggerated the threat against the Banyamulenge, claiming that massacres were taking place and that genocide was planned. Some members of the Banyamulenge community may have welcomed action by Nkunda and Mutebutsi, but others denounced the actions of the two renegade commanders, saying in a press statement that they had 'no need of these criminals for their defence'.[53]

Human Rights Watch researchers documented war crimes carried out by pro-government soldiers under the command of Mbuza and by forces under Nkunda and Mutebutsi. Soldiers of the 10th Military Region reportedly killed at least fifteen civilians, most or all of them Banyamulenge, between 26 and 28 May in Bukavu. They were said to have killed some of these civilians during searches for hidden weapons and Banyamulenge soldiers. In several cases they rounded up small groups of young Banyamulenge men and summarily executed them, in at least one case after having first detained them in a container located at Place de l'Indépendance, in the middle of town. Two witnesses told HRW that General Mbuza visited this site of detention on 27 and 28 May. MONUC later visited the detention centre and closed it down, freeing the remaining people still being held.

Soldiers of the 10th Military Region and some people who were not Banyamulenge suggested to HRW that the people killed were armed and preparing to fight on the side of Colonel Mutebutsi. This is doubtful, especially in the cases of women and children killed. Human Rights Watch reported a number of cases of abuse that occurred on 27 May, including the following:

- At around 10 a.m. soldiers brought four Banyamulenge university students including two student leaders, from their home to a major intersection in Bukavu. Soon after they brought two younger students, also Banyamulenge. Soldiers undressed them, tied them together, and beat them severely. Soldiers then brought them to a nearby field, apparently to prevent passing UN peacekeepers from seeing what was happening. They beat the students to death and threw the bodies into a shallow grave.
- Soldiers searched homes known to belong to Banyamulenge in the Nyawera neighbourhood, supposedly looking for weapons, and forced some fifty people to come from their hiding places. About twenty soldiers escorted these Banyamulenge civilians to the centre of town, claiming they were taking them to safety. There soldiers from another groups fired on the civilians killing a three-year-old girl, a thirteen-year-old boy and two adult men. At least five others were seriously injured, including two girls, one woman, and two men. Some fled, but the rest were taken to the empty home of a police officer, himself one of the Banyamulenge. The civilians were initially guarded and prevented from leaving the house but representatives of the group were later brought to General Mbuza, who agreed to release them to UN peacekeepers. They were taken to the border and crossed into Rwanda as refugees.
- About fifty people took shelter in a church compound on 26 May and were discovered by soldiers on 28 May. The soldiers demanded that the Banyamulenge whom they called 'Rwandans' pay money for their safety. The group then fled to the home of a local person not of Banyamulenge origin. Soldiers also appeared there and demanded more money, which was given by the owner of the house. MONUC evacuated the group the next day.

Representatives of the UNHCR reported that almost 3,000 civilians, most of them Banyamulenge, fled to Rwanda as a result of the violence in Bukavu. UNHCR reported that some of the refugees had suffered gunshot wounds and others had machete or knife wounds.

In several cases persons who were not Banyamulenge intervened to save those targeted by soldiers. These persons included a soldier who protected Banyamulenge against his fellow soldiers.

Mutebutsi and Nkunda claimed they took control of Bukavu to stop the killings of Banyamulenge people but their own forces also killed civilians and carried out widespread sexual violence and looting. As Nkunda's soldiers marched from Goma to Bukavu, they attacked numerous villages along the way. In the town of Minova local sources alleged that they killed two women and one young girl; while in Babamba they killed a further three people.

In Bukavu, rebel soldiers shot a fifty-five-year-old man in his home while looting it; the man reportedly died later in the hospital. Several other killings of civilians were reported during the period when these commanders had control of the town. International and local sources reported dissident forces going from house to house, raping and looting. Many women and girls were so fearful of being raped they went into hiding. In the neighbourhood of Kadutu, some one hundred women and girls took refuge in a local church, adding on additional layers of clothing as a disincentive to potential rapists. Another witness told Human Rights Watch:

> On Thursday June 3 two Banyamulenge soldiers came to my house. They pointed their gun at my head and asked for money. We were five men in the house, and my little sisters were in the back room. They asked for phones, and demanded $100 from each of the men. So I gave them $75 and a telephone, because we had heard there had been other killings ... Then they locked the men in a room and went to the girls' room. They attacked my seventeen-year-old sister. I heard her screaming ... One soldier came back into the room and said: 'Until you accept the Banyamulenge as Congolese, there will be no calm in Bukavu. Mbuza Mabe killed our mothers, sister and uncles. We leave you with that message.'

Human Rights Watch noted that Rwanda had been the chief supporter of the RCD-Goma since 1998 and that Nkunda had been trained in Rwanda. There were persistent reports about the continued involvement of Rwandan forces in eastern DRC. On 21 April 2004, a MONUC patrol in North Kivu was stopped by 400 Rwandan soldiers and asked to withdraw to its base.[54]

In Bukavu local sources alleged that elements of the Rwandan military were present during the Mutebutsi–Nkunda episode. They claimed to have identified commanders they knew from the previous Rwandan occupation and also claimed to have been able to distinguish vehicles, weapons and uniforms as those of the Rwandan army. President Kabila accused Rwanda of colluding with the rebels in their efforts to take Bukavu. The Rwandan government denied the accusation.

As Human Rights Watch pointed out, this combat conformed to a larger pattern in which rebellious factions of former rebel groups plus other armed groups that had not joined the transitional process were using violence to oppose integration into the new DRC army and to challenge the authority of the transitional government. Leaders of the former rebel groups apparently encouraged or tolerated these challenges even while taking part in the transitional government, perhaps seeking to keep all options open should the peace process not bring the desired dividends.

Human Rights Watch also argued that the abuses committed in Bukavu demonstrate what can happen when past crimes go unpunished. General Nkunda was a commanding officer over RCD-Goma soldiers who indiscriminately killed civilians, committed numerous rapes and carried out widespread looting in Kisangani in 2002.[55] Despite condemnation of these crimes by then UN High Commissioner for Human Rights Mary Robinson, neither Nkunda nor other officers were investigated or charged. On the contrary, Nkunda was proposed by the RCD-Goma to help lead the unified army, as were a number of officers from other former rebel groups who were implicated in war crimes and crimes against humanity over the past years. The national military leadership accepted the nomination of Nkunda. Although he did not take up the post, the message had been sent that authors of such crimes would be rewarded with government positions and not be punished.

MONUC negotiated Nkunda's withdrawal from Bukavu, and Mbuza Mabe re-entered the city to the acclamation of much of the population. Mutebutsi and his men withdrew south to the area of Kamanyola. There, MONUC fired on them (claiming that they had fired on its helicopter) and they fled into Rwanda. Nkunda withdrew to Minova, in the north-east corner of South Kivu, near the RCD bastion at Goma (North Kivu).

Following the events of May–June 2004 at Bukavu, the military command structure (10th Military Region) was under the orders of Kinshasa. A governor named by the so-called 'unarmed opposition', and two vice governors, one from the 'civil society' and the other from the RCD, administered the province. When I visited Bukavu early in 2005, the ethnic composition of this administration was being discussed, since the governor and one of his deputies were from the Lega community, while the other vice governor was a Munyamulenge. Some of the Shi, who consider that Bukavu belongs to them, apparently were unhappy.

Below the provincial level, the RCD-Goma 'government' partially remodelled the map of South Kivu. In 1998, it satisfied the long-standing demand of the Banyamulenge for a territorial base by creating a territory of Minembwe, at the expense of the neighbouring zones of Uvira, Fizi and Mwenga. Perhaps in order to camouflage this move or to make it harder to reverse, several other changes were made at the same time. Among the Shi living on the periphery of Bukavu, the 'commune urbano-rurale de Kasha' saw the light of day.

Kalehe Territory, in the north of the province, was the most seriously affected by RCD remodelling. Kalehe had a majority of Havu people, with minorities of Tembo and Rwandophones. It lost land and population in the west, as the RCD created a new territory of Bunyakiri. Creation of the new territory, with a majority population of Tembo, apparently was intended to reduce the level of opposition of the Maï-Maï militia to the RCD administration. It failed, since the Maï-Maï were not mainly fighting for a new territory but to get rid of the Rwandans and their allies.[56]

Within Kalehe Territory, the Buhavu Collectivity lost land and population as one of its constituent *groupements* became a separate collectivity. This *groupement*, Buzi, included both Havu and Rwandophones settled there during the colonial period.[57] The creation of the Collectivité-Chefferie de Buzi clearly was politically motivated. The chief of Buzi *groupement* had not welcomed the arrival of the AFDL forces in 1996, and in consequence his house had been pillaged. The chief was named head of civil aviation (Régie des Voies aériennes) by the RCD, apparently as a reward for his support. In return, he cooperated with RCD leaders by granting a vast land concession to a group of Rwandophone politicians, reportedly including the Munyamulenge Bizima Karaha, and Rwandan General Kabarebe. Before the statutory three-year delay for the concession to be permanent, a minister of the central government annulled it.

A third area of South Kivu (other than the Mulenge-Itombwe highlands in the south and the Buzi area in the north) has been the object of contestation between Rwanda and Congo over the years, and that is the island of Ijwi (or Idjwi), in the middle of Lake Kivu. The people of Ijwi are Kihavu-speakers, like those of Kalehe, on the mainland. Rwanda briefly occupied Ijwi at the end of the nineteenth century. Its status as Rwandan territory was never consolidated, and the final border agreement between Germany and Belgium, in 1910, left Ijwi as part of colonial Congo. To this day, ethnic nationalists such as Msgr Kanyamachumbi cite Ijwi as Rwandan territory lost due to the Berlin Conference.[58]

During the 1970s, when Mobutu's Rwandan Tutsi chef de cabinet Bisengimana Rwema wanted to create a Zairian or Congolese identity, he claimed to be from Ijwi. The claim apparently was false, but the fact that he made it testifies to the important but ambiguous place of Ijwi in the political culture of the Great Lakes region. Bisengimana went on to become a major coffee plantation owner on Ijwi, through the 'Zairianization' process. (He also reportedly acquired cattle ranches at Masisi, in North Kivu.)

The question of Ijwi and its supposed connections to Rwanda has arisen again and again. Recently, the Havu community of Ijwi met in Bukavu to deny that Ijwi people had voted in Rwandan elections. Rwandan citizens living in Ijwi had returned home to vote, it was explained, as indeed had Rwandan citizens from other parts of Congo. It was stressed that the chiefs of the two collectivities on Ijwi had in no way encouraged their subjects to vote in Rwandan elections. In a 2005 interview with a member of a chiefly family from Ijwi, I was assured that Ijwi was firmly in the camp of President Joseph Kabila for the upcoming elections.

Gatumba and beyond

After the withdrawal of Nkunda and Mutebusi from Bukavu, talk of a third war receded. The problems of South Kivu and the Banyamulenge were far from over, however. On 13 August 2004, armed fighters, the majority of them belonging to Burundi's Front National de Libération (National Liberation Front, FNL) massacred at least 152 Congolese civilians and wounded 106 others, in Gatumba refugee camp, near the Burundian capital of Bujumbura. The FNL was the most extreme of Burundi's pro-Hutu, anti-Tutsi movements. The victims were principally Banyamulenge but (argued Human Rights Watch) the massacre was more than another case of ethnic violence. It occurred at the intersection of the two 'fragile peace processes' in Burundi and Congo and 'underlined if not aggravated the climate of political tension that continues to exist' in the two countries. The contenders for power in these two countries, and the protagonists in the cross-border conflicts, immediately tried to use the massacre to serve their own political interests. In so doing, they augmented the chances of a new war and of further massacres of civilians.[59]

The soldiers of the UN peacekeeping mission claimed to have been unable to save the civilians because they were not informed of the attack. Burundi's soldiers and gendarmes failed to act, even though the attack occurred near their bases.

The governments of Rwanda and Burundi and the leadership of Congo's RCD quickly circulated an interpretation according to which the Gatumba attack had been organized and carried out by a force crossing from Congo, combining Congolese Maï-Maï, Rwandan Hutu 'Interahamwe' and FNL fighters. This version was rapidly taken up in the press, and was subsequently adopted by the UN Secretary General.[60]

The governments of Rwanda and Burundi threatened to invade Congo. In the case of Rwanda, the justification was unclear, since the crime had occurred on Burundian soil and the victims were Congolese. The position of Congo was equally politicized, in that the Congolese nationality of the Banyamulenge victims, contested during their lifetime, was reaffirmed in death.

Amid the intense emotion and manipulation, Human Rights Watch was a lonely voice, re-examining the evidence for the supposed international plot. HRW found that Banyamulenge men, including at least one connected with the RCD intelligence service, were watching over survivors in the hospital, and intervening in attempted interviews. Despite this interference, HRW was able to interview a man who was familiar with the official version but refuted a key point. Despite allegations that some of the attackers had spoken Kinyarwanda, Kiswahili, Kifulero, Kibembe and even Lingala, he said he had heard no language other than Kirundi.

On this point, the official version strains credulity. Supposedly some of the attackers were Maï-Maï, and thus connected to the Kinshasa government. But why would Maï-Maï in the Uvira-Fizi area, local youth, be using Lingala, language of the Congo military since the colonial era, in an operation in Burundi?

Other arguments for the involvement of Rwandans and Congolese in the attack fare no better. Tracts supposedly were circulating in the region, warning Ruberwa or the Banyamulenge that they were in danger. Despite repeated reports in the press, HRW was unable to find anyone who had seen such a tract at Gatumba.

Arguments on the other side were equally absurd. Persons wishing to justify the massacre claimed that Rwandan military personnel had been present, and that the attackers had clashed with these troops. A document circulated in the name of the Civil Society of South Kivu alleged that Ruberwa had visited the Gatumba camp on the eve of the massacre. The same document added a claim that Gatumba (Katumba) was in reality on Congolese soil, and called on the African Union to redraw the border to reflect this reality.[61]

The Banyamulenge have had an ambiguous relationship to the Congolese state and to their neighbours in South Kivu, for generations. The account of Weis, written in the 1950s before decolonization loomed on the horizon, is eloquent in this regard. Depelchin, writing in the 1970s (after independence and the 'rebellions'), provides further evidence of a people setting itself apart. As such, the Banyamulenge were an easy target for scapegoating on the part of a demagogue such as Anzuluni Bembe.

The war of 1996 found the Banyamulenge open to another form of exploitation, this time on the part of the RPF government in Rwanda. Some of them sided enthusiastically with Rwanda, while others like Ruhimbika and Commandant Masunzu opted for Congo.

The constitutional referendum of December 2005 and the elections of 2006 were supposed to put an end to years of confusion and bloodshed in Congo. Some 25 million Congolese registered to vote. In some areas of South Kivu, Banyamulenge reportedly were able to register with no difficulty. In 'their' area, the high plateau of Minembwe-Bijombo, where they form the majority, many apparently registered. Elsewhere, where Banyamulenge form a minority, they reportedly met with violence on the part of local people who did not want to see them register.

In any case, the new parliament is based on previous territorial divisions. New territories created under RCD rule – Minembwe territory for the Banyamulenge, and Bunyakiri territory for the Tembo – did not exist in the eyes of the Independent Electoral Commission.

Violence and intimidation against the RCD and its (perceived) supporters, Banyamulenge and others, were commonplace during the election campaign of 2006. The RCD office near Bukavu town centre was sacked. Participants in an RCD march were beaten. The majority of the population tacitly approved of this violence against those seen as accomplices of Rwanda during the two wars and the recent occupation of Bukavu by General Nkunda.

In the end, the elections of 2006 seem to have consecrated the disappearance of the Banyamulenge from the political scene in Bukavu and throughout the province. The campaign pitted a majority bloc, Swahili-speaking and aligned behind Kabila, against a minority bloc of Lingala-speakers backing Bemba.

As the time of writing, South Kivu remains suspended between war and peace. Some units of Interahamwe have returned home to Rwanda, but others continue their activities, mistreating and exploiting the local population. Rwanda periodically threatens to intervene against them, as it threatened to do during the Mutebutsi–Nkunda episode and in the immediate aftermath of the Gatumba massacre.

FIVE
War in North Kivu

§ The Tanzanian musician Mr Nice recorded a song called 'Rafiki' ('Friend'). His version goes as follows:

Unakula naye	You eat together
Unacheka naye	You laugh together
Kumbe mwenzako anaona gee	But he hates you, even though you considered him a friend.

Students of Goma invented a parody of 'Rafiki', according to which:[1]

Tunakula naye	We eat together
Tunacheka naye	We laugh together
Tuna-tricher naye	We cheat together
Kumbe mwenzako ni Rwandophone-ee	But now our friend says he is a Rwandophone

The rivalries among students had thus been reduced to a dichotomy, the Rwandophones or Kinyarwanda-speakers against the others, presumably 'authentic Congolese' who speak other languages. The expression 'Congophone' began to be heard, even though it literally makes no sense, since Congo as opposed to Kongo is not a language.

The process of reduction had several aspects: the Kinyarwanda-speakers had to overcome their internal divisions, between Hutu and Tutsi and between descendants of long-term residents of Congo and more recent arrivals. The 'authentic' Congolese had to overcome other divisions, notably between those who considered themselves authentic residents or *originaires* of North Kivu, those who were from other fragments of the former Kivu, and Congolese from elsewhere, e.g. Katanga or Kasai.

Two quite different types of conflict have been conflated: local-level conflicts involving land tenure and chieftaincy, in which Rwanda-speakers are pitted against so-called 'autochthonous' or 'native' populations, and regional-level conflicts pitting Rwanda-speaking elites against others, led by the Nande of North Kivu and the Shi of

South Kivu. Superimposed on these two levels and promoting changes on each is a third level of conflict, of international warfare waged on Congolese soil. To a far greater degree than in South Kivu, the 1996 war came into a province already at war.

Each of the key concepts on the various levels is problematic. What is a chief, for example, and what are his so-called customary prerogatives? What are the populations or ethnic groups present, and in what circumstances did they emerge (by what process of ethnogenesis)? Which groups are Congolese, and how does one identify them?

Bisected by the Equator, North Kivu lies along the border between DR Congo and its neighbours Uganda and Rwanda. Within Congo, it borders on Province Orientale to the north, Maniema to the west, and South Kivu to the south.[2] Like South Kivu, North Kivu represents a transition from the region of mountains and lakes in the east, to the Congo basin in the west. The highlands in the eastern portion of the province are densely populated, whereas the equatorial forests in the west are almost empty. According to 1984 census figures, the predominantly Rwandophone zones (territories) of Goma, Rutshuru and Masisi reported densities of 423.2, 126.2 and 109.6 inhabitants per square kilometre respectively. In the so-called Grand Nord, the zones of Beni and Lubero reported densities of 94.9 and 44.2 inhabitants per square kilometre. In contrast, the western forest zone of Walikale had just 6.2 inhabitants per square kilometre.[3] Raw density figures are misleading, since in recent years large areas have been given over to cattle, at the expense of cultivation, especially in Masisi.[4]

North Kivu is characterized by remarkable political and cultural homogeneity, as Willame writes.[5] All over the province there were tiny 'theatre states' governed by ritual and symbols rather than by power. Each possessed elaborate rules of succession, of access to the throne, and of royal funerals, as if these tiny units were somehow the equal of the much larger states to the east, i.e. Rwanda or Ankole.

North Kivu includes three major ethnic clusters, the Rwando-phones (Hutu and Tutsi) and Hunde in the south-east, the Nande in the north, and the forest peoples (Nyanga, Lega and others) in the west. The Nande, Hunde and Nyanga speak interlacustrine languages similar to Kinyarwanda, but there is little sign of ethno-linguistic solidarity.

North Kivu has a long history as an administrative subdivision of the former Kivu province. It enjoyed separate status as a province ('provincette' in the evocative expression used by the Congolese elite) from 1962 to 1968, when Mobutu re-created most of the former colonial provinces, and from 1988 to the present.

The Rwandophones of North Kivu

The 'autochthones' of North Kivu tend to claim that all the Rwandophones are foreigners. The Rwandophones tend to claim that portions of North Kivu were detached from Rwanda by colonial partition. Neither of these claims is valid.

There are several different sorts of Kinyarwanda-speakers in North Kivu. Some were pre-colonial residents of the area. Others came in during the colonial period, during decolonization, or even since the independence of Congo and Rwanda, in 1960 and 1962 respectively.[6]

The present Rutshuru territory has been inhabited by Kinyarwanda-speakers for centuries. It was known to Rwanda as 'Ubuhutu' (the country of the Hutu), because there were almost no Tutsi there.[7] The Hutu microstates of Rutshuru fit the model sketched by Pauwels, according to which the submission of Hutu territories on both slopes of the Congo–Nile watershed (i.e. in the present North Kivu as well as north-western Rwanda) was only nominal. These principalities, each headed by a mwami or muhinza, 'maintained a grumbling and turbulent attitude' towards the Rwandan monarch. 'These local rulers did not accept orders from anyone and continued an independent life.'[8]

Some of the current 'Rwandophone' areas of North Kivu were not under Rwandan domination in any sense. Dr R. Kandt, German resident at the Rwanda court, visited the Mokoto Lakes (present Masisi territory) in 1899. He wrote that 'several Watussi' visited him. He found them to be 'likable and simple' but 'not so handsome and elegant' as the Tutsi of Burundi and Rwanda, because these men had to work. They were not the 'sovereigns of the country', but lived in isolated villages as cattle raisers, alongside the first residents of the region, who were farmers. This was near 'Kischari', i.e. Gishari, where the Rwandophone *chefferie* would be created in the 1930s. The description of these Tutsi reminds one of the future Banyamulenge of South Kivu, who lived among the locals without dominating them.[9]

Vervloet, a Belgian officer who spent several years in the service of the Congo Free State in North Kivu at the beginning of the twentieth century, described Tutsi ('Watuzi') domination of the local people, from whom they extracted taxes that passed up the chain of command to the Mwami of Rwanda. The chief at each level kept a portion of the proceeds. Sometimes, when the court was dissatisfied with the quantity received from below, chiefs would attribute the low amount to taxpayer revolt. For the most part, according to Vervloet, the Tutsi were 'unloved' and often even 'manhandled' by their subjects. The Tutsi exactions can only 'fortify the antipathy of the Bahutu, too bent under the yoke, to try to free themselves, by use of force, from this domination'. Vervloet served in North Kivu at a time when the Free State territory extended east to the thirtieth meridian, and included Bufumbira (currently in Uganda) and Ruhengeri (in Rwanda). He refers to the local population as 'Warundi' and distinguishes several subgroups, including Kiga and Hutu. The Tutsi were foreigners, who dominated the locals. He calls the language of the Hutu 'Ki-rundi' as opposed to 'Ki-ruanda', the language of the Tutsi.[10] Ethno-national identities have evidently been transformed since then.

Vervloet finished his service in Congo shortly after the agreement of 1910, establishing the frontier between Congo and German East Africa. According to him, affinities of 'race' and 'native political units' helped determine the frontier between Belgian, German and British territory. In virtue of these principles, Germany received, in the Ruzizi basin, 'all of the Sultanate of Rwanda', some of which its agents were already occupying. It was important not to cut it in two, placing its territory in two different zones of European influence, Vervloet explained. From his perspective, the present Goma–Rutshuru–Masisi area was not part of the Sultanate or Kingdom of Rwanda.[11]

Over the years, the Belgian administration sometimes followed Vervloet in considering Hutu and Tutsi as constituting two separate groups. At other moments or in other contexts they were considered subgroups of a single group, the Rwanda or Banyarwanda. The Maes and Boone synthesis of 1935 refers to 'Baniaruanda', who are said to comprise 'three races': the Watutsi or *classe noble*, the Bahutu or 'people', and the Batwa or Pygmies. This may reflect Belgian thinking about Rwandans in general, rather than close observation of North Kivu. By the time Boone publishes her 1954 map, the Tutsi and Twa have disappeared and she refers only to Hutu. Cuypers (Vansina et al., 1966) refers to 'the Hutu of Rutshuru' but the accompanying map localizes 'Rwanda', i.e. Banyarwanda. The Hutu of Rutshuru are said to have arrived in the area before the Hunde and to have mixed with the latter. Cuypers's notions of who arrived in what order, however, are fatally flawed by his reliance on the fantasies of the colonial governor Moeller.[12]

Classifications such as those of Maes and Boone (1935) or Boone (1954) were based on administrative documents and were intended to serve the needs of administrators, among others. As regards the Banyarwanda, the Belgians pursued two quite different policies on the two sides of the border between Ruanda–Urundi and Congo. In their mandated territory, they continued the policy of relying upon and reinforcing the powers of the Tutsi-dominated states, to the detriment of the Hutu majority. In Congo, in contrast, they tended to define the Hutu as an ethnic community and to recruit chiefs from among their leaders. The policy became thoroughly incoherent when the Belgians decided to import Hutu labour from Rwanda and instal those men and their families on Congolese soil (mainly in Masisi). The consequences of that decision are still being felt. Rather than attempt to examine Belgian policy in detail, throughout North Kivu, I shall outline the main stages, and then focus on the two areas of Bwisha and Masisi.

In North Kivu, lengthy resistance to colonial rule delayed Belgian efforts to organize the region and begin economic exploitation. As of 1911, almost all the chiefs of Kivu were said to be *insoumis* (untamed, disobedient). None of the state posts had any influence beyond the adjacent villages. A major military campaign was launched, which led to the surrender of the populations living around the post of Kitofu (Masisi), the Mokoto Lakes and Bwito, in 1912. Populations living south of Lake Edward were conquered in 1913. Those living west of Lake Edward and in the plain of the Osso river remained independent.

In 1915, apparently taking advantage of Belgian involvement in the First World War, the people to the north-east of Rutshuru rose up; they were not conquered until 1919. The area west of Lake Edward was not 'pacified' until 1927, while the people of the Mitumba mountains surrendered 'definitively' only in 1934.[13]

Reorganization of local administration was begun at the end of the military campaign of 1912–13, and then was postponed until after the First World War. By then, Belgian native policy favoured not the restoration of traditional political units, but the unification of several traditional *groupements* within a given 'tribe'. When it was judged difficult to proceed directly to a *grande chefferie*, artificial units called 'sectors' were created as a transitional stage.

One of the first 'tribes' to be reorganized on this new basis was the Hutu of Bwisha. The Bwisha sector was created in 1921, regrouping the small *chefferies* whose chiefs (two Tutsi, two Hutu) had been deposed because of involvement in the uprising associated with the Nyabingi movement.[14] Other small *chefferies* of the Rutshuru basin were added to the sector, little by little, followed by those situated west of the Mitumba mountains (Bwito area). Much of the population of Bwito was not Hutu but Hunde. The sector was transformed into the *chefferie* of Bwisha, under Grand Chef Daniel Ndeze (a Hutu), in 1929. Amazingly, this chief remained in charge of the collectivity for the next sixty years. At his death, a family member succeeded him.

Other sectors were created among the Hunde, Nyanga and the Hutu of Bukumu (south of the volcanoes) in 1922. These were transformed into *chefferies* in 1930. Among the Nande, the process was slower, since resistance continued and the Belgians were unable to find effective and 'loyal' chiefs.[15]

Starting in 1933, there was a reorientation of 'native policy'. The sector was no longer seen as transitional; instead it was a non-traditional collectivity, uniting traditional units too small to stand alone. By 1942, North Kivu had been completely reorganized. It now included four territories, twelve *chefferies* and two sectors.[16]

This organization or reorganization reflects 'territorialization of ethnicity' as Vlassenroot calls it. There were two predominantly Nande territories, Beni and Lubero, including also ethnic minorities (Amba, Pere). Rutshuru was a Hutu (Rwandophone) territory, although there were some Tutsi and some Hunde as well. Masisi included one *chefferie* each for the Hunde, Nyanga and Kano (sometimes considered a branch of the Lega). It also included a separate *chefferie* of Gishari for transplanted Rwandans.

In 1944, many people in the Bapere, Banyanga and Bakano *chefferies* adopted the millenarian movement called Kitawala (a radical offshoot of the Jehovah's Witnesses) and some participated in a revolt.[17] That led the Belgians to transform these *chefferies* into sectors, to facilitate tighter administrative control.

Rutshuru was divided into two territories in 1953. The new Rutshuru territory corresponded to the *chefferie* of Bwisha while the *chefferie* Bukumu became the Territory of Goma. In the same year, Masisi was cut in two; the new Masisi included the *chefferies* of Bahunde and Gishari while Walikale included the Nyanga and Kano sectors.

The final changes of administrative structure of the colonial period came in 1957. Gishari *chefferie* was eliminated and its Banyarwanda population integrated into the Bahunde *chefferie*. Goma and Butembo, the two most important towns of North Kivu, each became *centres extra-coutumiers*.

Much of the disorder and bloodshed of the past half-century has swirled around Masisi. We shall have to examine in detail the factors underlying the creation and suppression of the Gishari *chefferie*. It must be said, however, that Belgian manipulation of population and administrative units was not limited to Gishari and Masisi but characterized North Kivu as a whole.

Rutshuru was apparently quite densely populated when the Belgians arrived, yet they proceeded to move people around in ways that greatly increased pressure on the land. They moved Rwandophone Hutu out, to clear space for European coffee planters (who received 60 to 70 hectares each) and to create, at the demand of the Institut des Parcs nationaux du Congo Belge (National Park Institute), the Virunga Park. The new park occupied half of Rutshuru territory and cut the Bwisha *chefferie* in half.[18] The people displaced by these major projects were resettled in *paysannats* or state farms, where they lived alongside Nande, whose home territory is further north. The Hutu and Nande were forced to grow coffee.[19]

Masisi territory was sparsely populated, mainly by Hunde; there were a few Tutsi pastoral communities. The Belgians decided to 'develop' it by bringing in Hutu from Rwanda to work on European plantations. They needed 'suitable', willing workers and the local Hunde people were both less 'suitable' in Belgian eyes and also less willing to work on Belgian plantations.[20] Another motivation on the part of the Belgians was to ease population pressure in famine-prone Rwanda. Rwandan Hutu were also sent to the mines of Katanga, where some of their descendants can be found to this day.

In 1937, the Belgian authorities in Rwanda and Kivu and the para-statal Comité National du Kivu signed an agreement to create a new body called the Mission d'Immigration des Banyarwanda (MIB). The MIB was given the authority to manage immigration of Rwandans to Masisi, from the formalities to perform upon their arrival, to their political organization, and the salaries to be paid to the plantation workers.

The Belgians had recently fused many tiny Hunde chiefdoms under a single neo-traditional mwami, Kalinda. They then persuaded the new mwami to cede a piece of Hunde land to the newcomers, in exchange for cash.[21]

The Belgians asked the Rwandan authorities to supply a certain number of their subjects as emigrants (and to ensure that these people did not return to 'over-populated' Rwanda). At the same time, they promised Rwanda's Mwami Rudahigwa that 'the emigrants would preserve close political ties with Rwanda'.

The Rwandan (and Congolese Rwandophone) version of the Masisi transaction has Rudahigwa negotiate the agreement with Kalinda and pay 24,000 (or 29,000) Belgian francs as purchase price or *prime* (i.e. bonus) for the land. Rudahigwa installed Bideri, a Tutsi, as chief of the mainly Hutu population of the new circumscription, Gishari, created on Hunde land.[22]

This version of events is incredible. The Belgians were very in-terventionist in Congo. It hardly seems likely that they would have allowed a paramount chief from one colony (Rudahigwa) to negotiate a deal with a lesser chief from a neighbouring colony. Rudahigwa had recently been installed as mwami, replacing his father (who displeased the Belgians) while (as explained) Kalinda had been appointed head of an artificial *chefferie*. Neither mwami could have defied the Belgians.

In any case, the Belgians were concerned that this transaction might lead to problems. Under international law, the mandated territory of Ruanda–Urundi and the Colony of Belgian Congo were absolutely distinct, even though the Belgians had attached Ruanda–Urundi to Congo, administratively. Belgium could not permit a conflict over the rights of the Rwandan mwami to lead to a call for annexation of part of Kivu to Rwanda. That would certainly draw unwelcome attention from the League of Nations, or later the United Nations.

The story of the agreement between the two bami (or mwamis) is ideological. It recasts a Belgian administrative decision as a decision taken by Africans. About the same time, the Abbé Alexis Kagame produced a version of Rwandan history according to which Rwanda had conquered vast portions of what would become eastern Congo, as early as the fifteenth century![23] Logically, the two arguments are incompatible: if Masisi had belonged to Rwanda since the fifteenth century, why did Mwami Rudahigwa need to negotiate an agreement with his subordinate, the 'mwami' of the Hunde? Practically, the two arguments are mutually reinforcing, in that they justify the implantation of Rwandan subjects in Congo.

More than 25,000 Rwandans were settled in Masisi between 1937 and 1945, and another 60,000 in a second wave between 1949 and 1955. As Kraler points out, 'many more may have come on their own accord, joining resettled relatives, friends and neighbours'.[24] At first, the Mwami of Rwanda and his associates seem to have tried to implement the new agreement by sending Tutsi pastoralists to Masisi. In 1939, the Belgians discovered that 72 per cent of the Rwandans in Masisi were Tutsi, compared with only 28 per cent Hutu. This was contrary to their intention of providing agricultural workers to the European settlers, and to a broader policy of discouraging Tutsi pastoralism in North Kivu. Steps were taken to reverse the trend, and Hutu soon became the majority.

The Rwandophones insisted on having their own collectivity on Hunde soil, and the Belgians accepted this for a while, in the form of the Gishari *chefferie*. The first significant conflict between Hunde and Banyarwanda arose when the latter tried to have their collectivity enlarged. In 1957, the Belgians abolished Gishari. The Rwandophone immigrants remained in Masisi but had to accept the authority of the Hunde mwami.

As the colonial era drew to a close, there were several Rwandophone majority circumscriptions in North Kivu. In addition to the Bahunde *chefferie* in Masisi, these included the Centre Extra-Coutumier of Goma (future Ville de Goma), and the Bwisha, Bwito and Bukumu *chefferies*. The chiefs of these units, and of the other circumscriptions of North Kivu, cannot be considered 'traditional' chiefs, ruling according to 'custom', although they were described as such.

The Tutsi refugees of 1959 and thereafter

Violence in Rwanda, before and after the overthrow of the monarchy, led many Tutsi to flee into Uganda, Tanzania, Burundi and Congo. The 'locals' tended to interpret this process in the light of previous experience. Relations between the Tutsi and the Nyanga, around Ihula (Walikale territory), were apparently good. In Masisi territory, in contrast, the refugees were settled despite fierce opposition from the locals. Under pressure from the UNHCR, Hunde notables granted provisional permission for the refugees to settle at Bibwe, but insisted that the land on which they settled remained Hunde property.[25]

Facing the hostility of the Hutu regimes first of Kayibanda, then of Habyarimana, back home, the Tutsi refugees had little choice but to seek to integrate themselves into their host country, Congo. For those Rwandophones already in Congo before independence, accession to citizenship was easy, despite the hostility of some locals. The presence of a large Rwandophone community made it easy for these refugees to 'melt in', especially since Hutu–Tutsi tensions were not as great as they would become later on. A series of changes in the law on nationality (see below), and the laxity of the administrators charged with enforcing the law, made it relatively easy for refugees having arrived after 1959 to gain Congolese nationality.

As Rukatsi notes, the behaviour of some chiefs, notably among the Hunde, likewise facilitated the integration of the Banyarwanda. If one believes that the importance of a chief depends on the number of his subordinates, then such a chief will tend to want to ensure that the newcomers remain and even have the right to vote, although not the right to be elected to office.[26]

In Masisi territory, the Rwandophones paid Hunde chiefs for access to land. Politically the Rwandophones were dependent on the Hunde, but economically, the Hunde were dependent on the Rwandophones.

The result, as Musoni stresses, was a mutual sentiment of injustice. The Rwandophones felt they already owned the land they cultivated, and did not see why they should continue to pay *redevances* ('custom-ary' rent or royalties) to the chief. The Hunde saw the Rwandophones as trying to escape from legitimate obligations. Musoni's Rwando-phone informants told him that these tensions built up, then exploded in ethnic conflict, culminating in 1963 in the revolt or war called 'Kanyarwanda', after a mythical ancestor of all Rwandans.

Recruitment of an African elite

Until independence, education and other social services were al-most entirely in the hands of the Catholic missions. The southern portion of the present North Kivu was included in the Apostolic Vicariate of Bukavu. This was the fiefdom of the White Fathers. The northern portion of the present North Kivu – the 'Grand Nord' in local terminology – was entrusted to the Assumptionist Fathers. As a result of the activities of these two missionary orders, primary and post-primary education were more developed in the 'Grand Nord', home of the Nande ethnic group, than in the southern portion of North Kivu (present territories of Goma, Rutshuru, Masisi and Wa-likale). Because the network of primary and post-primary schools was relatively less developed in the south, pupils from these territories had to go to Bukavu to pursue their education.

Within the southern portion of the present North Kivu, 'missions and schools were set up almost exclusively among the Banyarwanda'.[27] Prior to the arrival of the immigrants from Rwanda, there were three missions and eleven schools in Rutshuru, among the Banyarwanda, one mission and four schools in Masisi, among the Hunde, and no missions or schools at Walikale, among the Nyanga.

In 1960, after a large number of Rwandan immigrants had arrived, there were ten missions and 241 schools in Goma, Rutshuru, Masisi and Walikale, but the imbalance created earlier persisted. Five of the missions and ninety-six of the schools were in Goma–Rutshuru. In Masisi, which by then had a substantial number of Rwandophones, there were four missions and 115 schools. In Walikale, home of the Nyanga and of the Kano (Lega), there was only one mission and thirty schools.

Thus, there were two rival elites in what became North Kivu: the Nande in the north and the Banyarwanda in the south. The other groups, Hunde, Nyanga etc., were greatly disadvantaged.

These disparities show up clearly in data on participation in national and provincial politics. The one participant from North

Kivu in the Round Table Conference on Politics, held in Brussels in January–February 1960, was from the Banyarwanda community. Two Banyarwanda and one Nyanga took part in the Round Table Conference on Economics (Brussels, April–May).

The Lumumba government of 1960 included two Banyarwanda of North Kivu and one Nyanga. The Adoula governments (1961–64) included two Banyarwanda, one Nande and one Nyanga. At the provincial level, the Kivu government of Jean Miruho included four Banyarwanda, three Nande, one Hunde and no Nyanga.[28] The imbalance in the Catholic Church hierarchy was even more striking than in the political sector, as Musoni demonstrates.

Similar imbalances existed elsewhere in Congo, of course. The works of Mabika-Kalanda on the Luba–Lulua conflict in Kasai, and of Gérard-Libois on the Katanga secession, demonstrate the effects of such imbalances, as does my own work on the Tetela of the savannah and the forest.[29] All modernization is 'differential', after all. The Lulua, the 'authentic Katangans', and the forest Tetela all blamed their problem on the Belgians, who had favoured the outsiders over themselves. The conflict in North Kivu differed mainly in that the 'outsiders' were partly but not entirely from a neighbouring country and that their numbers were being augmented by new immigration.

The 'Provincette' of North Kivu

Conflict has been acute since Congolese independence in 1960, on the local and provincial levels. There are two questions on the local level: first, what are the boundaries of the units of local administration, and second, who is to head each unit (and thus to control the treasury and access to land).

Events in Rwanda since 1959 brought many Rwandans to eastern Congo, mainly to North Kivu. Rivalries between Rwandophones and others, both their immediate neighbours such as the Hunde and also the other highly 'modernized' community (the Nande), have dominated the region. When Congolese politicians decided to divide the six colonial provinces into smaller 'provincettes', there was great controversy around maintaining Kivu unity versus dividing it to create the 'provincette' of North Kivu. The Banyarwanda tended to favour Kivu unity, since they were dominant in Goma but also had important interests in Bukavu. The Nande tended to favour a North Kivu from which the Rwandophones were excluded.

Shortly after independence, land disputes between Hunde and Banyarwanda led to violent clashes. Hunde had replaced the Hutu administrators, put in place by the Belgians. As a consequence,

Banyarwanda started losing land, houses, shops, cattle and plantations. They tried to fight back to reclaim their rights. The resulting Kanyarwanda War, which lasted for two years, was the first sign of a spiral of unending violence at Masisi.

The Simba rebels never entered Masisi (their path having taken them from Uvira–Fizi to Maniema and on to Kisangani). The Hunde and others, however, accused the Banyarwanda of rebellion and obtained the aid of Mobutu's army to crush their enemies.

After taking power in 1965, Mobutu reunified most of the provinces, while stripping them of their separate governments. In 1988, he redivided Kivu and re-established North Kivu province.

The colonial system of land control and alienation continued after independence. The first major change came in 1973, under Mobutu, in the form of the so-called 'Bakajika Law'. All land – including that administered by chiefs – became state property. 'Customary law', as codified under colonial rule, ceased to be a legitimate source of land rights.[30]

The result of the Bakajika Law was the emergence of 'new networks of land control' based on alliances between new rural capitalists, politicians, administrators and representatives of the rural chiefs. The commercialization of rural space and relationships 'altered the social and economic structure. In Masisi, these processes produced a fragmented political economy, leading to land alienation and marginalization of large parts of the rural population, and eventually to violent conflict for access to land.'[31] Perhaps one should say it led to renewed violent conflict over access to land.

As Vlassenroot points out, this new situation had its origins in Kinshasa with 'the conversion of social capital built up in Mobutu's political entourage into economic property rights, as Mobutu rewarded political loyalty with the distribution of nationalized assets, including communal land that could now be expropriated without a preliminary investigation of vacancy'.[32]

Distribution of land as political reward was strongly felt in Masisi, where clientelist relations between chiefs, politicians and rural capitalists were prominent. The Banyarwanda – who had obtained citizenship under the law of 1972 – were major beneficiaries of the new distribution processes. These people were Mobutu's main allies in North Kivu, in part because of their vulnerability. Banyarwanda often bought their land rights in Kinshasa.

The National Conference of 1991 represented an important step in the development of democracy in Congo, as Nzongola explains.[33] What he fails to stress is that in Congo democracy is closely linked to demagogy and that the national conference provided a platform for various groups of 'autochthones' in North and South Kivu to reopen the question of nationality. In the end, the transition to democracy was aborted. One of the important consequences was an upsurge of violent conflict directed against the Rwandophones by those who saw them as usurpers occupying their lands. The genocide in Rwanda and the flight of Hutu into the two Kivus took place against a background of this conflict, and in turn contributed to it. Rwanda and Uganda invaded Congo and put Laurent Kabila in power, then invaded again when Kabila proved unable to provide security along Congo's eastern border.[34]

Conflict in North Kivu in the nineties

The Congo war of 1996 came to a North Kivu already in flames. The two regional wars (1996 and 1998) interacted with the ongoing war in the province. Through this interaction, losers in one round of fighting became winners in the next. As Bucyalimwe argues: '[North Kivu] is the only province in the DRC that suffered from an uninterrupted war in the last nine years [1993–2002]. The war itself is the result and/or the expression of "multilayered conflicts" although some outdo others in historical depth, scale and consequences. The actors are always the same. What changed in the years of war is only the stakes involved and the strategies set up to cope with them.'[35]

The various ethnic factions in North Kivu struggled to control the governorship. They sought support from the Kinshasa government. In addition, however, the Rwandophone Hutu and Tutsi sought support from abroad, accentuating the regional or transnational dimension to North Kivu conflicts, long before the AFDL war.

In 1989–90, Hutu of North Kivu formed the Mutuelle Agricole de Virunga (Agricultural Mutual Aid Society of Virunga, MAGRIVI), to defend their interests. Despite its banal title, this was a politico-military organization. About the same time, the predominantly Tutsi Rwanda Patriotic Front (RPF) allegedly became active in North Kivu, recruiting fighters and preparing a rear base for its campaign against the Habyarimana government. Between 1990 and 1992, there were localized conflicts in North Kivu, associated with the census or *identification des nationaux*. In Masisi territory, conflicts pitted Hunde against Hutu. In Rutshuru, Tutsi were aligned against Hutu in Jomba (Bwisha) and Kihondo (Bwito). In 1993, a full-blown 'Masisi War' broke out. It was not limited to Masisi Territory, but included the Wanyanga Collectivity in Walikale Territory, and Bwito Collectivity in Rutshuru Territory. Bucyalimwe explains that the broadening of conflict was due to manipulation from Kinshasa and to the actions of the 'transnational' Tutsi elite.[36] Later events, much more newsworthy, obscured these local conflicts without, however, supplanting them. These were the 1994 genocide in Rwanda, the seizure of power in Rwanda by the RPF and the flight of hundreds of thousands of Rwandan Hutu refugees into North Kivu province, and the 1996 and 1998 wars.

The transnational dimension of the North Kivu wars can be traced back to colonial labour migration, but in this context it is more useful to start with the period 1977–81, when the question of nationality was 'relaunched' in Congo/Zaire. Another aggravating factor was the decision of the Mobutu government to attempt to decentralize administration. The former Kivu was chosen as a test case. Thus Kivu was divided into three new provinces including North Kivu, and Goma became a provincial capital. At first, Mobutu continued his long-standing policy of entrusting administrative responsibility to people from other regions. At the beginning of the 1990s, however, as multi-party competition was allowed, a new administrative policy was begun. This was the policy that the Congolese call *la géopolitique* (geopolitics). This meant that governors and vice-governors would come from the local population.[37]

Mobutu attempted to hand North Kivu to loyal subordinates, headed by Enoch Nyamwisi Muvingi, whose party, the DCF/Nyamwisi, belonged to the Mouvance Présidentielle or coalition of parties backing Mobutu. In turn, Nyamwisi moved to reinforce the social base of his party. He named an associate, Jean-Pierre Kalumbo Mbogho, as governor of North Kivu and members of the DCF as heads of most of the administrative territories and provincial divisions of state services.

In 1991–92, the Sovereign National Conference (CNS) monopolized the attention of politicians, chiefs, religious leaders and leaders of NGOs. The nationality question was manipulated on a vast scale. Leaders claiming to represent each ethnic group did whatever they could to have a share of power in a major political, economic and social space. Perhaps influenced by ideas imported from Rwanda, Hutu of North Kivu began to talk about the '*facteur Hutu majoritaire*', which they hoped to use to win the elections the CNS was discussing. MAGRIVI would serve as a basis for political mobilization. Their slogan was 'The Hutu is one and indivisible', by which they seem to have meant that Hutu of Masisi and Bwisha (Rutshuru) should be united. In reaction, other ethnic groups, including the Hunde, Nyanga, Tembo, Tutsi and Nande, formed an anti-Hutu coalition.

This coalition was inherently unstable, as the province was racked by a series of rivalries, Hutu v. Tutsi, Banyarwanda (Hutu and Tutsi together) against non-Banyarwanda, Nande v. Hutu-Banyabwisha, and Nande v. Hunde.

About the same time as power was transferred to North Kivu leaders under *géopolitique*, Mobutu's troops rioted and pillaged Goma and Butembo, the two main towns in the province. Disorder spread, and with it (as Bucyalimwe argues) opportunities for politicians to pillage. He mentions the 'quasi-institutionalized' extortion from local people in Masisi and Bwito, the illegal trade in diamonds, coltan and coffee, the poaching of elephants and the smuggling of their ivory. This pillaging was facilitated by the decay of the MPR party-state that once had assured a degree of order, and of the 'customary authority' of chiefs who had for many years been the local extensions of the party-state. In this context, the struggles of pro-Mobutu and anti-Mobutu elements, pro-Nyamwisi and anti-Nyamwisi people, *originaires* and people from other provinces, overwhelmed the struggle for democracy. The result is characterized by Bucyalimwe as 'an indescribable cacophony'.

MPR-DCF dominance in Goma and North Kivu proved short-lived. The turbulent Nyamwisi was assassinated in January 1993 in his fiefdom of Butembo. This removed a key actor from the provincial scene and provided his rivals with a chance to replace him. The new coalition was led by UMUBANO, a predominantly Tutsi welfare association, formed when the Tutsi-led party CEREA was denied recognition by the CNS.

At the same time, the prosperity of Goma was declining, due to changes in the region. Its prosperity depended on that of its hinterland – Masisi and Bwito – and on trade with Kinshasa and other towns of Congo and of Rwanda. Goma's rival Butembo was doing better, owing both to the greater stability and dynamism of its immediate hinterland, the Nande country (Beni–Lubero), and its contacts with Kampala and Kisangani. The Masisi war, beginning in March–April 1993, further disadvantaged Goma.

Nande and Hunde were over-represented in the new political institutions coming out of the National Conference, both national (presidency, parliament, government) and provincial, whereas others, especially the Hutu of Masisi and the Tutsi of any territory, were excluded as *non-originaires*. This had happened, according to Bucyalimwe, in a national context of political paralysis, based on the cleavages between the old and new political generations and between supporters and opponents of Mobutu (*mouvance présidentielle–*

opposition radicale, in the vocabulary of the time). This bipolarization set off a series of violent confrontations in various provinces, especially Katanga, Province Orientale (Ituri), and North Kivu. In North Kivu, the confrontation took the form of the Masisi War of 1993. There was a vacuum of legitimacy, and the anti-democratic current triumphed.

On the national level, the National Conference had stripped Mobutu of power. Rather than go quietly, however, he and the interests that had profited from his years of power created a counter-government. The National Conference had chosen Tshisekedi as prime minister. Faustin Birindwa, a Shi from South Kivu, a leading member of Tshisekedi's UNDP, headed a counter-government of *mouvanciers*.

Within North Kivu, the larger ethnic communities (Nande and Hutu), confident that they could translate their numbers into electoral victory, pushed for rapid organization of elections. The Nande, however, had an additional weapon to use against their Hutu rivals and that was the label of 'persons of dubious nationality', as endorsed by the National Conference. That is why the Nande sought at any price to control the provincial electoral commission and to exclude the Hutu. All the other communities, especially the Hunde and the Tutsi, were unenthusiastic about elections, since electoral loss would mean the loss of the strong positions and enormous privileges they had obtained during thirty years of dictatorship of Mobutu and the chiefs. This being so, Bucyalimwe argues, it cannot be surprising that the Nyanga and the Hunde 'pulled the trigger' at the state post of Ntoto (Walikale) and at the headquarters of Masisi territory, respectively.

Bucyalimwe explains the political behaviour of the Tutsi of North Kivu, during the period 1990–96, by the need to protect their interests on several levels, provincial, national and regional. Within the province, they feared elections, since their numbers were few. Within the Great Lakes region, they wished to promote the RPF, which had launched its military campaign in 1990 from Uganda, and needed North Kivu as a secondary base.

The Tutsi created a political party, which they named after CEREA (Centre de regroupement africain), one of the important nationalist parties of 1960. Unlike the first CEREA, the new Centre de regroupement et d'échange africains was virtually an ethnic party of the Tutsi, according to Bucyalimwe. When the new CEREA was denied recognition at the National Conference, as not being a Congolese party, its leaders promoted Umubano, a '*mutuelle*' or NGO. UMUBANO became a member of the anti-Mobutu coalition, l'Union sacrée de l'opposition radicale (USOR) at Goma, despite not being a political party at all.

Simultaneously there was an attempt at rapprochement between the group headed by Nyarubwa, interim president of MAGRIVI, member of DCF/Nyamwisi and adviser to Governor Kalumbo, and the Tutsi leadership at Goma. While this rapprochement did not succeed in improving relations between the Tutsi and the Hutu, members of other groups took it seriously as an 'anti-Congolese plot'. The real problem, according to Bucyalimwe, was the RPF war, which poisoned relations not just between Hutu and Tutsi but also between the Tutsi and all the other communities.

When the 1993 war broke out at Ntoto (Walikale), the administration of North Kivu was in the hands of the DCF of Nyamwisi while men of Mobutu controlled the army and security police. Mobutu came to Goma in July 1993 and ordered the DCF/Nyamwisi regime dismantled, in favour of a new administration controlled by CEREA-UMUBANO. The province was heavily militarized, while at the same time the 'civil society' (NGOs and churches) promoted a province-wide pacification campaign.

The arrival of Rwandan Hutu refugees in July–August 1994 put Kivu in general and North Kivu in particular at the heart of a national and regional geopolitical struggle. The regional stakes obscured the local stakes of the war. The latter would emerge again in 1996, during the war of Uganda, Rwanda and the AFDL. The subsequent occupation of Kivu by the Rwandan and Ugandan armies did not profit the 'Banyamulenge' Tutsi in whose name it was waged, nearly so much as it did the Tutsi refugees of 1959 and thereafter, and/or their sons.

Bucyalimwe criticizes those who stress the role of disorganized bands and pillagers in North Kivu during the period 1990–96, thereby neglecting the more organized forces that played a decisive factor in the rising violence. Mobutu and his men, disturbed by the turn of events, attempted to maintain control. Local politicians, often cut off from their social base, and the so-called 'customary authorities' were obliged to play their own cards in order to hang on to their posts or to reposition themselves in the ongoing struggle. These various sorts of politicos manipulated the diverse organizations that occupied the political field, including the NGOs, the political parties, the churches and the ethnic mutual aid associations. Instrumentalization of these bodies was easy, since some of the men of power were at the same time leaders of the associations. These 'leaders' or 'men of power' had years of experience in the 'system of shambles and skulduggery' that was Mobutu's MPR. Despite their public commitment to change it was not at all clear that they were capable of leading these associations towards a healthy management of the political space and the society in transition. From above, Mobutu had recruited his 'destabilizing agents', including Nyamwisi Muvingi of North Kivu and Anzuluni Bembe of South Kivu, from this category of 'leaders'. From below, the people attempted to use these same 'leaders' to take power.

Ethnicity was more politicized in North Kivu than elsewhere in the east of the country, as Bucyalimwe notes. 'Every political calculation was made in exclusively ethnic terms.' During more than forty years he had never seen an inclusive and progressive political programme put forward during an election campaign. Instead, there came to the surface on each occasion, the question of nationality. This could be seen in the annulled elections of 1987, and in the so-called census of 1991: 'What is bizarre in this fundamental question [Bucyalimwe writes] is that the heart always takes the place of the brain. For every Hunde, Nande, Nyanga and Tembo, the Hutu and Tutsi without exception are not qualified for the elections or for exercise of power because they are considered to be foreigners, en bloc.' Some Hutu politicians and intellectuals of Bwisha had contributed to this tendency, since 1982, by putting all Hutu of Masisi and all Tutsi in the same sack, as 'foreigners'. In other words, intra-Rwandophone and intra-Hutu conflict, motivated by electoral considerations, reinforced anti-Rwandophone tendencies on the part of other ethnic communities.

Bucyalimwe suggests that people in North Kivu were coming to accept the idea, already well established elsewhere in the Great Lakes region (especially in Rwanda), that an election was a kind of ethnic census, designed to determine who constituted the numerical majority and thus had the right to rule. This led the Tutsi to abandon democratic politics, Bucyalimwe argues, in favour of the military option, by participating in the RPF war starting in 1990, then in the AFDL war from 1996.

Control of the governorship was an end in itself and a means to an end for the various contending groups. Basembe Emina, who served until 1991, was the last governor from outside the province, under Mobutu's long-standing policy. Kalumbo, a Nande, succeeded him, with Bamwisho, a Nyanga, as vice governor (1991–July 1993). This administration was put in place by Nyamwisi and did not long survive his assassination.

Moto Mupenda, a Kano (Lega of Walikale) replaced Kalumbo, just after the outbreak of the Masisi War. Supposedly a peacemaker, he served as 'interim governor' until the AFDL took over, in 1996. Indeed, he passed the power to the AFDL because one of his advisers, the Tutsi Léonard Kanyamuhanga, took over under the AFDL and served also under the RCD, until his death from cancer.

Self-identified 'autochthones' or real Kivutians dominated the Kalumbo–Bamwisho administration. The Nande, largest of these groups, held the post of governor, mayor of Goma, administrator of four out of six territories, not to mention several provincial administrative services and the universities or higher institutes that were created. The three territories where the Masisi War took place – Walikale, Masisi and Rutshuru – were all directed by Nande. Members of other ethnic groups, including Hunde, Nyanga and Hutu of Bwisha, shared power with them. Most of them were members of DCF/Nyamwisi. In Kinshasa, the Nande had the same strong representation. Theirs was the only ethnic group of North Kivu represented in all the governments from May 1990 to April 1993.

To maintain their hegemony, the Nande needed to perform two tasks. The first was the exclusion or marginalization of their rivals, the Banyarwanda, and in particular the Banyabwisha Hutu whose claim to Congolese nationality was the most solid, and the Tutsi, the main political and economic rivals of the Nande. The second task was to organize the DCF Youth Wing, on the model (according to Bucyalimwe) of JUFERI in Shaba/Katanga. This youth wing or part of it later became the 'Bangilima' militia, one of the first of the Maï-Maï youth militias. In 1991, Nyamwisi had predicted a civil war in the near future. The Ngilima were recruited throughout the DCF zone, from Goma to Kisangani. They fought alongside the Hunde in Bwito (Rutshuru territory) from the beginning of the so-called Masisi War.

Genocide in Rwanda led to a massive exodus to neighbouring countries, especially Zaire/DRC. The UNHCR estimated that there were 850,000 Rwandan refugees in the Goma area.[38]

The refugees in the camps were under the control of the former authorities, to a large extent. In September 1994, Hutu infiltrators clashed with the Rwandese Patriotic Army, in Cyangugu prefecture, across from Bukavu. In December, larger-scale fighting occurred in Gisenyi prefecture, across from Goma. Fighters based in the camps also attacked Tutsi civilians living nearby.

The ex-FAR and Interahamwe brought to North Kivu the idea that the 'solution' to the many problems of the region lay in killing Tutsi. They worked hard to convince local Congolese Hutu of this, according to the London-based NGO African Rights, and for some time it seemed they had succeeded. They found North Kivu 'fertile ground for their ideology of exclusion' in the words of Samuel Gakuba, apparently a Tutsi from Bwito in Rutshuru, who became a refugee in Rwanda in 1995. Gakuba argued that the Congolese Hutu had already been exposed to the ideology of the former regime in Rwanda through the agricultural cooperative, MAGRIVI:

> MAGRIVI had worked hard at spreading hatred of the Tutsis. The Interahamwe told the Congolese Hutus and the other North Kivu ethnic groups that the Tutsis had seized power in Rwanda and planned to take control of Kivu. They said everyone should unite to fight the Tutsi invaders. They were dismayed at their Hutu brothers in Kivu, saying in so many words: 'We have exterminated the Tutsis, so how dare you keep them alive in your country?' They used to leave their camps to spread this propaganda among the peasants.[39]

The Interahamwe carried out their threats, according to Gakuba. 'They killed a lot of Tutsis, especially near Ngungu in Masisi.' According to African Rights, Gakuba and his companions were surprised by ability of the Interahamwe 'to erase, in a matter of months, a long history of peaceful co-existence'. The tension and violence increased until most Tutsi left for the safety of Rwanda. Hutu and Hunde friends protected some Tutsi but the propaganda that depicted Tutsi as 'a regional peril' had taken root. This claim of surprise is disingenuous; Hutu and Tutsi of North Kivu had been at daggers drawn for years.

One of the few Tutsi to remain in the village of Bushuhe in Masisi was Ntagara, sixty-eight years old in 1999–2000, and a farmer. Interviewed by African Rights, he emphasized the military training that accompanied the exhortation to kill or deport Tutsi.

> We have lived through very hard times since the refugees arrived. Before they came, the local people didn't know how to kill. But when the Interahamwe arrived, they taught them now to use guns. Most of the refugees had close relatives in the Congo. They gave them guns, saying, 'Take these! They'll help you get rid of the Tutsis one day.' That was when it all began. The Interahamwe had no hesitation in driving the Congolese Tutsis from their farms, telling them to go back to 'their Rwanda'. These statements were followed by ethnic cleansing of the Tutsis, which continued until Kabila's war in 1996. They retreated into the forests and came out to kill civilians.

Again, there seems to be an effort to put all the blame for violence in North Kivu on the ex-FAR and Interahamwe. They certainly were violent, and attempted to enlist the Hutu of North Kivu in their anti-Tutsi campaign, but they came into a province already at war.

The 1996 war was launched by Rwanda, with help from Uganda. The AFDL, supposedly an alliance of Congolese groups opposed to Mobutu, provided cover to an invasion. One of the four components of the AFDL, the Alliance démocratique des peuples, apparently represented Banyarwanda. Déogratias (Douglas) Bugera, a Tutsi from Rutshuru, was the leader; Manassé (Müller) Ruhimbika, from the Banyamulenge community of South Kivu, was a prominent member and occasional spokesman.

The AFDL established a provincial government at Goma, thereby altering the political balance within North Kivu. As Willame points out, the AFDL had not defeated the army of Mobutu. Instead, the latter had fled, along with most of the civilian authorities. The AFDL named new authorities, who may or may not have been consulted prior to nomination. There was an apparent effort to establish the credibility of the new team by including all major ethnic groups: Hunde, Nande and 'Banyarwanda'. Initially, the AFDL paid part of the back salaries of civil servants; by the end of 1996, civil servants were more or less forced to attend 'political training' and to provide three months of unpaid public service.[40]

The contradiction between the revolutionary rhetoric of Kabila and the AFDL, carried over from the Lumumbist rebellions of the 1960s, and the pillaging of the local economy, struck the population. What Willame calls 'mafia circles' came in from Burundi, Rwanda and Uganda, and carried off coffee, tea and papain (extracted from papaya) from North Kivu, as well as sugar from Kiliba (South Kivu). This was the first stage in pillage. Later, the emphasis shifted to minerals, especially coltan (columbo-tantalite), used in the production of mobile phones and other high-technology consumer goods. This new trade or plunder drastically modified political competition in Masisi, in particular. In the past the position of collectivity chief had been crucial, in that such so-called 'customary authorities' derived power and wealth from their ability to distribute land. In the new situation, coltan and other mineral wealth could be extracted using hand tools. Transfer from the miners to middlemen often happened at the barrel of a gun.

In 1998, the second war put North Kivu and a major part of eastern Congo under the control of the RCD. Goma became the seat of the RCD's so-called 'government', which claimed to govern the entire rebel zone. It remained the capital of the province of North Kivu. Various forces attempted to impose a governor favourable to their cause. Dr Emile Ilunga, head of the RCD-Goma after the dismissal of Professor Wamba dia Wamba, reappointed the Tutsi governor, Kanyamuhanga. Wamba, as head of RCD-Kisangani, attempted to name Kaisazira Mbaki, a Butembo-based (presumably Nande) politician as governor but lacked the means to impose his choice.

In 2000, at the death of Kanyamuhanga, Rwanda intervened to choose as his successor Eugène Serufuli. (The Tutsi politicians of RCD-Goma are unlikely to have made such a choice on their own.) Serufuli is a Hutu from Rutshuru. He was a founder of MAGRIVI, and remains closely identified with the Congolese Hutu 'hard-line' element. According to Amnesty International, Serufuli's 'power and considerable independence in relation to both the official RCD-Goma leadership and the transitional government was an added factor in the problematic political and entrenched ethnic dynamics of North Kivu'.

Under the RCD-Goma, two institutions were added to the usual array of Congolese organizations, probably at the instigation of Rwanda. One was the Local Defence Force (LDF), the other a 'parastatal NGO' (Vlassenroot's terminology) called All for Peace and Development (Tous pour la paix et le dévéloppement).

The LDF was established in 1998 or 1999 under Governor Kanyamuhanga. His successor Serufuli presided over the development of that organization as well as the TPD, described by Amnesty as 'a politico-military organization': 'Initially established to promote the repatriation of Hutu refugees to Rwanda, the TPD has also allegedly been active in the clandestine repatriation to North Kivu of Congolese Tutsi refugees in Rwanda, in arming a largely Hutu militia in North Kivu, the Local Defence Forces (LDF), and more recently, in distributing arms to Banyarwanda civilians in North Kivu.' The LDF was a paramilitary force of several thousand young men, mostly Hutu, under the personal command of the governor. The foreign origin of the institution was highlighted by use of the English label Local Defence, as in Rwanda. The LDF enabled Serufuli 'to hold a political position – and a potential military one – that was largely independent of the RCD-Goma leadership, and has enabled him to retain power as governor throughout the transition, despite his often overtly hostile attitude towards the transition and despite being named by the UN Group of Experts as having violated the UN arms embargo on the DRC'.[41]

In interviews with Amnesty International, Serufuli maintained that the LDF had been disbanded in 2003, in preparation for national unification, with members integrated into the ANC or disarmed.

Former LDF members were believed to comprise a significant part of the 11th and 12th FARDC Brigades in Masisi and Rutshuru. Serufuli reportedly retained extensive influence over these troops, paying them, and organizing logistics for their operations.[42]

Parallel state structures

The ceasefire and establishment of a transitional government left North Kivu divided. Congolese had to navigate between 'parallel' or duplicate structures in the military and other areas of public administration, with one structure loyal to central government and the other to the locally dominant armed group. The lack of real national unification and continuing rivalry between the RCD-ML and RCD-Goma, and between these two groups and the government, prevented cooperation on almost every level.

Parallel structures were especially pronounced in the military sector. The former FARDC commander of the 8th (North Kivu) Military Region, General Obed Rwibasira, a Tutsi from North Kivu, appeared to stall consistently on implementing orders from FARDC headquarters in Kinshasa. Deputy regional military commanders drawn from pro-government contingents, whose authority was not respected by ANC troops in North Kivu, were marginalized and left dangerously exposed. On several occasions, the deputy commanders' bodyguards and ANC soldiers clashed. After the events of December 2004 (see below) General Gabriel Amisi replaced General Rwibasira. Although Amisi also was drawn from the RCD-Goma (ANC) officer corps, he was apparently more favourable to military integration in North Kivu. Nevertheless, his appointment did not entirely resolve the problems of parallel chains of command. The 8th Military Region Command reportedly had only limited authority over some FARDC (ANC) units in North Kivu, especially some located in Rutshuru territory.

The security situation in North Kivu was closely tied to the struggle for economic supremacy. Minerals, timber, agriculture and cattle raising all are important. Both Goma and Beni are important customs clearance points for goods arriving from Rwanda, Uganda and further afield in East Africa, and the import taxes and other duties collected in the two cities are substantial. Control or a share in the profit of these resources represents the economic lifeblood of armed groups in the area, who have used the money generated to equip their forces, prosecute conflicts and embed themselves in power.

The process of national reunification, which aimed to place all these resources at the disposal of the national treasury, represented a real threat to the survival of the armed groups, and they went to considerable lengths to protect their sources of income, according to Amnesty International.[43] In late 2004, for example, the transitional government sent customs officers to Beni to take control of collection of import duties from the RCD-ML. The customs officers were subject to a campaign of intimidation, including being barricaded in their offices by RCD-ML soldiers, preventing them from doing their work and eventually forcing them back to Kinshasa.

Millions of dollars were at stake. As the process of national fiscal integration proceeded and gained strength, informed local sources reported 'a visible reduction' in tax receipts being recorded from the RCD-ML-controlled territories of Beni and Lubero, from $6,500,000 in 2003 to $4,500,000 in 2004, of which only $3,500,000 was transferred to the national treasury, according to Amnesty International interviews. The rest, according to these sources, was diverted to RCD-ML political or military figures, for their private profit or for politico-military uses. A portion of the tax loss was also attributed to RCD-ML officers accepting bribes from traders to organize the passage of their goods through customs without paying duties. In February 2005 four soldiers abducted a customs official in Beni and beat him severely. A RCD-ML officer (allegedly a Ugandan national) was believed to have organized the attack after the customs official objected to the illegal importation of unspecified goods from Uganda by the officer.

North Kivu, nominally under a unitary provincial authority in Goma, was fiscally split between north and south. The RCD-Goma, through its Office pour la Protection des Recettes Publiques (OPRP), Office for the Protection of Public Revenues, imposed 'import' taxes on traders attempting to move goods from the RCD-ML to the RCD-Goma zone. The OPRP existed to rectify the anomaly whereby revenues received in Beni and Lubero should be administered by the provincial authorities in Goma, something that the RCD-ML and Nande business elite have rejected. Salaries paid to public officials from central funds in Kinshasa were frequently delayed or did not arrive at all, and public officials such as judges working in the RCD-ML zone experienced the additional problem that their salaries were sent to the provincial authorities in Goma, who then deducted arbitrary 'transfer charges' from the salaries before forwarding them north.

Some government officials allegedly had a hand in this corruption. Commissions of inquiry established to conduct financial assessments of tax receipts across the country were blocked at senior government levels. 'Kinshasa is not making much effort ... As long as Kinshasa still gets its cut, everyone is satisfied with the status quo,' one official told AI, before remarking that the country could make much greater progress if there were clear and accountable government control of public revenues.

Brassage or integration of the army

A prerequisite to free and fair elections (most observers agreed) was the integration (in French, *brassage*) of former armed groups and former government forces into a new national army, the FARDC, and the demobilization of those who are surplus or unsuited to the needs of the new integrated army. In reality, integration proceeded in fits and starts, and elections were held before the process had been completed. President Kabila retained a Garde républicaine (formerly Groupe spécial de sécurité présidentielle), loyal to him. They were scattered across the national territory, particularly at all the borders. Bemba had military units of so-called 'Bangala' (Lingala-speakers) loyal to him. The situation of the Rwandophones was more complex. Ruberwa had a small personal guard of some thirty Banyamulenge. The bulk of the Tutsi officers, most prominently Laurent Nkunda, considered Ruberwa a traitor to their politico-ethnic cause.

Steps taken towards military integration included the creation of a unified senior command structure, down to the level of regional (provincial) command and deputy-command positions. A number of military integration sites (*centres de brassage*) were opened across the country and accepted their first intake of military units in February and March 2005. The various military forces, however, were reluctant to enter wholeheartedly into the process and kept their best forces away from the integration camps.

Military commanders did not reveal the real size of their units, because they benefit financially from a massive overstatement of the forces under their command.[44] Commanders reportedly resisted the individual identification of soldiers coming forward for integration, although this is essential to the success of the programme, providing the needed reassurance that, for example, foreign fighters were not entering the DRC's national army. Fundamental requirements for human rights protection were also missing: many of those entering the integration process are suspected of having committed human rights abuses, or have been named as alleged perpetrators.

Coordination between the integration process, led by the military, and the demobilization, disarmament and reintegration (DDR) process, led by a civilian governmental organization CONADER (Commission Nationale de Désarmement et Réinsertion) was poor. Integration and DDR were supposed to take place simultaneously.

Yet, while the integration camps were accepting troops, facilities were absent or not yet operational for those soldiers who chose or were selected for demobilization and reintegration.

The process was under-resourced, with non- or minimal payment of salaries to military personnel, and insufficient supplies of food, water and medical equipment to the *centres de brassage*, many of which had poor facilities. These factors left civilian populations around the camps at great risk of human rights abuses.

The issue of military integration contributed to two major military and political crises centred on South Kivu in June 2004 (see above) and on North Kivu in December 2004. Mutebutsi and Nkunda apparently were supported both by the Rwandan government and by the RCD-Goma authorities of North Kivu, including the province's FARDC regional commander, General Obed Rwibasira, and the RCD-Goma Governor of North Kivu, Eugène Serufuli, both of whom took no action to prevent the march south to Bukavu of Nkunda and his military force. Some reports allege that Serufuli's support went further, and included the provision of trucks and other equipment, or even troops.[45]

The bulk of Nkunda's men rejoined their units in North Kivu without sanction. Mutebutsi's withdrawal took him south of Bukavu and into Rwanda. Both sets of forces committed human rights abuses during their withdrawal. Transitional government and FARDC military authority, this time without any RCD-Goma military component, was established throughout South Kivu while that of the RCD-Goma became restricted to North Kivu.

In mid-December 2004, civilians at Kanyabayonga, Buramba and Nyabiondo in North Kivu were killed, tortured and raped. In the course of the military operations in those locations, military forces carried out intentional attacks on civilians. The troops responsible for the killings, rapes and other abuses in these places were all officially part of the integrated national army, the FARDC, and theoretically subject to a single command structure.

These events highlighted the vulnerability of the civilian population to attack, particularly in a context of heightened ethnic tensions and a lack of an integrated and accountable national army. The victims came almost exclusively from the Hunde and Nande ethnic groups. Many appeared to have been deliberately targeted on the basis of their ethnicity and their supposed loyalty to an opposing military group, according to Amnesty International.[46]

The military operations and attacks on civilians took place in the context of an escalation of political and military antagonisms between

Kinshasa and the RCD-Goma since the Bukavu events of June 2004. In late November, in response to an alleged rocket attack on its territory by the FDLR based in North Kivu, Rwanda protested that efforts by the DRC government and MONUC to disarm the FDLR had failed. The Rwandan president, Paul Kagame, said that Rwandan government forces might already be in DRC undertaking 'surgical strikes' against the FDLR. In late November a Rwandan government force of unknown strength reportedly entered North Kivu, crossing through the province apparently to attack FDLR positions and in the process allegedly reinforcing and resupplying RCD-Goma (ANC) units. At least thirteen civilians were reportedly killed and houses pillaged and burned in twenty-one villages by the Rwandan government forces. The Rwandan government denied this incursion, but evidence provided by MONUC and the UN Group of Experts and local eyewitness accounts, indicates otherwise.

After an international outcry, the force apparently withdrew, but not before President Kabila had announced on 30 November the dispatch of a further 10,000 FARDC troops to the east to counter the threat.[47] These forces were deployed in a military operation which began on 11 December and consisted of a two-pronged offensive against RCD-Goma (ANC) positions in North Kivu, one along a north–south axis from Beni and the second on a roughly west–east axis from Kisangani towards Walikale, with the capture of Goma its apparent ultimate objective. This offensive was called Operation Bima, a Lingala word that translates approximately as 'get out'. The FARDC forces comprised troops from the former DRC government (FAC), the MLC, the RCD-ML (APC) and Maï-Maï.

Operation Bima had as its stated objective to restore Congolese government control over North Kivu and secure the frontier between the DRC and Rwanda. Operational orders asserted the continuing presence of Rwandan government forces in Rutshuru territory without interference from the FARDC (ANC-controlled) 8th Military Region. Its only major success was the capture of Walikale from RCD-Goma (ANC) forces. Along the northern front, at Kanyabayonga, the FARDC operation failed through a combination of mismanagement and alleged corruption at senior levels as well as mistrust and poor coordination between the different units involved, each of which operated under separate chains of command. MLC forces were sent into the front line at Kanyabayonga, although these were reportedly among the least well-equipped troops, while better-equipped FAC (former government) troops were held in reserve.

The FARDC troops also suffered from a lack of equipment and

food. Without transport, many units had to walk long distances to the front lines and a number of soldiers reportedly died en route from exhaustion and malnutrition. Government forces reportedly hijacked vehicles belonging to four international humanitarian NGOs operating in the region, for the transport of troops and munitions. Soldiers looted from the local population. According to soldiers wounded in the fighting and interviewed later by Amnesty International, many soldiers deserted and some units even fought each other for access to ammunition and food.

The military build-up in the east dramatically worsened the already tense ethnic relations in North Kivu. Some Rwandophone leaders opposed the arrival of government forces, accusing Kinshasa of planning the 'expulsion' of the Banyarwanda, and alleging that the military forces sent by Kinshasa included Rwandan Hutu members of the FDLR. In turn, other communities accused the Banyarwanda leadership of plotting genocide against them, citing an extensive operation to arm Banyarwanda civilians in the province that had been taking place since October 2004. Demonstrations organized along ethnic lines in Goma in early December became violent.

On 11 December 2004, fighting broke out between RCD-Goma (ANC) and other FARDC forces at Kanyabayonga, a strategic town straddling Lubero and Rutshuru territories, on the border of RCD-ML and RCD-Goma zones of control. The confrontation followed an attempt by pro-government FARDC forces to take control of the town from the RCD-Goma. Fighting continued for nine days until a ceasefire was agreed on 21 December.

Throughout the fighting and afterwards, members of pro- and anti-government forces committed systematic acts of rape and pillaging. The human rights abuses and fighting spread north from Kanyabayonga to Kayna and Kirumba as government forces retreated or deserted. Inhabitants were chased out of their villages prior to the destruction or pillaging of property and the burning of their houses, schools and hospitals. A number of unlawful killings of civilians were also committed, including the apparently politically motivated killing by RCD-Goma (ANC) soldiers of the eighteen-year-old son of an RCD-ML official at Kirumba.

Among the range of abuses committed by all forces, the majority of rapes appear to have been committed by RCD-Goma (ANC) against women and girls of mainly Hunde and Nande ethnicity. Both Hunde and Nande groups were considered by the RCD-Goma to be supporters of the government forces. A subsequent MONUC investigation found that ANC forces had committed eighty-one rapes and that ANC forces 'used rape as a means to terrorize the civilian population'.[48] A local human rights organization reported to Amnesty International that they had documented around 160 cases of rape from Kanyabayonga and at least forty-four from Kirumba. More than 150,000 civilians were displaced in appalling conditions, as humanitarian NGOs were also forced to withdraw from the area.

On 17 December, RCD-Goma (ANC) forces belonging to the FARDC 123rd Battalion of the 12th Brigade killed dozens of civilians, mainly Nande but also including some Hunde, in and around Buramba in Rutshuru territory. In the days leading up to the massacre, RCD-Goma (ANC) troops in the area reportedly had been harassing civilians, stealing crops from the fields and robbing people at gunpoint along the roads. At around midday on 17 December, a group of fifteen ANC soldiers entered Buramba, firing into the air, apparently to frighten locals into handing over their property. A unit of 'Colonel' Jackson Kambale's militia heard the shooting and came running towards the village.[49] In the ensuing engagement, three of the ANC troops were killed. The remaining ANC fled towards their base in Nyamilima, around 4 kilometres away.

Hearing of the fighting, many Buramba residents fled. One group heading in the direction of Nyalima were intercepted by RCD-Goma reinforcements returning to Buramba. The soldiers reportedly let the women in this group go but held the men. At least two of those held reportedly were killed later that afternoon a short distance from Buramba. Shortly afterwards, gunfire erupted from all directions as RCD-Goma (ANC) troops came along different paths leading to Buramba. Some of the remaining population managed to flee, but others were trapped in their homes, where they were reportedly hunted down and killed by the soldiers, who then looted the houses. In all, at least thirty people, including women and children, were killed and probably many more according to the findings of a subsequent MONUC investigation.

A witness Thomas (pseudonym), aged fifty-seven, spent the night of 17/18 December hiding close to the village. He told Amnesty International that the shooting in and around Buramba continued through the night. The next morning, after the gunfire had stopped, he emerged from his hiding place and started walking towards Nyamilima. He encountered group of around fifteen ANC soldiers walking towards him, who initially let him pass, but shortly afterwards a vehicle came past and an officer got out. He ordered the soldiers to turn back towards Nyamilima and then demanded to see Thomas's identification papers. Examining the identity documents, the officer remarked, 'How can a man of your age not know where Jackson is hiding?' and ordered his arrest.

Shortly after, at around midday, they were joined by a further group of RCD-Goma (ANC) holding another civilian, Théophile Kalilikene (real name), whom Thomas knew. The enlarged group set off along the road to Nyamilima, but after a few hundred metres the officer gave another order and Thomas and Kalilikene were bundled off the road and towards a hut by an RCD-Goma (ANC) soldier. According to Thomas:

> The soldier shouts at whoever is inside to open up. There's only an old sick man. The soldier asks his name. The soldier demands money, but the old man has none, so he pushes him down into a corner of the hut. Then Théophile and I are ordered to lie down on the bed, side-by-side, and I knew that our moment had come. The soldier shoots several times: at the level of my head, and at the heart. This was at almost point-blank range. By some miracle one bullet grazes my neck and the second goes through my arm. Then the soldier goes out, closing the door behind him. This was around midday. Théophile is hit, his body twisted over me and across the bed by the bullets. He is whimpering, then he cries out suddenly and I know that he is dead. I was covered in blood, and lost consciousness.

Ethnic tensions and lack of integrated political and military structures are two aspects of a single situation. By mid-December, ethnic and military tensions had been rising in the area around Nyabiondo, a town in Masisi territory, for some time. A distribution of arms to Banyarwanda civilians in Masisi had given rise to armed incidents in the territory. For some days also, RCD-Goma (ANC) troops had been retreating eastwards from the government military offensive in Walikale. Villages in the path of this retreat, populated mainly by Hunde, had been attacked, looted and in some cases burned to the ground by the retreating RCD-Goma (ANC) forces. RCD-Goma (ANC) troops abducted civilians, forcing them to carry the looted goods. Maï-Maï of the 13th FARDC Brigade, based in Nyabiondo, reportedly carried out reprisal attacks on Banyarwanda villages in the area and killed unarmed civilians.

The retreating RCD-Goma (ANC) men were heading towards the headquarters of the 11th FARDC (ANC) Brigade in Masisi. In between lay Nyabiondo and its Maï-Maï battalion. The attack by the 11th FARDC (ANC) Brigade came from at least two directions in the early morning of Sunday 19 December. There were also reports that armed Banyarwanda civilians were among the attackers and that they took part in the killings and looting that followed. The initial attack claimed very few civilian lives, as under the protection of the dawn mist most of the population fled to the fields and forest. For several days afterwards, however, RCD-Goma (ANC) troops pursued civilians hiding in the villages, hills, forests and fields surrounding Nyabiondo, apparently searching for Maï-Maï soldiers but failing to make any distinction between them and civilians. Scores of civilians were killed. Local officials claimed that as many as 191 civilians were killed in the Nyabiondo area.

A man from Katale village, near Nyabiondo, told Amnesty International that RCD-Goma (ANC) soldiers had arrived in his village early on 21 December. He immediately fled with his wife Stéphanie and their four children, including a baby girl, carried by Stéphanie. Stéphanie was shot dead in the back as they ran across the fields. The husband and the other children made it into the forest. 'Along the edge of the forest there were many bullet-riddled bodies. After a few hours I went back to the village to see my wife's body – I had to be sure she was dead – and find the baby,' he told Amnesty International. He was able to recover the infant from a woman who had picked her up and sheltered her. Another witness described how Loashi, a town at the border of the RCD-Goma and Maï-Maï zones of control, was 'strewn with bodies'. RCD-Goma (ANC) soldiers reportedly tied up and burned alive a Maï-Maï fighter they had captured.

Many of the killings by the RCD-Goma (ANC) in and around Nyabiondo appear to have been ethnically motivated. The victims were mostly civilians belonging to the Hunde community. The step-mother of a local Hunde chief told Amnesty International delegates how close members of her family were killed:

> When they attacked my village, I could not run, because I am too old. So, I stayed with my husband in the village. My husband went to plead with the soldiers. I suddenly saw him running back to us, shouting and gesturing at us to flee. While he was running, the soldiers shot him in the back. We fled into the bush but we wanted to go and bury the body of my husband. We went to ask to my husband's son, who is the local chief, to come and help us bury my husband. After six days, we heard that the RCD-Goma (ANC) soldiers had taken my stepson and some of his colleagues because he was a Hunde chief. This was told to us by some of his colleagues who managed to escape and who joined us in the forest. They told us that my stepson was killed after having been tortured …

Willy, aged fifteen, a Hunde from Bukombo, told Amnesty International:

> The soldiers came in vehicles and on foot, killing and pillaging. Some were in uniform but others wore civilian clothes. Some came from the direction of Marambara, some from Nyange colline. The population fled straight to the forest. I was in a group of fifteen, with my mother, neighbours and other relatives. The soldiers found us and made us lie on the ground, where we were beaten with rifle butts. Baroki, the *chef de localité* (local chief) was with us. The soldiers came and took him away, I saw that. Then I saw his body afterwards, a week later, on 25 December. He had taken a bullet in the head. Had been tied up and whipped. The body lay on the ground.

The Hunde chiefs apparently were targeted.

RCD-Goma troops also reportedly raped several dozen women and girls as young as eight. As the health centres in the region had been pillaged and destroyed, many victims were left for weeks without care and medical help.

The attack on Nyabiondo displaced more than 25,000 people, the majority of whom fled in the direction of Walikale territory, while thousands also found refuge in the forest and neighbouring hills. At constant risk of further attacks by RCD-Goma (ANC) forces, the living conditions of these displaced were extremely difficult. Many returned home only in late January. On return, many found that their belongings were gone and their houses had been destroyed.

Nyabiondo and surrounding villages were systematically looted by RCD-Goma (ANC) troops, even to the extent of tiles being removed from the roofs of buildings. Schools and hospitals were treated similarly, including the Caritas Centre de Transit et d'Orientation (CTO), a rehabilitation centre for former child soldiers. The children fled into the forest. The warehouse of the German humanitarian NGO Agro Action Allemande (AAA) in the town was looted of material and equipment worth an estimated US $300,000.

The looting lasted until 26 January when, after negotiations, the RCD-Goma (ANC) were persuaded to abandon the town and the Maï-Maï brigade was reinstalled. Although Governor Serufuli and the Administrator of Masisi territory, Paul Sebihogo, both from the RCD-Goma, were informed of the looting, neither appears to have taken any action to stop the thefts.

A number of individuals in Nyabiondo questioned the role played by the RCD-Goma territorial administration. Prior to the 19

December attack, many local people had begun sleeping away from their homes because of the ANC activity in the area. On 16 December, a delegation from the territorial administrator had visited Nyabiondo apparently to reassure the population that the fighting in the area had ended and they were not at risk. This encouraged many to return to their homes and, on 18 December, to hold the usual Saturday market that took place in Nyabiondo. As a result, on Sunday morning, when the attack came, there were many people in the town.

Colonel Bonane, Commander of the 11th FARDC (ANC) Brigade responsible for the attack on Nyabiondo, admitted to Amnesty International that his troops had attacked civilians and raped women and girls. He claimed that these abuses were committed by undisciplined troops.

On 21 December, MONUC peacekeepers established a temporary 'buffer zone' between the FARDC and RCD-Goma forces over a 10 kilometre radius between Kanyabayonga and Lubero, aimed at facilitating humanitarian access to the civilian population and preventing further violence and human rights abuses. This measure, however, was inadequate. Amnesty International delegates were told during a visit to the region in February 2005 that the 'buffer zone' was ineffective and porous, consisting only of scattered MONUC posts established along some roads, together with occasional daytime patrols between these points. One staff member of an international humanitarian NGO in the area commented that the 'buffer zone' was no more than a 'no-man's land'. Soldiers from both sides were still reportedly entering the zone to rape at the time of Amnesty International's visit.

None of the RCD-Goma (ANC) troops and officers allegedly involved in the abuses at Kanyabayonga, Nyabiondo and Buramba has been prosecuted, despite the fact that the units and their commanders involved have in most cases been identified. The abuses have been investigated by MONUC, whose findings have been submitted to the DRC government and military authorities at national and provincial levels. Although Governor Serufuli established a commission of inquiry into the killings at Buramba, composed of local security officials, the commission's January 2005 report recommended no prosecution against those suspected of responsibility for the killings.

In February 2005, twenty-nine FARDC (pro-government) military personnel were found guilty of offences ranging from looting, indiscipline and rape to murder in connection with the Kanyabayonga abuses. Twenty-one of these were sentenced to death after what Amnesty calls 'a summary and unfair military trial'. Those sentenced were all of low military rank, and were reportedly mainly from MLC forces. They have appealed against the sentences. There were allegations that these soldiers were punished in order to cover up for the mismanagement of the Kanyabayonga offensive by the senior FARDC command. The majority of the pro-government forces, including commanders, allegedly responsible for the abuses at Kanyabayonga have not been brought to justice.

On 25 August 2005, the Congolese press published extracts of a letter apparently from Nkunda in which he accused what he called the 'Kabila clan' of organizing a 'plan for ethnic cleansing in North Kivu under the cover of military integration'. He urged 'concrete acts of resistance' and the use of 'all necessary means to force this government to step down'.[50]

Early in 2006, the linked problems of *brassage* and demobilization were dramatically illustrated in Masisi territory, where a demobilized soldier was reportedly beaten to death before being 'crucified' on a tree by soldiers of the FARDC 83rd Brigade. The victim was reportedly killed because he 'deserted the army and left the RCD'.[51]

In July 2006, Nkunda promised to allow the elections to proceed in the area under his control, and apparently kept his promise. The tense situation in North Kivu, in the aftermath of the elections, was illustrated in press reports on an incident at Sake, about 25 kilometres from Goma. Agence France-Presse reported that one Congolese officer had been wounded on 5 August, in an exchange between soldiers of two different brigades of the Congolese army.

The two units involved were the 94th Battalion of the 9th integrated Brigade and the 843rd Battalion of the 83rd Brigade. The 9th Brigade was undergoing integration into the new Congolese army. The 83rd Brigade had not yet begun integration. Some of the men of the 3rd Brigade reportedly were loyal to Nkunda. A MONUC spokesman told AFP that there had been a 'misunderstanding' with some men on each side believing that the other unit had forcibly disarmed some of their men.

Reuters presented a more alarmist version of the same incident, according to which two soldiers had been killed at Sake, and thousands of civilians had fled. Nkunda himself apparently was 100 kilometres away from Sake. He was demanding negotiation with the winner of the election, to obtain the peaceful return of 50,000 Kinyarwanda speakers from Rwanda to their homes in DRC.[52]

The Rwandan and Ugandan governments continued to provide support to Congolese armed groups in eastern DRC, in breach of the UN arms embargo on the DRC. Rwanda reportedly launched occasional military incursions into North Kivu, most recently in November 2004.

Under the terms of the 2002 peace agreements between the three governments, the DRC government undertook to disarm and repatriate these foreign groups, but has not done so. The failure to resolve this issue is perhaps the major impediment to the normalization of relations between the three states.

Rwanda and Uganda's security concerns notwithstanding, the disarmament and repatriation of these foreign groups is essential to prevent further human rights abuses against Congolese civilians. The insurgent groups have been responsible for crimes under international law and other human rights abuses in eastern DRC. Their presence in the Kivu provinces has also led to the impoverishment of the civilian population in the areas in which they operate, through pillage and extortion.

Human rights defenders targeted

In North Kivu, civil society and human rights NGO revelations of the distribution of arms to civilians led to a spate of death threats against them and a number were forced to flee the DRC. On 6 January 2005 the director general of the human rights organization Action Sociale pour la Paix et le Développement (ASPD) fled Goma after spending several days in hiding. He had received anonymous threatening phone calls and a visit to his home by security agents. He was reportedly told: 'You have become a politician. Be careful because you risk paying dearly.'

Another human rights defender, the director general of the Centre de Recherche sur l'Environnement, la Démocratie et les Droits de l'Homme (CREDDHO) also fled in January 2005 after receiving repeated threatening phone calls. One of these calls reportedly warned him in stark terms: 'If you think you are protected you are wrong. We have a programme to kill you.' On 3 January 2005 three men, believed to be local military intelligence agents, visited his neighbourhood asking to be shown his house. A third activist and spokesperson for a coalition of human rights organizations was forced to flee after receiving repeated threats. One phone call threatened, 'We will shut you up for good.' His home was visited on 31 December 2004, while he was away, by three armed men who demanded to know his whereabouts.

North Kivu and the transition

North Kivu has been the stage on which national political and military antagonisms play out. Far from improving the security climate in North Kivu, the DRC's transitional authorities at government and provincial levels have permitted deterioration in the situation, including an inflammation of ethnic tension. This in turn threatened to destabilize the fragile peace process in the DRC and to erode further the already poor human rights situation in North Kivu and the country as a whole.[53]

In December 2004 a large-scale military confrontation between different military units in North Kivu, all of them officially part of the FARDC, almost led to the collapse of the transition. In the course of the confrontation, hundreds of civilians in North Kivu were victims of killings, acts of torture, rape and other human rights abuses. As had become typical of the DRC's tragic recent past, the perpetrators of the human rights abuses committed during the December fighting were left unchallenged and the victims quickly forgotten by political leaders. The fighting gave way to a grudging standoff, as the government and international community tried to chart the DRC's way out of crisis.

Political power in North Kivu retained its ethno-territorial base. The Rwandophone-led RCD-Goma controlled the capital Goma and the territories of Rutshuru (bordering Rwanda), Nyiragongo and most of the territory of Masisi. Since December 2004, Walikale and the westernmost part of Masisi territory (formerly held by the RCD-Goma) were under government control. Beni and Lubero territories, which border Uganda, were controlled by the RCD-ML, headquartered in the city of Beni. The RCD-ML, primarily Nande-led, had two ministerial posts in the transitional government, one of which was occupied by the RCD-ML President Mbusa Nyamwisi, younger brother of the assassinated Nyamwisi Mavungi. The RCD-ML had its base at Beni, one of the two economic poles of the province and of eastern Congo.

RCD-Goma had its base at Goma, the other main economic pole. Its political strength depended to a large extent on its ability to maintain Tutsi–Hutu unity.

The other two major ethnic groups in North Kivu, the Hunde and Nyanga, had little in the way of political power or representation in North Kivu, and were largely marginalized by the Nande and Banyarwanda. Before armed political groups came to dominate politics, the Hunde and Nyanga controlled portions of the 'Petit Nord' (southern North Kivu) through the collectivity chiefs. This 'customary' authority was waning. Militarily, relatively weak and incoherent Maï-Maï militia units represent both communities.

During its rule, the RCD-Goma also ensured its officials controlled the civilian administration system, in the process replacing a number of collectivity chiefs with Banyarwanda. The RCD-ML similarly ensured that its loyalists controlled northern North Kivu. The new structures ensured RCD-Goma and RCD-ML control over land, natural resources and lucrative customs revenues in their respective zones, all of which were directed towards the continuation of conflict and the private profit of leading officials.

Recognizing the centrality of the issue of nationality to the successful pacification and reunification of the country, the international community pressurized the transitional government to reform this law. In November 2004, after a hotly contested passage through the DRC's parliament, a new nationality law was promulgated which confers the right to Congolese nationality on all people – and their descendants – who were resident in the DRC on or before 30 June 1960, the date of independence. Dual nationality is not permitted.

It is no coincidence that ethnic pressures in North Kivu, incited and manipulated by the political elite, were building up while preparations for national and local elections and the process of army integration were under way. The various leaders, aware that these developments, if successful, would jeopardize the benefits they garnered from military, political and economic control, moved to consolidate and if possible extend their ethnic base. RCD-Goma and RCD-ML, intent on maintaining their military, political and economic hold over North Kivu, but with little prospect for anything other than limited local success in the national elections, were resisting integration of national structures. Both had some interest in delaying the electoral process or pushing it off track.

RCD-Goma and RCD-ML leaders have enriched themselves with the natural resources of North Kivu, have become owners of large tracts of land, or have vested themselves with profitable positions in state enterprises or the public administration. Revenues from taxation and economic exploitation have funded the RCD-Goma and RCD-ML's military and political growth, and have benefited from the trade network dominated by the RCD-Goma and their Rwandan connections, or the RCD-ML and their Ugandan connections. The hostile relationship between the pro-Rwandan RCD-Goma and the presidential *clan katangais* was perhaps the main factor driving insecurity in North Kivu. The role of the RCD-ML, however, which held effective control of the upper half of the province, was also an important element in the poor human rights situation, not least because the two ethnic groups – the Nande and the Banyarwanda – with which the RCD-ML and the RCD-Goma respectively were aligned, were competing for economic and political domination of the province.

For the government in Kinshasa, the riches of North Kivu also represented a powerful lure. The vested interest of the *clan katangais* close to President Kabila to maintain Luba–Katanga control of power in the DRC marries with a strong nationalist reflex. This taps in turn into the deep resentment felt towards Rwanda and the RCD-Goma by large sections of the Congolese population for their occupation of the east. However, unable to defeat the RCD-Goma militarily and wary of Rwandan military might, Kinshasa instead resorted to a strategic erosion of the RCD-Goma's hold on North Kivu, aimed at undermining the RCD-Goma's power base, military cohesion and political credibility bit by bit. According to Amnesty International, this strategy took a number of forms, including paralysing local decision-making through the recall to Kinshasa for long periods of RCD-Goma provincial administrative and military officials, and undermining the more moderate RCD-Goma leaders in the transitional government in decisions relating to security issues and reform of the army. It also includes demonising ethnic Tutsi through pro-government media.

The main interests of the RCD-Goma were to retain political and military control of its remaining bastion in Masisi and Rutshuru territories, and the economic benefits accruing from this control. This involved maintaining the cohesion of its ethnic base and holding government forces as far as possible from the centre of its power, Goma. The group retained its commercial, political and military links to Rwanda. Many RCD-Goma members were sceptical of the transitional process, and its hard-line wing was inclined to rely on armed force as the guarantor of their political interests.

The deliberate inflammation of ethnic tensions by political leaders of different communities, through radio broadcasts, public meetings and street tracts or demonstrations, was itself intimately related to the question of who would hold ultimate political and military control over North Kivu. This ongoing mobilization of ethnic populations for political ends left North Kivu teetering dangerously on the edge of renewed warfare.

On 9 December 2004, these tensions worsened in Goma when an unauthorized 'Rwandophone' protest march took a route through a district of the town inhabited primarily by people of non-Banyarwanda ethnicity. The Hutu moderate mayor of Goma, François-Xavier Nzabara Masetsa, told Amnesty International he had refused permission for the march because authorization had not been sought in time and because of concerns at its planned route. The organizer of the march, François Gachaba, claimed in an interview with Amnesty International that this district lay unavoidably between the Banyarwanda areas and Goma city centre, where a rally was planned.

The march, which demanded that Kinshasa reverse its decision to send 10,000 troops to the east, was joined by a number of RCD-Goma officials and ANC soldiers, and also reportedly contained several civilian protesters brandishing firearms. A counter-demonstration in support of Kinshasa's decision was organized, and the situation degenerated into violence in which two demonstrators were killed and a number wounded.

Many Banyarwanda moderates refused to take part in the 'Rwandophone' march. Many Banyarwanda would reportedly welcome the extension of DRC state authority to North Kivu and resent attempts at manipulation by some of their pro-Rwandan community leaders. On the other hand, many Banyarwanda, even those who are Congolese nationalist in outlook, have reason to doubt the sincerity of central government. They were looking forward to elections as an opportunity to choose representatives who faithfully reflect their position.

Amnesty International found it disturbing that moderate RCD-Goma politicians, who see the transition as the only viable way forward to the satisfactory representation of their interests, appeared to have lost ground in North Kivu to the more hard-line actors. In part, this failing was the government's, since little has been done by the DRC's political leadership to allay the genuine fears of the Banyarwanda community that a continuation of nationalist government policies will not again lead to the exclusion of and discrimination against the most vulnerable ethnic minorities.

Ethnic manipulation was especially evident in the case of the RCD-Goma Tutsi leadership, who sought to co-opt a reluctant and largely suspicious Hutu population to their cause by fusing the Congolese Hutu and Tutsi communities under the 'Rwandophone' label. This was widely viewed as a Tutsi stratagem to co-opt the larger Hutu population into a position of supporting RCD-Goma control in North Kivu and thus to deter attack by Kinshasa. This view reflects a political mindset (on both sides) that was again separating Banyarwanda from Congolese national identity and allying it more closely with perceived Rwandan interests in eastern DRC. One aspect of the 'fusion' of Hutu and Tutsi identity is that the perceived threat of genocide against the Congolese Tutsi in the DRC, often stated by Tutsi spokespersons, might be extended to the Congolese Hutu, with clear attempts being made by Tutsi leaders to convince Hutu that forces in Kinshasa were intent on their 'extermination' also.

For other actors, there was a temptation to take advantage of the attitude of students and others, pitting 'Congophones' against 'Rwandophones'. At the same time, the fragility of the 'Rwandophone' coalition was evident to all concerned. As elections drew near, Professor Sekimonyo, a prominent Hutu from North Kivu, suggested that the label 'Rwandophone' be abandoned.[54]

The Kabila camp needed a base in North Kivu. It apparently was unwilling to commit Mobutu's error of relying on the Tutsi alone, or on the Nande alone. A better strategy might be to rely on the Nande and Hutu, provided the Hutu could be divorced from the Tutsi. There was some evidence that such an approach was being pursued. Sekimonyo, first leader of MAGRIVI and number two at the state-owned mining company Gécamines, apparently became a Kabila favourite. Was he being used to undermine the position of Serufuli, or to try to win over his Hutu 'brother'?

Manipulation was evident, too, among the Nande, where the RCD-ML was keen to maintain its economic and military control over the Grand Nord, and among Hunde chiefs who relish the possible demise of Banyarwanda political leaders as a chance to recover lost privileges. Leaders in these communities reinvigorated old fears about the creation of an autonomous Banyarwanda homeland in North Kivu (if not an outright annexation of the province by Rwanda) and the fantasy of a Tutsi-Hema 'empire' extending from the Kivus to Ituri.

SIX

Congo and the 'international community'

> *Nazali matako ya zungu*   I am the bottom of the pan,
> *Naganga ka moto te*   I am not afraid of the fire.

(William Lacey Swing – in the aftermath of the elections
of 2006, a Congolese musician came out with a sympathetic
but sarcastic portrayal of Swing. Wearing a white wig and
moustache to impersonate 'Koko Souing' (Grandpa Swing),
he sang in French with a strong American accent, 'Me Koko
Souing. I want peace and calm in the city of Kinshasa ...'
See: <news.bbc.co.uk/1/hi/world/Africa/617739.stm>.)

§ Ambassador Swing's self-proclaimed fearlessness has stood him
in good stead. As head of MONUC (Mission de l'Organisation des
Nations Unies au Congo, United Nations Mission in the Congo), he
has had a hot time. Some of the criticism has concerned abuses on
his watch, notably a series of charges of sexual abuse of Congolese
women and children by UN peacekeepers. Other attacks have been
personal. Swing is a CIA agent, according to a Congolese journalist,
and as such reports to the regional head of the American spy agency,
President Paul Kagame of Rwanda.[1] I detect no sarcasm. The journalist apparently was attempting to explain two supposed 'facts' by
linking them: first, the presence of an American at the head of the
UN mission, and second, the perceived and otherwise inexplicable
favouritism of the UN mission, i.e. favouring the Rwandan aggressors
over their Congolese victims.

This Congolese view contrasts with that of the Rwandans. Far
from being happy with the supposed pro-Rwandan bias of the United
Nations, the Kigali authorities complain with apparent sincerity about
how badly they are treated by the international body. Their complaints
focus, in particular, on the series of reports by UN 'experts', alleging
Rwandan pillage of Congolese resources and smuggling of weapons
into Congo.[2]

Both Congo and Rwanda have some legitimate grievances against
the international body. The UN has been as much a part of the

problem in the Great Lakes region as it has been a leader in solving that problem or set of problems. The resources made available probably have been insufficient and the mandate has been ill adapted to the situation. The deficiencies of the organization itself, increasingly visible since the Rwanda catastrophe of 1994, have played a part.

The Congo wars involved a great number of actors. As combatants, in addition to the Democratic Republic of Congo itself, there were Rwanda, Uganda, Burundi, Angola, Zimbabwe, Namibia and several other African states. South Africa, Zambia, Tanzania, Gabon and other states of the region took part as mediators, facilitators and so on. Extra-continental actors, including the United States, Britain, France, Belgium, Russia and China were involved.

In addition to the state actors, and the various Congolese 'rebel' movements supported by one or another state actor, the international governmental and international non-governmental organizations (IGOs and INGOs) were prominent. These bodies have attempted to play major roles in ending abuses and/or bringing about an end to the Congo wars.

At the centre of this tangle of state and non-state actors sits the United Nations. The fact that William Swing is so well known in Congolese political circles testifies to the perceived centrality of the UN in shaping recent events in the Congo.

IGOs and INGOs in Congo: a long history

International organizations have been involved in Congolese politics since the beginning. They have shaped the Congolese state. Recently, they have shaped the catastrophic situation prevailing in that country.

The international system has undergone a series of transformations, conducted under the influence of the winners of major struggles. Major regimes include the congress system of the nineteenth century, created by the British and other winners of the struggle against Napoleon; the League of Nations, created by the Americans and other winners of the First World War; and the United Nations, created by the Americans and other winners of the Second World War.[3] Congo has evolved within these three frameworks.

The Congolese state was created during the period of the congress system. 'It didn't happen at Berlin,' as Katzenellenbogen points out, i.e. Africa was not partitioned at the Berlin West African Conference.[4] Congolese and Rwandan elites, however, believe that their border was established at Berlin, and debate questions of territory and citizenship within a common framework of error. It is true that Leopold

II, King of the Belgians, used the conference to obtain recognition of his personal colony, much as he had exploited the movements for exploration of Africa and against slavery. One might say that Leopold got what he deserved when the 'international community' under the influence of the Congo Reform Association publicized his abuses and forced the transformation of the personal colony into a more orthodox structure, the Belgian Congo, in 1908.

The First World War ushered in a new international order, incarnated by the League of Nations. Belgium, as an ally of the United Kingdom, had occupied portions of German East Africa, but was not allowed simply to convert the conquered territory into a colony or annex it to Belgian Congo. Ruanda–Urundi (the present Republics of Rwanda and Burundi) was united administratively with Congo, and its governor had the status of vice governor general of Belgian Congo. But Ruanda–Urundi was held under a League of Nations mandate, and Belgium was obliged to report on its administration of the territory to the League, an obligation it did not have as regards Congo. We have seen, in the discussion of organized migration from Ruanda–Urundi to Congo's Kivu province, that the Belgians looked over their shoulder to see if the League was watching. When the Second World War led to the creation of the United Nations, the League of Nations mandate was transformed into a UN trusteeship. The difference was real. The UN was more directly involved in the decolonization of Ruanda–Urundi than was the case for the Congo, until newly independent Congo invited in the UN.

Again, elite beliefs about these matters have influenced political choices. Patrice Lumumba and other elites of 1960 tended to believe that Ruanda–Urundi was part of Congo that was being detached by the Belgians during decolonization. More recently, 'Rwandophone' intellectuals including Professor Ndeshyo have invoked the administrative unity of Ruanda–Urundi and Congo to argue that Rwandan immigrants to Belgian Congo were not foreigners.[5]

In 1960, when Belgium's *pari congolais* (gamble on Congolese independence) started going badly, the UN was called in. President Joseph Kasavubu and Prime Minister Patrice Lumumba agreed on the necessity to call in the international body in the face of Belgian military intervention immediately after independence. ONUC (Organisation des Nations Unies au Congo) quickly became a major political force in the fragile new state. The UN Secretary General Dag Hammarskjöld came to share the Western antipathy for Lumumba, and the international body collaborated or at least acquiesced in the elimination of the prime minister who had sought its intervention. In

1964, withdrawal of ONUC forces was followed almost immediately by an insurrection launched by partisans of the murdered Lumumba.[6] Among the insurrectionists was a young man named Laurent-Désiré Kabila; he and his close associates certainly had not forgotten the role of the UN in the early 1960s, and their hostility towards the international body influenced their decisions in 1996 and thereafter.

The Congo crisis of 1960 was a formative event in African international relations. It led to the division of African states into hostile blocs, the so-called moderates of the Brazzaville group (later enlarged to form the Monrovia group) versus the so-called radicals of the Casablanca group. This division was papered over when the Organization of African Unity was created in 1963, but persisted in fact for decades.[7]

When the struggle for liberation of white-ruled Africa heated up in the 1970s, the self-proclaimed 'front-line states' including Tanzania led the struggle, while Congo (by now known as Zaire) was widely considered to be an enemy of liberation. This split between supporters and opponents of the liberation struggle would carry over into the Congo wars, when Tanzania welcomed the war against Mobutu in 1996, and Zimbabwe and others supported Laurent Kabila, in 1998.

The Congo wars of the past decade have occurred in yet another stage in transformation of the international system, i.e. the post-Cold War era. Unlike the other transition points – 1815, 1918 and 1945 – the end of the Cold War has yet to yield new institutions to replace those born after the Second World War. The OAU, born in the Cold War era, has given way to the AU (African Union). It may yet prove to be the case that the Congo crisis of the 1990s and early 2000s, along with other crises in Somalia, Liberia, Ivory Coast and elsewhere, leads to new approaches to conflict management and resolution. For the moment, however, the institutions and practices in this area seem ill adapted to the challenges.

The Congo wars clearly are linked to the Rwanda genocide. For some analysts, the linkage is linear. American journalist Lynne Duke, who attempted to locate Rwandan refugees who fled camps in eastern Congo, is one such. She notes the problematic nature of the concept 'refugees':

> ... the very word suggested innocence and victimization. Of the 1 million Rwandan refugees who lived in those eastern Zaire camps in the care of the United Nations, perhaps most were indeed victims. But among them, too, were scores of thousands of stone-cold killers: soldiers, militiamen, and civilians who'd slaughtered their

countrymen in the Rwandan genocide of 1994, then fled en masse across the border. The Zaire war of 1996 was a direct result of that genocide, whose domino effect would claim Mobutu, embolden a new clique of African leaders, rearrange power politics in the region, and expose, yet again, the international community's ambivalence and prevarication over the value of African life. From Africa to Europe to the Americans and the United Nations, diplomats debated the number of refugees and whether their plight warranted rescue. It had been this way for two years, since the genocide whose repercussions were shaking much of Africa.[8]

I argue that Rwanda's role in 1996 was 'a direct result of that genocide' but Congo/Zaire was heading for a catastrophe in any case. The events in the various states of the Great Lakes region are best understood as 'convergent catastrophes', as David Newbury has put it.[9]

The UN role in the convergent catastrophes

Setting aside Burundi for the time being, the convergent catastrophes are (a) in Rwanda, the war of the RPF, beginning in 1990, followed by attempt at a negotiated solution (the Arusha accord of 1993), the genocide of 1994, and the flight of more than a million Rwandan Hutu into eastern Congo, and (b) the decline and collapse of the Zairian/Congolese state, which permitted the Hutu to continue their struggle against the RPF from Congo and the RPF to attack them, in 1996.

The convergent catastrophes are linked also in terms of international response or lack thereof. The UN and the 'international community' failed lamentably to prevent the Rwandan genocide, as Michael Barnett among others has made clear.[10] The same community failed to act between 1994 and 1996 in response to the crisis generated by the flight of Hutu Rwandan authorities, troops and civilians to eastern Congo, even though the danger of international war was obvious. There were various reasons for this inaction, but a major one was the rivalry between France on the one hand, which was backing Mobutu, and the United States, which wanted to replace its former protégé. This relationship had shaped the catastrophes in the Great Lakes region at least since 1990, when the West began pressurizing the dictators Habyarimana, Mobutu and their neighbours to democratize. As often as not the USA and France were pulling in opposite directions, preventing effective international intervention.

When one says that the UN failed in Rwanda, or is failing in Congo, who or what is being criticized? Does this mean that the member states in general and the permanent members of the Security Council in particular failed to use the UN to best advantage? Does it mean that the Secretary General, the Secretariat and/or the Department of Peacekeeping Operations failed to perform their duties, as Barnett suggests? The UN is at once a forum for member states and an actor in its own right. It is not a single forum or locus of decision, but a set of forums; the General Assembly, in which all member states are equal, contrasts with the Security Council, in which leading states occupy privileged positions. The United Nations is material (the buildings in New York, Geneva and elsewhere, and the personnel occupying offices inside those buildings or in the field). This material UN, however, reflects the immaterial; as Barnett writes, it is 'the bureaucratic arm of the world's transcendental values'.[11]

Given the multiplicity of meanings of the term UN, and of the structures to which that label refers, it is more useful to break down the organization into its components, and compare the role of each in the Rwanda and Congo situations. These include specialized bodies dealing with human rights and refugees, as well as the Secretariat and Security Council with their broad political responsibilities.

The UN has given increased attention to human rights since the end of the Cold War, and has been given institutions to deal with this sensitive area. A week after the Arusha accords were signed by the Rwandan government and the internal and external opposition (4 August 1993), the UN special rapporteur on extrajudicial, summary or arbitrary execution released his report on the situation in Rwanda. The special rapporteur, Maître Waly Bacre Ndiaye of Senegal, noted, 'the victims of the attacks, Tutsis in the overwhelming majority of cases, have been targeted solely because of their membership in a certain ethnic group, and for no other objective reason ... ' Noting the definition of genocide in Article II of the Genocide Convention, Ndiaye asked whether these acts might not be considered to be genocide. As Barnett points out, Ndiaye reported to the UN Human Rights Commission. His report never came before the Security Council; had it done so, it probably would have discouraged UN intervention. The UN was trying to promote a transitional government and the logic of that operation conflicted with the logic of combating human rights abuses, even genocide.[12]

By 1994, as Rwanda was falling into the abyss, the UN stepped up its institutional commitment to human rights. By coincidence, the first High Commissioner for Human Rights, Jose Ayala-Lasso of Ecuador, took office on 5 April, the day before Habyarimana's plane was shot down, setting off the genocide. Ten days later, Ayala wrote to Secretary General Boutros Ghali, offering his assistance. On 11–12 May, more than a month after the genocide had begun, Ayala visited Rwanda and appealed to 'both parties to stop the human rights violations immediately and to work for a negotiated settlement of the conflict'. This curiously even-handed intervention presumably reflected briefings received in Geneva or New York. I share Barnett's doubt that a more vigorous intervention by Ayala could have prevented the genocide.[13] In any case, the UN's human rights machinery proved irrelevant to the massive violations of human rights occurring in Rwanda. Recognition of this irrelevance seems to have conditioned activities in Congo, where the UN attempted unsuccessfully to act more vigorously in defence of human rights.

Refugees and internally displaced persons played major roles in the Rwandan crisis, since the RPF was based on the Tutsi refugees of 1959 and thereafter, while the Interahamwe militia drew heavily on Hutu displaced by the RPF invasion. The UN High Commissioner's office had been participating in negotiations with the Rwandan and Ugandan governments, on the eve of the RPF invasion in 1990, regarding the plight of Rwandan refugees in Uganda. The UNHCR complained (in vain) to the Rwandan government, when the MRDD (ruling party) began recruiting Burundian Hutu refugees into the Interahamwe militia.[14] Once the genocide broke out and refugees fled to neighbouring countries, some of the UNHCR staff displayed an inclination to believe stories told by Hutu of their victimization at the hands of Tutsi. For the most part, however, the UNHCR problem was more basic: how to cope with huge numbers of refugees, mixed together with and under the influence of people who had carried out the genocide. The UNHCR was unable to resolve this problem, and contributed thereby to the outbreak of war in 1996.

The biggest problems for the UN in Rwanda came in the politico-military area. As in Congo a few years later, there was a problem of the mandate of the international organization and another concerning the resources (men and equipment) needed to carry out that mandate. The problem of neutrality or impartiality – visible in the declaration of Ayala-Lasso, cited above – continuously weighed on the UN.

This difficulty was compounded by what Human Rights Watch calls the problem of obtaining 'accurate information about what is happening on the ground'. As the human rights organization points out, the governments most involved in Rwanda – France, Belgium and the United States – had substantial information about the situation on the ground but shared this information with only a few others. Non-permanent members of the Security Council – with the exception of Rwanda, itself a non-permanent member in 1994 – depended for information on the UN Secretariat. From the field, the head of the UN peacekeeping force in Rwanda, General Roméo Dallaire, and the representative of the UN Secretary General, Jacques-Roger Booh-Booh, sent very different descriptions of events to the Secretariat in New York.

In preparing briefings for the Security Council (HRW continues), the Secretariat favoured Booh-Booh's interpretation, which gave no sense of the systematic and ethnically based nature of the killing. Relying initially on this information, the non-permanent members agreed to withdraw most of the peacekeepers. But when they later learned of the extent and genocidal nature of the slaughter, they pushed the Security Council to send a second and stronger UN force to Rwanda.[15]

In terms of the UN structure, this communication problem can be seen as a conflict between the special representative and the military head. Something of the flavour of that troubled relationship can be gleaned from books by Dallaire and Booh-Booh. Dallaire's book was called *Shake Hands with the Devil*, Booh-Booh entitled his *Le patron de Dallaire parle: révélations sur les dérives d'un général de l'ONU au Rwanda* (Dallaire's Boss Speaks: Revelations on the Drifting of a UN General in Rwanda). Dallaire considered Booh-Booh too sympathetic to the Hutu regime in Rwanda, while Booh-Booh considered Dallaire too sympathetic to the RPF. Booh-Booh alleged that Dallaire was unable to accept working under an African. Booh-Booh subsequently was called to testify for the defence in the trial of Colonel Théoneste Bagasora, alleged mastermind of the genocide, before the International Criminal Tribunal for Rwanda.[16]

Barnett demonstrates the convergence between the viewpoints of the United States and the United Nations, despite tense relations between the Clinton administration and the Secretariat under Boutros Ghali. He shows how the 'Somalia syndrome' made the United States put pressure on the UN to oppose intervention in Rwanda. With the USA opposing intervention, and the French continuing to back the Hutu regime even after the death of Habyarimana, there was no way for a UN consensus to emerge in favour of intervention. The failure of Boutros Ghali to make a forceful case for intervention was a contributing factor.

American opposition to intervention led the Clinton administration to refuse to recognize genocide, which would have required action. On the basis of 'Rwanda's absence of strategic relevance' the USA called the events in Rwanda 'civil war'. The UN adopted a similar position. Under the principle of 'neutrality, impartiality, and consent' in peacekeeping, the UN characterized the situation in Rwanda as civil war instead of 'ethnic cleansing', as Dallaire, the UN's senior military commander in Rwanda, was calling it from the field. Inside the Security Council, 'several council members made thinly veiled charges of double standard that the powerful were willing to expend unlimited resources on "losing propositions" in Europe but ready to fold at the first hint of trouble in Africa'.[17]

One of the most damning criticisms of the UN is a decision-making process in which important differences of opinion could be papered over. UNAMIR was sent to Rwanda in a grey area, operating somewhere 'between Chapter VI' of the UN charter, where peacekeeping occurred with the consent of all parties, and 'Chapter VII' under which force could be used. General Dallaire went out to Rwanda thinking that his recommendations on terms of engagement had been endorsed when they had not. UNAMIR was 'naïve' and 'undernourished' from the beginning, according to Barnett.[18]

From his vantage point at the US mission to the UN, Barnett describes 'the fog of genocide', under which the UN Secretariat and the Department of Peacekeeping Operations demonstrated indifference in dealing with the situation after the genocide began. He highlights the irresponsibility of the United Nations decision to pull out UNAMIR peacekeepers after Rwandan forces killed ten Belgian peacekeepers. Adding insult to injury, the United States showed 'Rwanda's absence of strategic relevance' by pushing for non-intervention on the grounds that it was civil war, despite Dallaire's letters to the DPKO about 'a very well-planned, organized, deliberate and conducted campaign of terror initiated principally by the Presidential guard'.[19]

I hesitate to place too much blame on the UN or its Secretary General, given the heavy influence of state actors. France attempted to promote an intervention that would save its client Rwanda, while the USA attempted to avoid engagement, both before and after the genocide. Only when the two agreed was action possible; the USA acquiesced in UN sponsorship of Operation Turquoise, by which France provided a chance for its Hutu clients to regroup and flee to eastern Congo. As Duke puts it:

> The whole Hutu state fled: government ministers, generals of the ex-FAR, the Interahamwe, plus national bureaucrats and town and village officials. They took cars, trucks, buses, tankers, documents, currency, and arms. In effect, the Hutu state transplanted itself, using ordinary Hutu people as convenient cover. People fled in the same

village or commune formations in which they had killed … And the United Nations mounted a massive humanitarian rescue mission for the Hutu 'refugees', who included a significant number of killers … The United Nations housed and fed them in a network of forty U.N. refugee camps up and down the frontier in the Zairian region of Kivu, along a vast lake of that name.[20]

The Rwandan Hutu flight to eastern Congo led to the wars of 1996, 1998 and even later. Yet these events should not be seen as inevitable. As Lanotte explains, the UN responded to a series of political and humanitarian crises in the Great Lakes region since 1994 with a 'long litany of non-decisions and non-interventions'. This included the challenges of the 'humanitarian sanctuaries' granted to Hutu power in the Kivus from 1994 to 1996, the problem of the remaining Rwandans after the invasion of 1996, and the problem of the second Congo war. Lanotte blames the UN for the misuse of the label 'refugee' and for keeping the genocidal militias so close to the Rwandan border: 'The crisis of 1996 thus was only the consequence of the attitude of non-decision of UN machinery that provides only humanitarian responses to problems requiring political solutions.'[21] This judgement is rather harsh, in my view. The High Commissioner, Sadako Ogata, was well aware of the problem posed by the presence of armed men from the former Hutu regime among the refugees, but lacked the means to separate the two. She eventually was obliged to hire a number of soldiers from Mobutu's armed forces. Derisively known as 'Ogata's army', this force helped maintain order in the camps but was not useful in terms of protecting refugees from intimidation.

Pottier offers further insights into the UNHCR mindset. Much as the Tutsi elites tended 'to substitute collective guilt for individual responsibility, and to affix the label *génocidaire* to the Hutu community as a group', Pottier sees the UNHCR and the international aid effort as carrying out a similar, essentialist oversimplification. Aid organizations 'habitually label "the refugees" as an amorphous mass of people-in-need; a labelling which, in the case of the Rwandan camps, made the notion of collective guilt – and hence disposal – more acceptable'.[22] He goes on to argue, 'The aid community's refusal to approach refugees as differentiated individuals, as professionals, as people prepared to take an active part in the everyday running of the camps, reinforced the legitimacy of an essentialist stereotyping through which blame for the 1994 genocide was apportioned to "the Hutu" collective.'

Lumping the Hutu refugees together, the UNHCR and the implementing NGOs ignored the presence among them of people with potentially useful skills. Moreover, the refugees were treated as if they had come from a 'unified Rwanda'; most aid workers were unaware of the north–south split so important in Rwandan history, in Pottier's view. Finally, lack of differentiation led to a dangerous oversimplification: '… although aid workers recognised that the majority of refugees were not guilty of any actual killings during the genocide, they all came to be labelled as "hostages" collectively trapped under the claw of unrelenting extremists'.[23] In the place of discussion of 'the refugees' and whether 'they' could be or should be repatriated, Pottier presents cases of refugees who had returned home, evaluated the situation there on a local level ('we heard my mother-in-law had been killed by Inkotanyi' i.e. RPA solders) and returned to the safety of the camps in Congo. Supposedly, some eighty people were returning to Kibumba camp, near Goma, each day. Facing pressure from different funding sources, UNHCR and its NGO partners including MSF evaluated the same situation in diametrically opposed fashion. Carol Faubert of UNHCR declared that 'the intimidation of "ordinary" refugees' by leaders of the old Rwandan administration 'no longer occurs' while the same day, MSF declared that the 'instigators of the genocide are taking control of the camps in an increasingly systematic way, and block the return of the refugees …'[24]

Such stereotyping led indirectly to the massacres of refugees in 1997, according to Pottier. After the attacks on the camps late in 1996, some 700,000 refugees returned home to Rwanda. The US military declared that only 'the warring parties' remained.[25] The Rwandan ambassador to Belgium explained: 'Rwanda estimates the returning refugees to be about half a million. That means more or less everyone. What remains in Zaire are the criminals.' Paul Kagame said that 'no one has ever known how many refugees were in those camps, but I guess – and my guess is just as good as anyone else's – that most refugees have now returned to Rwanda'. The Americans released aerial photos supposedly supporting the Rwandan government view, and the American ambassador endorsed that view. All of this assured the Rwandan and others in the Great Lakes region that the USA was supporting the new Rwandan government.

The UNHCR, unable to treat as a humanitarian crisis the highly politicized problem of Rwandan Hutu in eastern Congo, had been let off the hook. But the problem of the disappearing refugees did not itself disappear. UN Human Rights Rapporteur Roberto Garréton attempted to report on it, as will be related below. Not until the Americans, British and other backers of the first war turned against

Kabila did the question of alleged massacres in the forests of Congo return to the international agenda.

The Security Council vote in November 1996 of Resolution 1080 (1996) authorizing the sending of a multinational force to aid the Rwandan refugees and displaced populations in distress showed that the UN was conscious of the gravity of the situation, as Lanotte writes. But the return of perhaps 600,000 refugees the same day – after the AFDL/RPA attack on the camps – called into account the decision. The rescue mission never was sent.

During the following months, numerous calls were made for intervention on behalf of the surviving Rwandan refugees. Emma Bonino, EU Commissioner for Humanitarian Affairs, went so far as to accuse Laurent Kabila of having transformed eastern Zaire into a 'veritable slaughterhouse'.[26]

Eventually, not having been able (or willing) to prevent the massacre of many of the refugees, the UN decided to establish an investigatory commission to shed light on the 'presumed massacres'. After considerable obstruction from the Kabila government, the commission finally completed and turned in a report, according to which the AFDL and its external allies had committed acts that could be called 'genocide'.[27]

When the second war broke out in August 1998, the UN was no quicker to respond. It took nearly a month for the Security Council to take up the question, reaffirming the 'obligation to respect the territorial integrity and national sovereignty of the Democratic Republic of Congo'.[28] It asked all states of the region (without naming them) 'to refrain from any interference in each other's internal affairs'.

Early in 1999, the UN supported the mediation process undertaken by the OAU and SADC, and again asked unspecified foreign states to put an end to the presence of 'uninvited' forces in Congo. Lanotte sees the word 'uninvited' as another proof of UN ambivalence. I suspect that it was inserted at the insistence of the Congolese, to distinguish Angola and Zimbabwe, who were supporting Kabila, from Rwanda and Uganda who were not.

The Congo crisis unfolded on the watch of Boutros Ghali, from 1994 to the end of 1996. The new Secretary General Kofi Annan assumed his post at the beginning of 1997, which means that the slow process of UN engagement in Congo can be attributed in part to him. Not until the Rwanda–Uganda coalition broke down did Annan and the Security Council become more active on the Congo question. Annan pushed to give priority to withdrawal of foreign forces over promotion of the inter-Congolese dialogue. The Security Council gradually abandoned its silence on violation of human rights and pillage of Congo. By its Resolution 1291 of 24 February 2000, the council authorized a MONUC of 5,537 men, with a mandate referring to Chapter VII of the Charter. This took a long time to materialize, however. In April 2000, there were still only 111 UN military men, deployed in capitals of east-central Africa.

Many of the millions of people dead since 1998 have died since MONUC was deployed. The United Nations is responsible for some of these deaths. These include people killed by MONUC troops (relatively few), people killed in the presence of MONUC troops (many more), and more generally, many of those who died due to perpetuation of the war. In a series of widely publicized reports, the International Rescue Committee has estimated several million 'extra' deaths due to the war, starvation, disease, etc.[29] Such deaths continue.

The size of the UN mission has been augmented on several occasions, and its mandate has been strengthened. From the beginning, however, the mandate included the possibility of action to defend civilians. MONUC has carried out this mandate only sporadically.

Two episodes clarify the limitations of MONUC. The first is the so-called Interim Emergency Force sent by the European Union, which in this case mainly means France. The operation was given the label 'Opération Artémis'.[30] The international community in general and the UN in particular had been pressurizing Uganda to withdraw its troops from Ituri district, in conformity with the peace agreement. Ituri had been Uganda's 'wild west', a French-speaking province, and so on, where a number of high-ranking Ugandan officers were becoming very rich. The district was governed by 'divide and rule', with the Ugandans backing various factions in the bloody militia combat. The situation grew more and more confused and deadly, as the Rwandans and the Kinshasa government each backed their own contenders.[31]

By withdrawing in a hasty manner, the Ugandans virtually ensured that chaos would ensue. MONUC had neither the mandate nor the resources to provide security in Ituri, but had been obliged to deploy a battalion of Uruguayan guards (URUBATT) to protect UN personnel participating in the Ituri peace process brokered by MONUC one month earlier.

As the last Ugandans left Bunia on 6 May 2003, 'Lendu-based militias' and the 'predominantly Hema Union of Congolese Patriots (UPC)' fought to take control of Bunia. Thousands of civilians fled from the town; thousands of others clustered around MONUC sector two headquarters and their airport where the Uruguayans had established their base. On 13 May, two UN military observers were murdered in Mongbwalu (a gold mining town 30 kilometres from Bunia), and their bodies mutilated. The situation was 'spiralling out of control'.[32]

On 15 May, Secretary General Annan called for 'the rapid deployment to Bunia of a highly trained and well equipped multinational force ... to provide security at the airport as well as to other vital installations in the town and to protect the civilian population'. Annan telephoned Jacques Chirac, who expressed France's readiness to deploy a force to Bunia. At that point, it was not clear that the operation would be authorized by the European Union, which had never undertaken an autonomous military mission outside Europe. Its decision was presumably made easier by France's willingness to serve as 'framework nation' and main contributor of military personnel.[33] The European Council asked its Secretary General/High Representative for the Common Foreign and Security Policy (former NATO Secretary General Javier Solana) to undertake a feasibility study. He reported back and the EU council approved the mission. On 30 May 2003, the UN Security Council authorized the deployment, with a mandate lasting until 1 September.

In short, the Artémis intervention demonstrated that it was possible to intervene more rapidly and more effectively than the UN had done. There is no clear lesson to be learned, however. Artémis probably was too big for the European Union and too small for Congo. As the UN's own Peacekeeping Best Practices Unit concluded: 'In coming to the assistance of the UN mission, the IEMF proved its effectiveness. But, at the same time, it was only a very short-term expression of international support while MONUC is the long-term commitment of the United Nations and must be made to work.'[34] Another 'lesson' is the fact that (as during Operation Turquoise in 1994) France is willing to practise geopolitics behind a screen of humanitarianism. That is, its motivation apparently was in part to consolidate its influence in Kinshasa rather than helping war victims in Ituri.[35]

The ineffectiveness of MONUC was further illustrated the following year. Mutinous soldiers linked to the RCD-Goma fought forces loyal to the Kinshasa government for control of Bukavu, the capital of South Kivu province. As recounted in Chapter 4, both sides committed war crimes against civilians, according to Human Rights Watch.[36] The extent of direct Rwandan involvement is debatable; the passivity of MONUC is not.

Kinshasa was attempting to bring the province of South Kivu, hitherto controlled by the RCD rebels, under its control. When fighting broke out at Bukavu between 'Banyamulenge' troops led by Colonel Jules Mutebutsi and troops loyal to Kinshasa, MONUC apparently attempted to reach a negotiated solution to the threat to the peace. It obtained an agreement from Mutebutsi to confine his troops to quarters, without disarming. MONUC declined to use force when a second force of Kinyarwanda-speakers, under General Laurent Nkunda, moved south to threaten Bukavu. Instead, it attempted to persuade Nkunda not to seize Bukavu. Mutebutsi's men left their quarters and, together with Nkunda's men, occupied the city. After many committed murders and rapes at Bukavu they eventually withdrew, and General Mbuza Mabe, loyal to Kinshasa, took control of the city.

MONUC had substantial warning of the arrival and behaviour of Nkunda and his men. As Nkunda's soldiers marched from Goma to Bukavu they attacked numerous villages along the way. They reportedly killed a UN observer, several government troops and numerous civilians.

MONUC must have known about Nkunda's long record of human rights abuses. He was a commanding officer over RCD-Goma soldiers who indiscriminately killed civilians, committed numerous rapes and carried out widespread looting in Kisangani in 2002.[37] Despite condemnation of these crimes by then UN High Commissioner for Human Rights Mary Robinson, neither Nkunda nor other officers were investigated or charged.

As Human Rights Watch notes, UN forces rescued hundreds of individuals who were under threat of violence by relocating them, but failed to take further action under their Chapter VII mandate.[38] The UN Security Council mandated MONUC to, among other tasks, 'protect civilians and humanitarian workers under imminent threat of physical violence' and 'use all necessary means to fulfil its mandate'.[39] MONUC forces carried out limited patrols in Bukavu but took no military action to stop the renegade commanders from taking control of the city. With only some 700 troops present in Bukavu MONUC officers gave a narrow reading to the Chapter VII mandate.

Once Nkunda had withdrawn from Bukavu, a MONUC official claimed, 'the withdrawal took place because of pressure from MONUC'. He said MONUC force commander General Iliya Sumaïla spent a lot of time obtaining the withdrawal of Nkunda and Mutebutsi's troops.[40]

There has been no blow-up over Congo, equivalent to that over the Rwanda genocide, to provide insight into problems within the UN mission. Tensions between civilians and military within MONUC probably have not have been as severe as those in Rwanda between the Secretary General's representative Booh-Booh and General Dallaire. But there are indications of military dissatisfaction with the limitations within which they had to work. Shortly after withdrawing from Bukavu, Mutebutsi's men were fired upon by a MONUC helicopter, causing them to flee. MONUC claimed that the Banyamulenge rebels had fired at the helicopter and that they were only returning fire.[41]

Subsequently, the UN provided MONUC with highly professional officers drawn from Europe. Dutch General Patrick Cammaert was named commander of the eastern zone, including North and South Kivu. Even more interesting was the appointment of General Christian Houdet of the French Foreign Legion as MONUC chief of staff. Houdet had served in Congo in 2003, during the brief Opération Artémis, in Ituri. One wonders whether this appointment was not meant as a message to Uganda and Rwanda.

Sex scandals in Congo

While the United Nations has struggled to define its mission in the Congo and to assembly the requisite forces, the international organization has had to deal with accusations that its personnel had been guilty of massive sexual misconduct. At the beginning of 2005, the UN High Commissioner for Refugees, former Dutch Prime Minister Ruud Lubbers, resigned under pressure; an ABC News report revealed an internal UN investigation corroborated allegations of sexual harassment brought by women who worked for or with Lubbers. The report concluded that Lubbers lacked 'the requisite integrity'.[42]

ABC's follow-up investigation revealed hundreds of allegations that UN peacekeeping soldiers had raped Congolese women and girls, run prostitution and paedophile rings, and actively consorted with prostitutes in direct violation of the UN Code of Conduct.

The scandal threatened to bring down a second major UN official, the head of MONUC, Ambassador Swing. UN and US State Department officials told ABC that Swing would resign. He was not accused of any personal misconduct. 'He was asked to stay on and institute a crackdown,' a UN source told ABC. 'But he said he was not the kind of person who could do that. He's too much of a gentleman.' Swing told ABC, 'We are not at a 100 per cent compliance with zero tolerance, but we will get there.'

The sexual abuse question illustrates the extreme slowness of the UN machinery to respond to stimuli. Allegations of sexual abuse or misconduct by UN staff stretch back at least to the 1990s, to operations in Kosovo and West Africa. In 2002, a coalition of religious organizations sent a letter to Secretary of State Colin Powell urging the United States to send more human rights monitors into Congo. The UN responded by introducing a 'code of conduct' to help prevent future abuses, including prohibitions against sexual activity between staff and children and the exchange of money or food for sex.[43]

In 2003, the MONUC office in Kindu reportedly sent a memo to its headquarters in Kinshasa, detailing suspicions of sexual exploitation. There was little apparent follow-up, however. Between September 2001 and January 2004, MONUC's security branch investigated only sixteen cases of alleged exploitation or abuse.

The issue of sexual abuse by UN personnel caused damage to the reputation and influence of the international body, in Congo and abroad. Internationally, opponents of the UN used the issue to argue for withdrawal of MONUC. In contrast, human rights NGOs such as Human Rights Watch argued for the reinforcement of MONUC and the improvement of its capacities. As Anneke Van Woudenberg of HRW told the US House Committee on International Relations:

> Some have claimed that providing more funds and resources to MONUC at a time when a number of its troops stand accused of sexual abuse is wrong. Human Rights Watch strongly disagrees. We believe that the U.N. needs to take urgent action to deal with those accused of sexual abuses, but it is important that this issue does not overshadow the important role that MONUC must play in helping to bring about peace in the DRC through a process of democratic elections. As we have seen in Iraq and Afghanistan, the lead up to elections can be violent and there are many side issues which can weaken the resolve of the international community. The U.S. government and others must not allow MONUC to be further weakened and must take action to ensure it is capable of doing the job for which it was created.[44]

Ambassador Swing did not resign. The US government and the 'international community' in general do seem to have taken more seriously the abuse charges, in the aftermath of the public scandal. Allegations of child prostitution resurfaced in 2006.[45] Little has been done to aid victims of abuse.

UN 'experts' on pillage and arms traffic

Soon after the beginning of the second war, the government of Laurent Kabila charged that Rwanda and Uganda were motivated not by security concerns but by desire to exploit Congo's economic resources. The UN Security Council took these accusations seriously, to the extent that it established a so-called Panel of Experts to investigate the charges.

The panel produced an interim report in January 2001, which Secretary General Annan duly submitted to the Security Council. The interim report summarized the responses of the various governments interviewed. The DRC government alleged that the 'occupying forces' (Rwanda and Uganda) were plundering gold, diamonds and colombo-tantalite (coltan) from eastern Congo. The Rwandan government and General James Kabarebe denied that Rwanda was plundering Congo. Rwanda's troops were moving around. Because of that they could not carry out economic exploitation. Kabarebe implausibly denied any economic motive or interest lay behind recent clashes between the Rwandan and Ugandan armies in Congo. Instead, the conflict was due to a dispute as to who were the best soldiers. The Zimbabwe government said the panel should not concern itself with Zimbabwe's role in Congo since it was there as an ally of the Congolese government.[46]

The panel's (first) final report, in October 2002, was much more specific and much more damning. The panel identified 'elite networks' within Congo, centring on the Rwandan and Ugandan occupation zones and on the Kinshasa government. Eighty-five foreign companies were cited as participating on the illegal exploitation of Congo's resources. The panel lacked subpoena powers and some of its data were shaky. In my view, however, the broad outlines of the system of exploitation described by the expert panel are valid. In particular, I accept the distinction established between the Ugandan system of plunder (decentralized, with a great role of political and military leaders close to President Museveni) and the Rwandan system (allegedly operating through a Congo office, attached to the presidency).

The panel was kept on for another year, and charged with pursuing its task. The 2003 report was censured, a section presenting detailed information on the elite networks and the foreign companies being presented to the Security Council but not to the public. Predictably, it was leaked soon thereafter.

On the basis of the report, the Security Council seems to have decided to shift its emphasis from illegal exploitation of Congo's resources to the wars that are financed by illegally obtained resources and in turn facilitate the illegal exploitation. The council passed a resolution calling for an arms embargo. A new expert panel would investigate the arms flow.

Rwanda continued to refuse to cooperate with the UN's experts' panel and to criticize its conclusions. Eventually, this led to a bizarre episode in which William Church, a former staff member of the UN Panel of Experts, disagreed with his superiors, got fired, and turned up in Kigali to publicize his disagreements with the panel. It seems that on the particular information being discussed, Church is at least partly right. The panel does seem to have exaggerated the evidence for direct Rwandan support for Nkunda and Mutebutsi, in May–June 2004. Rwanda found Church's arguments very helpful and seems to have encouraged him.[47]

The United Nations and the end of the Congo war

As Congo moved towards the elections that would finally end the transition and give the country a more nearly legitimate government, the UN was everywhere. Its troops were carrying out joint operations with the FARDC (Congolese armed forces). It was training magistrates, in conjunction with Lawyers without Borders. It was feeding hundreds of thousands of displaced Congolese, with the cooperation of a variety of non-governmental organizations. It was even providing Congo with a modern, professional radio network, again in cooperation with an international partner. Despite its evident deficiencies, the UN was proving essential to Congo and the Congolese.

Although its tasks were daunting, the MONUC was far from alone in providing international assistance. In particular, it worked with and was supported by a variety of international actors, many of them assembled under the banner of the International Committee in Support of the Transition (Comité international d'accompagnement de la Transition, CIAT). The CIAT had been created in December 2002, in Pretoria, to provide a framework through which the 'international community' could guide the Congolese actors as they moved from war to peace. Its composition reflected the process as it had developed. CIAT included the five permanent members of the Security Council (USA, UK, France, Russia and China). Belgium, the former colonial power, was included. So too was Canada, well known as a 'mid-range' power and a bilingual state that participates in the Commonwealth and in *la Francophonie*. Four African states were included. South Africa and Zambia had hosted important meetings as part of the peace process (meetings at Pretoria, Sun City and Lusaka). Portuguese-speaking Angola and Mozambique were members of CIAT, Angola being the only belligerent in the Congo wars to be included.

Notably missing from CIAT were representatives of Francophone Africa and of African regional or sub-regional bodies (AU, SADC, COMESA, CEEAC and the like). At an earlier stage, some of these organizations had played major roles. In particular, Laurent Kabila's choice of steering DRC towards SADC had provided him with key allies in the fight against Rwanda and Uganda. As we have seen, three SADC states intervened on Kabila's behalf. Three others – South Africa, Botswana and Zambia – eschewed the military option and instead worked for a negotiated settlement.

The OAU/AU had been recognized in the Lusaka accords and the AU was to share joint responsibility with the UN for the Joint Military Commission, charged with overseeing the ceasefire and the withdrawal of foreign forces. From the beginning, however, the UN overshadowed the AU, which had little military capacity. MONUC came to play the major part in policing the transition.

CIAT was active during the run-up to the elections of 2006. In March it criticized the Electoral Commission's interpretation of its relations with the legislative and executive branches of the transitional government. In July, the CIAT called on all candidates to respect the rules of the election and to promote national reconciliation as they campaigned.[48]

In the aftermath of the first round of elections, when members of Kabila's presidential guard clashed with Bemba's men in Kinshasa, the CIAT ambassadors including Bill Swing were 'under the bombs' (as Colette Braeckman puts it). They had to be rescued by troops from the European Union force (EUFOR), sent to back up MONUC in just such an emergency.[49]

Finally, yet another international body was added to the mix, on the eve of the first round of elections. Former President Joachim Chissano of Mozambique told a press conference that the Comité International des Sages (International Committee of the Wise) was not intended to replace the CIAT. Rather, he explained, it would complement the CIAT much as EUFOR was complementing MONUC. The other sages included Madame Madior Boye, former prime minister of Senegal, Judge Lewis Makame, former president of the Independent Electoral Commission of Tanzania, and another former president, Nicéphore Soglo of Benin. The intention clearly was to reinforce the specifically African support for Congo's electoral process.[50]

DRC could not have completed the transition from open warfare to the elections of 2006 without substantial international support. Paradoxically, however, this strong support became a political problem. A number of opposing candidates, and people associated with the major non-candidate Tshisekedi, claimed that the international community was imposing its choice, Kabila. The argument was widely supported, particularly in Kinshasa, and seems to have contributed to Bemba's electoral victory there.

SEVEN
After the war

Mimi ninalya, uruma
Kwa uchungu, uruma
Kwa kuona, uruma
Ginsi wameuwa, uruma
Wa défenseurs des droits humains
Uruma

I am crying for you
(our hearts ache)
for all the suffering.
To see
how they kill
human rights defenders

(Extract from a lament song for Pascal Kabungulu
Kibembe, written and performed by human rights
group SOFAD All-Stars)[1]

§ The presidential elections of 2006 were supposed to represent a decisive step in war-torn Congo's transition to peace. They did so, to an extent, but also indicated how much work remained to be done. Many Congolese voted for peace but their votes led, paradoxically, to a second round choice between the two leading warlords. The elections were supposed to put an end to 'partition and pillage' but territorial reunification was far from complete when the elections were held, and pillage continued. Incumbent president Joseph Kabila won, in the second round, but only after a first round that revealed a Congo deeply divided between east and west.

Registration, a political process

The elections themselves occasioned new waves of violence. The process of registering voters met with emblematic difficulties when 'Maï-Maï' militiamen in North Kivu kidnapped electoral commission workers, who then had to be rescued by the army.[2]

Registration, far from being a technical step preliminary to the election itself, became a political phenomenon in its own right, in part because of its perceived linkage to the nationality question. Refugees in the neighbouring Republic of Tanzania returned to Congo in droves, apparently in response to a rumour that those who did not have the voter registration card would be deprived of their citizenship.

Many Kinyarwanda-speakers crossed over from Rwanda, as did some from Burundi, to register to vote in the Congolese elections. In Rwandophone majority areas, such as Minembwe in South Kivu and Rutshuru in North Kivu, these people were able to register without difficulty. In mixed areas, such as Uvira (South Kivu) and Goma (North Kivu) fighting broke out, as self-styled 'autochthones' attempted to prevent what they saw as registration by foreigners.[3]

The relative security enjoyed by Rwandophones during the registration process was swept away, prior to the elections of 2006. The Independent Electoral Commission (Commission Electorale Indépendante, CEI) announced that it was taking no account of the new administrative subdivisions created under the RCD – including the territories of Minembwe and Bunyakiri – since the national institutions in Kinshasa had not approved these changes. This deprived the Banyamulenge of a relatively sure legislative seat from Minembwe.

Etienne Tshisekedi, a one-time Mobutu loyalist who had become the leader of the unarmed opposition, chose to boycott the registration process. His hope, apparently, was to force a renewed national dialogue before the elections. As had happened in the past, he miscalculated. In the absence of a national census, the registration process served not only to put individual voters on the rolls, but also to apportion legislative seats among the various provinces. Congolese turned out heavily to register in the east, which meant that North and South Kivu, in particular, would be heavily represented in the new parliament. Tshisekedi's boycott call was heeded especially in his home area of Kasai Oriental and to a lesser extent in Congo's sprawling capital of Kinshasa. Since the Kivus were strongholds of support for Kabila, whereas Kasai Oriental and Kinshasa could have been expected to provide many votes to Tshisekedi, both the presidential and the legislative electoral processes were slanted in favour of Kabila.

Forty-six years of politics, recapitulated

After collecting declarations of candidacy and deposits ($50,000 per candidate), the CEI published a list of thirty-three presidential candidates.[4] Six stood as independent candidates, including Joseph Kabila. The remainder stood with party labels. (The vast number of candidates reflected, in part, strategies dictated by the electoral rules, according to which a second round would be held if no candidate obtained more than 50 per cent of the votes. See the French presidential elections of 2002, in which far-right candidate Jean-Marie Le Pen edged out Socialist Lionel Jospin in the first round, only to be crushed by Jacques Chirac in the second round.)

The thirty-three presidential candidates recapitulated the political history of Congo since independence. One found among them representatives of the major political tendencies of 1959–60, when Patrice Lumumba emerged as the leading figure in Congo's first political generation, and of 1964–66, when followers of the assassinated Lumumba revolted against the pro-Western government in Kinshasa. The thirty-plus years of the Mobutu dictatorship were on offer, as was opposition to the dictator (although the most important opponent, Tshisekedi, remained on the sidelines). The wars of 1996–97 and 1998–2003 provided another set of candidates, including the president and three of the four vice presidents of the infamous 1 + 4 settlement that emerged from internationally sponsored negotiations.

Some observers noted the presence of four second-generation politicians among the thirty-three would-be presidents. Apart from Joseph Kabila, whose father Laurent Kabila had been a leader of Lumumbist insurgents in the 1960s, these included children of Lumumba himself, of Congo's first president, Joseph Kasa-Vubu, and of General Mobutu, who overthrew first Lumumba and then Kasa-Vubu.

Guy-Patrice Lumumba, the youngest son of Patrice Lumumba, was born after his father's murder. He spent most of his life abroad and most Congolese knew little about him. (His older, better-known brother, François Lumumba, '*s'est ruiné*' [went broke] trying to finance his campaign, first for the presidency and then for the legislature, according to Belgian journalist Colette Braeckman.[5] A third brother, Roland, won two thousand votes as an unsuccessful legislative candidate from Katako Kombe, home territory of the Lumumba family.)

Mobutu Nzanga studied in Belgium, returned to Congo, and then went into exile with his dying father. Like the younger Kabila and the Lumumba brothers, he must have a superficial knowledge of the country. On the other hand, he seems to have deeper pockets than most of his rivals.

Justine M'poyo Kasa-Vubu, daughter of Kasa-Vubu, briefly served as a minister and ambassador under Laurent Kabila. She soon resigned and wrote a book, denouncing the president's abuses. (One could also include Gaston Diomi Ndongala, son of Gaston Diomi, head of the Province of Kongo Central in 1961.)

Joseph Kabila, Guy Lumumba, Mobutu Nzanga and Justine Kasa-Vubu, however, were not the only candidates of 2006 who reflected the political divisions of 1960. Those parties had varied along two axes: from radical to 'moderate' or pro-Belgian, and from national to ethno-regionalist and federalist. Patrice Lumumba's Mouvement National Congolais (MNC-L) was the clearest example of a party that was both radical and nationalist (even pan-Africanist). The Parti Solidaire Africain of Antoine Gizenga was equally radical but regionally based. The Parti National du Progrès was Congo-wide but very 'moderate' while the Confédération des Associations Tribales du Katanga (Conakat) was both regionalist and 'moderate', i.e. reactionary.

The venerable Gizenga, Lumumba's deputy prime minister, stood in 2006 as candidate of the Parti Lumumbiste Unifié (Unified Lumumbist Party, PALU). This was one of the few of Congo's 'historical' parties to take part in the elections. PALU had enjoyed a shadowy existence as an opposition force from 1964, when Gizenga declined to join Mulele, Soumialot and Kabila in their violent revolt against the pro-Western government in Kinshasa. Gizenga was in exile for much of the Mobutu period, but returned to revive PALU when multi-party activity resumed in the 1990s. Despite the ambitious programme suggested by its name, PALU never was able to reunify the Lumumbist movement. The party remained popular in Kinshasa and in Gizenga's home province of Bandundu.

In 2006, at least three candidates claimed the heritage of Lumumba's radical nationalism. Claims were made that Joseph Kabila was the heir to Lumumba, Mulele and 'Mzee' (the old man) Laurent Kabila, despite Joseph's exceedingly moderate public discourse.[6] Guy Lumumba attempted to articulate a message of economic nationalism but drew little support. (The turbulent Joseph Olenghankoy, a Tetela like the Lumumbas and an opponent first of Mobutu, then of the Kabilas, could also be considered a candidate in the Lumumbist mould. His message included charges that unnamed persons were giving away Congo's wealth.)

Kasa-Vubu, the country's first president, had attempted to link intransigence on liberation (he called for immediate independence before Lumumba), Congolese nationalism and ethno-regional solidarity of the Kongo people. The Kongo are strongly represented in the educated elite of DRC but seem unlikely to regain the prominence they enjoyed in 1959–65. Whereas the majority of the Kongo people supported Kasa-Vubu's party ABAKO in 1959–60, in 2006 they were faced with an array of choices. Including Justine Kasa-Vubu, they could choose among at least six Kongo candidates, three of them women. Wivine Nlandu, widow of former Prime Minister Nguz a Karl-I-Bond (a Lunda from Katanga) was a presidential candidate, as was her own sister, Marie-Thérèse N'Landu Mpolo Nene, former *chef de cabinet* of Nguz. (The sisters apparently cannot agree on anything, not even how to spell their family name.) Other Kongo presidential aspirants included Diomi and Matusila. All of these Kongo elite candidates (unlike Joseph Kasavubu) are somewhat out of touch with the masses. The separatist Bundu dia Kongo (Kingdom of Kongo movement), twelve members of which were killed in Matadi shortly before the elections, may better represent mass aspirations than the politicians.[7]

For more than thirty years, Mobutu monopolized political space in Congo/Zaire. In the 1990s, renewed multi-party competition led to the emergence of two vast, ill-defined political 'tendencies' or 'families', the presidential tendency and the 'sacred union' of the opposition. In 2006, the presidential tendency was still visible, but (like the movements of Lumumba and Kasa-Vubu) it had fragmented. There was the biological heir, Mobutu Nzanga, but also a variety of figures from Mobutu's home region of Equateur and/or considered to have been 'barons' of the Mobutu regime. Nzanga stood as candidate of the 'Union des Démocrates Mobutistes' (Union of Mobutist Democrats, UDEMO) and used the familiar light green banner and red torch of the Mobutist party-state, the MPR, in his electoral propaganda. Voters nostalgic for the MPR, however, had an alternative choice. They could support Madame Catherine Nzuzi wa Mbombo, presidential candidate of the MPR 'Fait Privé', the transformed former party-state.

Another form of continuity with the Mobutu era was available, through the candidacy of Pierre Pay-Pay, former president of the national bank. Mobutu had invoked Pay-Pay without citing his name, when he explained the massive public debt run up under his rule. When he wanted to travel abroad, the president said, he would ask an aide to get him a million dollars in cash. The aide would pass on the message, adding a million to the total being requested. By the time the request reached Pay-Pay at the national bank, the total had risen to four million. Pay-Pay would withdraw five million, pocket one million, and pass the remainder to the president through the same intermediaries, each of whom took his cut.

Several other barons of the Mobutist regime were present on the ballot, including two former prime ministers. These were Professor Lunda Bululu, 1990–91, and Professor (and former general) Likulia Bolongo, who served briefly before Mobutu fled into exile in 1997.

Confronting the Mobutists, however defined, were several types of oppositionists. Gizenga represented continuity in opposition, from the 1960s onwards. The 'sacred union' of the early 1990s, which had wrung a series of concessions from the dictator but had been unable to assume power, was not directly represented, since Tshisekedi and the UDPS had chosen to boycott the process. Laurent Kabila, who had considered Tshisekedi to be part of the Mobutist political system, whereas armed insurgents such as himself were the only true opposition, was represented by his (supposed) biological successor, Joseph Kabila. Joseph may not have much support as the ideological successor to Lumumba, Mulele and Laurent Kabila. It seems clear that he combines two kinds of support: ethno-regional support as the successor to Laurent Kabila, son of the Luba–Katanga ethnic community, and nationalist support as the incarnation of opposition to the Rwandans and Ugandans and their Congolese allies. The latter support is particularly strong in the heart of the former Rwandan occupation zone, North Kivu and South Kivu.

The transitional government formed after the war (1 + 4) provided several candidates, starting with President Joseph Kabila. Three of the incumbent vice presidents were candidates. Azarias Ruberwa Manywa, a Munyamulenge from South Kivu, was the candidate of the Rassemblement Congolais pour la Démocratie (Congolese Rally for Democracy, RCD or RCD-Goma), which had begun life as the vehicle for Rwandan intervention against Laurent Kabila, in 1998. Jean-Pierre Bemba Gombo of Equateur was the candidate of the Mouvement de Libération du Congo (MLC, Congo Liberation Movement), the Uganda-backed branch of the anti-Kabila rebellion.

The third vice president standing as a presidential candidate was Arthur Z'Ahidi Ngoma, a Lega from Maniema, who had left the RCD to become nominal head of the unarmed opposition and its principal representative in the transitional government. (Perhaps one should say that Z'Ahidi had been adopted by various groups of the unarmed opposition who wished to block the accession of Etienne Tshisekedi to a vice-presidential post.) Z'Ahidi Ngoma had founded a party called the 'Forces du Futur' but preferred to stand for election as candidate of the 'Camp de la Patrie', the label adopted by those who supported Kinshasa against the Rwandans and Ugandans and their allies, during the Sun City talks.

Two other candidates represented splinters from the original RCD of 1998. These were Roger Lumbala, whose RCD-National became the 'Rassemblement des Congolais Démocrates' for the presidential elections, and Antipas Mbusa Nyamwisi, whose RCD-Mouvement de

Libération gave way to the 'Forces du Renouveau' (Forces of Renewal), where he was allied to Olivier Kamitatu.

Candidates Kabila, Ruberwa, Lumbala and Mbusa all could be considered 'warlords' in that their candidacy was based on an armed faction from the wars of 1996–97 and 1998–2003, and that wealth derived from plunder was diverted into the electoral campaign. Only Vice President Z'Ahidi is an exception. Events would reveal a major gap between the military-security capabilities of Kabila and Bemba, however, each of whom had kept some of their best men out of the reintegrated army, and all the others. Ruberwa was considered a traitor by many of the former RCD officers, who refused his leadership. Dr Kashala was prevented from establishing even a small security service.[8]

The age range of the candidates is striking. Kabila's backers had struggled to establish the constitutional age limit at thirty rather than forty, so that their man would be eligible. In so doing, they made possible the candidacy of Mobutu Nzanga (age thirty-six). Ten candidates were between forty-one and fifty years old, twelve more between fifty-one and sixty, and seven between sixty-one and seventy. By far the oldest were Gizenga (aged eighty-one) and Mukamba (aged seventy-five).

The Kabila camp blocked the adoption of a minimum educational requirement for president. In so doing, they once again kept their man eligible. Many of the other candidates are university graduates, and there was a strong sentiment in favour of limiting the presidency to those holding university degrees. The new constitution bars military officers from holding political office. This led Kabila to resign his commission.

The new constitution also guarantees gender equality. There were four women candidates for president, which represents progress by comparison with Congo's past. All four female candidates were veterans of the political class; none came out of the recent expansion of 'civil society' or non-governmental organizations.

Journalist Octave Juakali Kambale labelled the Congo presidential poll of 2006 the 'elections of the rich', at least partly because the $50,000 deposit screened out anyone who was not rich or backed by those who were, in a country where unemployment is widespread and the average person earns perhaps a dollar a day.[9] Beyond that, one can say that most of the candidates are members of the Congo's political class. Many hold degrees in law or social science, particularly those who began their political careers in the 1980s or earlier.

Apart from the professors and lawyers that one has come to expect in Congolese political circles, there are newcomers. Several medical doctors stood for the presidency. Even more striking is the heavy representation of clergymen. Christian clergy were involved in Congolese politics at earlier stages. Father (Abbé) Athanase Djadi was a major figure in the politics of the Province of Sankuru (Kasai Oriental) in the 1960s; he was defrocked, or left the clergy. Protestant pastor Isaac Kalonji and Catholic Bishop Monsengwo Pasinya presided over the National Conference in 1991–92, presumably on the grounds of their impartiality. Father Apollinaire Malumalu heads the National Electoral Commission in 2006, again presumably on the basis of his impartiality, although he has been attacked as pro-Kabila.

In 2006, however, one also finds an *abbé* (Catholic priest) defying his church to run for president. Father Rigobert Banyingela was suspended from his priestly functions but remained an active candidate. His suspension was announced together with that of 'Mademoiselle' Noëlle Wetchi, a nun or former nun who ran for a parliamentary seat from Maniema, still wearing a habit.[10]

On the Protestant side, there were several clergymen, including Vice President Azarias Ruberwa. Candidate Moleka is an evangelical pastor in Kinshasa. Candidate Mukungubila, an ardent polygamist, announced himself the 'unique candidate of the Eternal' and a 'Prophet'.

Perhaps one should not be surprised at the number of pastors. Evangelical and prophetic churches represent a growing force in Congolese society. More basically, as Schatzberg suggests, the line between the domains of religion and politics is indistinct in what he calls Middle Africa (including DRC).[11]

Finally, while all regions of the vast country were represented among thirty-three candidates, the representation was very uneven. The eastern provinces, predominantly Swahili-speaking, where Kabila could expect to do well, provided only 10 candidates: Province Orientale 3, North Kivu 2, South Kivu 1, Maniema 1 and Katanga 3, including Kabila himself. In contrast, there were 23 from the western provinces, including 6 from Bas-Congo, 5 from Bandundu, 3 in Equateur, 4 in Kasai Occidental, and 5 in Kasai Oriental. As a result, votes in these provinces were very dispersed.

Kabila's campaign was organized on two tiers. He stood for president as an independent. His party, the PPRD, campaigned aggressively to elect him and its various candidates to the national legislature. At the same time, a coalition called the Alliance de la Majorité Présidentielle (Alliance for the Presidential Majority, AMP) gathered together twenty-nine other political parties as well as several dozen 'independent political personalities'. The various parties presented their own legislative candidates, and many of the personalities stood as independent candidates.

The website of the AMP presented the platform of the alliance, starting with 'Who is Joseph' and his 'Genealogy', thereby signalling that the attacks on Kabila had had a certain effect. His accomplishments were summarized. His vision was presented under five subheadings: consolidation of the nation, restoration of the state, economic development, the struggle against poverty, and culture, sports and leisure.[12]

The activities of the alliance would include rallying and mobilizing Congolese women and men to feed the flame of patriotism and to safeguard Congo's territorial integrity, unity and sovereignty. Second, members of the alliance would work together in order to win the presidential election and the other elections, so as to govern under the leadership of Kabila and a common will to build the nation. The programme referred also to participative democracy, to reconciliation of the various elements of the society, to strengthening the structural and institutional reforms carried out by Kabila, to reconstruction of the infrastructure, and to combating negative values such as corruption, hatred, tribalism and political violence.

Its announced strategy was to ensure the election of Kabila in the first round of voting, by putting the *rouleau compresseur* (steamroller) in motion. The target of a first-round victory was not achieved.

The effect of the AMP at the level of the legislative elections is unclear. Logically, some AMP candidates should have desisted to ensure the victory of one of their number, but this usually did not happen. At Katako-Kombe (Kasai Oriental) for example, Christophe Lutundula was elected as a candidate of his Mouvement de la solidarité pour la démocratie et le développement (MSDD), with 15,972 votes. Close behind was Nembalemba, candidate of FONUS, Olenghankoy's party. Third place went to Omatuku of the PPRD and fourth place to Diheka, of Mende's CCU party. Roland Lumumba, son of Patrice and brother of candidates Guy and François, won 2,579 as candidate of MNC-Lumumba. The MSDD, PPRD and CCU all were AMP members.

Kindu's only parliamentary seat went to Alexis Thambwe Mwamba, independent candidate. He finished well ahead of another independent. The PPRD candidate finished in third place. Thambwe Mwamba was a notable of the Mobutu regime, before becoming a prominent founder of the RCD. In 2006, he reappeared as an individual member of the AMP. At one point, he was very unpopular at

Kindu because of his close association with the Rwanda-organized RCD. Presumably he was able to recoup his position by investing heavily in his campaign.

At Lubumbashi, eleven deputies were elected, including five PPRD candidates. Also elected were Kissimba Ngoy Honorius of UNAFEC (Union des Nationalistes fédéralistes du Congo) and independent candidate Banza Mukalay. UNAFEC was an organizational member of AMP, Banza an individual member.

Bemba had a coalition or alliance of his own, the Regroupement des nationalistes congolais (RENACO). Approximately twenty parties and a number of prominent individuals signed on. Three of the presidential candidates – Bemba of course, but also Jonas Mukamba and Christophe Mbosso – came from this bloc. Another important party was the MDD of Kisombe, which presented twenty candidates, mostly at Kinshasa.

After the AMP and RENACO, the third 'bloc' was a single party, Gizenga's PALU, with thirty-four deputies. PALU's legendary discipline stood Gizenga in good stead, as he negotiated with the rival leaders. Other would-be kingmakers, e.g. Pay-Pay with his CODECO and Mobutu Nzanga with UDEMO, had too few votes to have much impact by themselves. The Bemba camp talked of '*tous contre Kabila*' (TCK, everyone against Kabila) but it seemed clear that they lacked enough posts to promise to groups that might join them to be able to catch up with Kabila, let alone reach the 251 needed for a parliamentary majority. In the end, successful negotiations with Gizenga and Mobutu Nzanga led to a parliamentary majority for the AMP, and Kabila's second-round victory over Bemba.

Conduct of the elections

The elections went well, according to the United Nations, the European Union and the Government of South Africa, all of which had a stake in such being the case. The Carter Center, with less to prove, issued a more balanced assessment.[13]

Just as it is difficult to evaluate at a distance the effect of resources poured into the campaigns, so too is it difficult to evaluate the effect of violence and threats of violence. Human rights defender Tshiswaka Hubert fled Lubumbashi after threats against his life, apparently from people associated with Kissimba Ngoy.[14]

While 31 July passed quite peacefully, there were major incidents immediately before and after election day. The presidential campaign ended in a wave of violence, in which the armed forces of three major candidates clashed in the streets of the capital, Kinshasa. A soldier from the personal guard of Vice President Ruberwa was shot dead, and another seriously wounded, by members of the presidential guard. The incident took place at Ndjili Bridge, on the road to Kinshasa's international airport. A presidential motorcade, returning from the airport, met Ruberwa's motorcade, heading in the opposition direction. The vice president told reporters that two vehicles of his motorcade had passed, when the third came under fire without warning. President Kabila was present, according to Ruberwa, as 'probably' was the chief of staff of the army. From this he concluded that the attack was premeditated.[15]

Events surrounding Vice President Bemba were even more bizarre and more costly in human life. Two French Mirage F-1 jets of the European Union force flew over Kinshasa. About the same time, a fire broke out in Bemba's compound. 'Radio Trottoir', Kinshasa's rumour mill, quickly linked the two phenomena and many residents of the capital 'learned' that the Europeans had bombed Bemba's compound. That same day, after Bemba addressed a crowd at Tata Raphael Stadium, some of his followers battled with the police and set fire to the office of the Haute Autorité des Medias (High Authority on the Media, HAM).[16]

In the provinces, some of the pre-electoral violence seems to represent proxy warfare. Lodja is the capital of Sankuru district (Kasai Oriental province), homeland of the Tetela people. At Lodja, followers of Defence Minister Onusumba, a Tetela and former president of the RCD-Goma, apparently clashed with followers of Lambert Mende of the Convention des Congolais unis, itself a member-organization of the Alliance de la Majorité Présidentielle, supporting Kabila. In a separate incident, presidential candidate Olenghankoy (another Tetela) was prevented from flying into Lodja; it is unclear whether this was the work of pro-Kabila or pro-RCD forces.

Armed assailants prevented would-be voters from going to the polling place in two of the most troubled regions of eastern Congo, namely Ituri and North Kivu. In the last few weeks of the electoral campaign, a series of violent incidents took place in North Kivu province. On 7 July, armed men ambushed teams campaigning for Kabila's PPRD and the RCD-Goma, in separate incidents. Four people were hospitalized with gunshot wounds. 'The attackers stole money and essential campaign equipment, such as mobile phones.'[17]

On 14 July, security forces injured three people while breaking up a peaceful demonstration by supporters of the Movement of Congolese Patriots (MPC) in Goma. They also arrested eight alleged participants in the demonstration. The MPC had provided twenty-four hours' notice of the demonstration, as required by law, which raises questions (according to Human Rights Watch) 'about why security forces had intervened'. The probable explanation lies in rivalries within the 'Rwandophone' community. Goma was administered by the RCD-Goma under Hutu governor Eugène Serufuli; the president of the MPC is Tutsi businessman Victor Ngezayo Kambale. Over the past several years, Ngezayo has been involved in a series of conflicts with the RCD over the mining business in the province.[18] In Bukavu, capital of South Kivu, youths backing Kabila reportedly attacked supporters of the RCD-Goma.

Perhaps the most egregious use of state force against a candidate concerned the Luba-Kasai oncologist Oscar Kashala, who had returned from twenty years in the USA to stand for president. His American, South African and Nigerian security personnel were detained on suspicion of preparing a coup d'état, and then expelled from the country. This action had the presumably unintended effect of attracting attention to Kashala, hitherto almost unknown.[19]

Violence was reported from most regions of the country, generally against ethnic or political minorities and against observers such as journalists and human rights activists.

Parties and candidates published programmes, but much of the 'debate' during the campaign consisted of personal attacks. In a rally in Kamina (Katanga) opposition candidate Joseph Olenghankoy criticized certain unnamed Congolese for aiding foreigners to 'pillage the country's natural wealth, especially in Katanga'. The attack clearly referred to Kabila, whose father hails from Katanga, where foreign firms have in recent years won mining contracts that offer particularly attractive taxation rates.[20] Bemba said he would demand renegotiation of such contracts. The argument could be taken to imply that Kabila is a Congolese who aids foreign pillagers, or that Kabila is himself a foreign pillager, who is aided by Congolese accomplices. Longtime Mobutu associate Honoré Ngbanda led the attack on Kabila and on Ruberwa as 'foreigners'.[21]

The Kabila camp tended to ignore the charges of pillage. They lined up support from the Luba Katanga community, which endorsed Joseph as their 'son'. They spent little time attacking Bemba as an agent of Uganda. Instead, they attempted to associate Bemba with abuses committed by his men, including alleged acts of cannibalism against Mbuti or 'pygmies' in Ituri. When Bemba criticized Kabila for having done nothing during a campaign appearance in Bukavu and asked residents what he could do for them, they reportedly shouted (according to a pro-Kabila source), '*Utukule*' (Eat us).'[22]

After the war

On Election Day, millions of people voted in relative calm. In Mbuji Mayi and several other towns in Kasai Oriental and Kasai Occidental, however, the boycott call of the UDPS led to stone throwing and even arson of polling places. The polls were reopened the following day, in Mbuji Mayi and Mweka, under the protection of government forces, but the turnout remained low.

Immediately after the polls closed, various parties began launching accusations of fraud. In particular, Vice President Ruberwa alleged that in North and South Kivu, his supporters had been chased away from the polls, while supporters of Kabila had stuffed the ballot boxes.[23] I suspect that such incidents did occur, but doubt that they substantially affected the outcome. For many people in the Kivus, the elections offered a chance to vote against war and that meant voting against the RCD.

Much more serious abuses took place in Kinshasa during the counting period. Reuters reported:

> A suspicious fire at a major Kinshasa election center during a third day of chaotic poll-counting Thursday deepened concerns over the transparency of the results of Congo's first free elections in more than 40 years. Used and unused ballots were burned, along with other election material, outside an election office that was meant to process one-quarter of the capital's votes.
>
> At the center in N'Djili, a popular neighborhood in the capital, election workers said they had burned empty ballot boxes to clear up rubbish ...
>
> But a Reuters reporter saw the remains of burned ballot papers – some used, others unused – in the ashes outside a room littered with voting material.
>
> 'It would appear that something serious has taken place here. The key question is what is the size of the problem?' one international election observer said.
>
> 'It certainly raises concerns about the credibility and transparency of the process,' the observer said. 'It plays into the hands of those who question this process.'[24]

On 18 September, less than six weeks before Kabila and Bemba were to face off in the second round of voting, a large fire broke out at Bemba's party headquarters. Two television stations owned by Bemba, housed in the headquarters building, were taken off the air by the fire. As firefighters worked to contain the blaze, UN forces arrived and Bemba supporters gathered and chanted: 'Things are going to get hot today! Those who think Bemba will die are wrong!'[25]

Post-electoral tension in North Kivu appears in press reports on an incident at Sake, about 25 kilometres from Goma. Agence France-Presse reported that one Congolese officer had been wounded on 5 August, in an exchange between soldiers of two different brigades of the Congolese army. Citing MONUC, the press agency reported that a Congolese officer had been wounded and taken to the military hospital in Goma.

The two units involved were the 94th Battalion of the 9th Integrated Brigade and the 843rd Battalion of the 83rd Brigade. The 9th Brigade was undergoing integration into the new Congolese army, designed to replace the separate armies of 1998–2003. The 83rd Brigade had not yet begun integration. Some of the men of the 3rd Brigade reportedly were loyal to renegade General Laurent Nkunda. A MONUC spokesman told AFP that there had been a 'misunderstanding' with some men on each side believing that the other unit had forcibly disarmed some of their men.

Reuters presented a more alarmist version of the same incident, according to which two soldiers had been killed at Sake, and thousands of civilians had fled. Nkunda himself, apparently, was 100 kilometres away from Sake. He had promised not to interfere in the elections and it is claimed he kept his promise. He was demanding negotiation with the winner of the election, to obtain the peaceful return of 50,000 Kinyarwanda-speakers from Rwanda to their homes in DRC.[26]

Three interrelated problems remained: creation of an integrated army, ending the impunity of Nkunda and others responsible for war crimes in DRC, and resolving the long-standing problem of nationality and citizenship in the Kivus. A second-level problem was whether one should minimize such incidents, as MONUC and AFP did, or highlight them as Reuters did. Which approach makes it easier to solve the problems?

The first round of presidential voting concluded with Kabila well ahead of the others but well short of the 50 per cent plus one vote needed to avoid a second round of voting. These results reflect the divisions in Congo society. The splits between the zones of DRC's four main vehicular languages have been politicized as never before. The Kikongo zone remains marginalized, as can be seen in the multiple Kongo candidates, discussed above. Bemba did quite well in Bas Congo province, particularly in the port city of Matadi. This victory may represent an anti-Kabila vote by the Kongo community. Their willingness to support Bemba, however, suggests a major evolution in thinking since the 1950s and 1960s, when the 'Bangala' (Lingala-speakers such as Bemba) were seen as the main rivals of the Kongo.

Bandundu province, where State Kikongo (Kikongo ya Leta) is the vehicular language, voted heavily for its native son Gizenga.

The Tshiluba zone supported the UDPS boycott call to a large extent, and marginalized itself. Because so few people registered in that zone, the absent Tshisekedi had made it impossible for anyone else from his ethnic community or region to do well. Dr Kashala served as a kind of surrogate for his co-ethnic Tshisekedi, and finished fifth overall, but his potential was limited by the boycott of the registration process.

That leaves the zone in the west, where Lingala is the main vehicular language, and the Kiswahili zone in the east. When Laurent Kabila and his Rwandan backers invaded eastern DRC in 1996, Mobutu's army justified its flight by claiming that the conflict was the affair of the locals, i.e. that Kivu people and Rwandans were the same.[27] When Kabila and his backers, speaking Kiswahili and sometimes English, took over in 1997, people in Kinshasa had the impression that they were being invaded. The Lingala zone in the west is considerably more suspicious of Kabila than is the Kiswahili zone in the east. People in Kinshasa, and apparently in the west in general, are willing to believe the story that Joseph Kabila is not really the son of Laurent Kabila, but instead a Rwandan or Tanzanian. They are sympathetic to the argument that he is the candidate of foreigners.

Putting Humpty Dumpty together again

From a strong and united state on 30 June 1960, today the DRC is broken up into several entities. At Kinshasa, the capital and seat of all the institutions, a government directed by Joseph Kabila controls a portion of the territory. If this government masters completely two provinces, Bandundu and Bas-Congo, it controls only a part of Equateur, of Kasai Occidental, of Kasai Oriental and of Katanga. In other terms, the government shares the management of these last-mentioned provinces with rebel movements and has nothing to say about the others, notably Orientale province, South Kivu, Maniema and North Kivu.[28]

For the Congolese journalist, state collapse was a reality in 2001, since the war that began in 1998 led to the break-up of Congo into three (or more) microstates. Conceived of in that way, state collapse might be relatively easily remedied, by merging the microstates, or by one of them conquering the others.

Following that narrative line, state collapse had not been completely reversed by the time of the elections in mid-2006. The RCD rebel regime survived in attenuated form, through the provincial government in Goma. Some army units had not been absorbed into the FARDC. Substantial areas of the east remained out of central government control, notably in Ituri (Province Orientale) and in North Kivu, where Laurent Nkunda continued to control territory and issue ultimatums.

Many political scientists do not limit 'state collapse' to control of territory. They maintain that the Congolese state collapsed because it could no longer perform the functions required for it to pass as a state.[29] Such a definition focuses on three functions, according to Zartman: '... the state as the sovereign authority – the accepted source of identity and the arena of politics; the state as an institution – and therefore a tangible organisation of decision-making and an intangible symbol of identity; and the state as the security guarantor for a populated territory'. The various functions are so intertwined that it becomes difficult to perform them separately, Zartman adds. It is difficult to establish a threshold of collapse.[30]

The Congolese political class generally agrees that Congo is a country and the Congolese state is or should be the sovereign authority. There is much less consensus regarding federalism, or the partial decentralization of the political arena and the decision-making process. The state has been unable to guarantee the security of the population, but most people seem to think that it should do so. In short, there is a deficit in the accomplishments of the state, more so than a rejection of the state by the population.

Weiss, who argued that the state had not (yet) collapsed in Zaire/ Congo in the early 1990s, also argued that the *society* had in fact collapsed: 'The infrastructure, roads, means of communication have disappeared, the universities are closed, the hospitals have become mortuaries, the campaigns to fight the great epidemics are suspended and one no longer measures the ravages of AIDS.'[31] Maintenance of roads and of universities and fighting against epidemics had been state functions. Perhaps what happened is better seen as drastic curtailment of state functions rather than collapse of the society.

A decade and more later, after two wars and countless attacks by militias, some of the same societal conditions are present. Universities are not closed. Higher education limps along under the aegis of the state, with student fees providing most of the budget of the various institutions. At the secondary-school level, the *examen d'Etat* (state school leaving examination) was conducted on a national level. Pupils in the occupied east were able to participate in the national examination, thanks to logistical help from the United Nations.

Health services are in a catastrophic state, but decay is uneven. When Ebola fever struck Bandundu province (south-western Congo) health services were functioning there. Outsiders arriving to combat the disease found trained personnel with whom they could work. In much of the former rebel zones of the east and north, the medical infrastructure indeed has been destroyed, and many of the nearly four million casualties of the years since 1996 are due to the lack of basic healthcare.

The holding of elections in 2006 is a major element in the restoration of the Congolese state. The elections are not the end but the beginning of the process, however. The primary task of the new government will be to give the state the capacity to defend the population and provide basic services.

Writing early in the second war, Prendergast and Smock evoked the children's rhyme of 'Humpty Dumpty' to refer to DR Congo. Their narrative differs from that of the journalist or of Zartman et al., in that what must be 'put together again' is not the Congolese state, but peace in Congo.[32] Stability and state construction in Congo were dependent on (successfully) addressing three issues: 'a more equitable distribution of political and economic power throughout the Congo; a more effective counterinsurgency campaign against the nonstate actors that continue to feed off the Congolese vacuum and destabilize neighboring countries; and a more coherent strategy for addressing the boiling cauldron called the Kivus … ' The years of fighting, since the Lusaka ceasefire and the Prendergast–Smock article, might be attributed to the failure of the Congolese and other governments and the so-called international community to address these issues. Certainly, the distribution of political and economic power through the Congo remains highly inequitable. Portions of South and North Kivu and of the Ituri district of Province Orientale continue to boil. The non-state actors, especially those comprising Rwandans and Ugandans, continue to cause trouble, particularly to Congolese and Ugandan civilians; it is unclear that the regimes in Rwanda and Uganda really are destabilized by their activities.

Two 'issues of international principle' collided in Congo, according to Prendergast and Smock. The first was the international obligation to counter the threat to international peace and security – and the threat of genocide – posed by the Rwandan and other militias operating from Congolese soil. The second was 'the need to uphold the sovereignty and territorial integrity of the Congo and other states in the region'. The second point is strangely put: which other states saw their territorial integrity threatened by the events unfolding in eastern Congo?

The Prendergast–Smock narrative balances the internal aspects (the three issues mentioned above) and the international ones (the two issues of principle, namely threats to peace v. sovereignty). In that respect it is preferable to narratives that cast the Congo crisis as a civil war. Moreover it notes the importance of the economic dimension:

> The free-for-all over Congo's vast natural resources fuels the conflict. Some belligerents are using state military budgets to finance their involvement in the war while individuals close to the leadership plunder the vast resources of the Congo. This amounts to state subsidization of personal enrichment. Even for those that are not benefiting personally, all parties to the conflict are exporting mineral to help defray war expenses ... [33]

The authors also claim that 'self-financing of the war effort also reduces the potency of donor leverage for peace'. Are they trying to suggest that Britain, the United States and other donors had made serious efforts to rein in Rwanda and Uganda, as of 1999?

Prendergast and Smock were writing in a conflict-resolution mode, one that leads them to look for mutually acceptable solutions. They point out, astutely, 'All sides in the conflict think that the others need to be pressured to implement the [Lusaka] agreement in good faith, so a package of transparent pressures and incentives should be constructed multilaterally.' The details of their suggestions are somewhat out of date. It is striking, however, that Congo arrived at the elections of 2006, the supposed end of the transition, without having resolved the problems that they identified back in 1999.

New constitution, same old problems?

In May 2005, Congo's bicameral legislature completed a draft constitution, to be approved by referendum. Approval of the constitution, and the election of new leaders under its terms, would mark the end of the democratic transition, begun in the early 1990s, interrupted by the two wars, and begun again under the agreements of Lusaka, Sun City and Pretoria.

The United States 'applauded' the new DRC constitution, described by State Department spokesman Richard Boucher as establishing 'a balance of powers between the branches of government', ensuring 'protection and development of minorities', and providing for 'a limit of two presidential terms'. The USA noted 'the flexibility shown by all members of the transitional Congolese government in reaching this agreement' and expressed the hope that 'the national constitutional referendum will take place as soon as feasible, followed by national elections within the time frame mandated in the Sun City Accords of 2003'.[34]

Not all commentary was as flattering. Writing in a Kinshasa newspaper, Professor Mukadi Bonyi criticized the draft, judging it vague both as regards the form of state – unitary or federal – and the form of regime – presidential or parliamentary.[35] It does seem true that the legislators, divided on these two matters, resolved the problem by not adopting a clear-cut position.

As regards nationality, a motive or a pretext for so much conflict over the years (as Prendergast and Smock among others suggest), the constitution adopts the following language: '*Est Congolais d'origine, toute personne appartenant aux groupes ethniques dont les personnes et le territoire constituaient ce qui est devenu le Congo (présentement la République Démocratique du Congo) à l'indépendance.*' (Is Congolese by origin, any person belonging to the ethnic groups whose persons and territory constituted what became the Congo [presently the Democratic Republic of Congo] at independence.) This was a considerable concession to the Rwandophones, in that no reference was made to 1885. No doubt one should welcome also replacement of the old-fashioned term 'tribe' by 'ethnic group'. But difficulties are foreseeable. Nationality is still defined in terms of one's community, and the communities divided by the frontier (Rwandophone, Lunda, Kongo and the rest) all include some people (and their descendants) who were in Congo at independence and others who have arrived since. The door is still open to conflict based on nationality.

Not mentioned by the Americans or by Professor Mukadi were two other matters of equal importance that had drawn considerable attention in Kinshasa and indeed throughout Congo and the Congolese diaspora. As already mentioned, the question of the minimum age required of candidates for the presidency, presented as a matter of principle, had in fact been the object of arm-wrestling between backers of President Joseph Kabila and his opponents.[36]

Another matter of great significance slipped through, apparently without much debate. That was the question of the creation of new provinces. The 2003 *avant-projet* (draft) had specified in Article Three, 'The Democratic Republic of Congo is composed of eleven provinces possessing "*la personality juridique*" [legal personality, i.e. ability to undertake certain commitments, such as administering a budget]. These provinces are: Bandundu, Bas-Congo, Equateur, Kasaï-Occidental, Kasaï-Oriental, Katanga, Maniéma, Nord-Kivu, Province Orientale, Sud-Kivu and the city of Kinshasa.'[37]

As Tshiyembe points out, the 'inter-Congolese dialogue' had been a battle of men and not a battle of ideas. The questions of what kind of republic and what kind of democracy the Congo needed were not addressed. No durable solution was proposed to the 'crisis of state legitimacy' or to the 'crisis of representation and of redistribution of responsibilities'. The cleavage between populists and federalists, pitting partisans of strong central government against those of local autonomy, was not debated, even though it has 'structure[d] the Congolese political field since 1960'.

In the place of such a debate, proponents of the creation of new provinces put forth the argument that some provinces were too big and therefore their authorities were too far from the people. A provincial governor wishing to tour his province faced a far more manageable task in Bas Congo Province (area 53,920 square kilometres) than his counterpart in Province Orientale (area 503,239 square kilometres).[38] On this basis, civil society spokesmen proposed to substitute for the eleven existing provinces a new structure that was eventually adopted by the legislature (see Table 7.1). The basis was the existing division of the Congo into districts, although the Tshilenge district of Kasai Oriental did not become a province on the basis that its area was too small. The three provinces of the former Kivu – Maniema, North Kivu and South Kivu – were left intact, apparently on the basis that the Kivu of 1960 had already been divided.

The unspoken dimension of the debate, if one can call it such, was the ethno-regional dimension of the proposed new provinces. For example, re-creating Sankuru (which had been a province from 1962 to 1966) would give the Tetela 'their own' province, free from Luba–Kasai domination. Bas Congo (always a kind of play on words, since the French Bas Congo or Lower Congo is pronounced the same as Bakongo) was relabelled Kongo Central, like the provincette.

No existing provincial border was altered, although the possibility was left open. A new province of Lomami was recognized, corresponding to the district of the same name, but it remained to be seen whether the Songye people – divided between Katanga, Kasai Oriental and Maniema – would get 'their' province, equivalent to the Lomami provincette of 1962–67. In North Kivu, it seems likely that the Nande will demand separate status for the 'Grand Nord', separating them from the Rwandophones.

There could have been a serious debate as to whether DR Congo ought to be considered as a federation of ethnic groups, as advocated by Tshiyembe and Kabuya among others.[39] My own opinion is that this is a recipe for disaster, given the ethnic wars of the 1960s and the 1990s, but the topic should be debated, and it has not been.

TABLE 7.1 Post-election provincial structure

11 existing provinces	26 proposed provinces
Kinshasa	Kinshasa
Bandundu	Kwango
	Kwilu
	Maï-Ndombe
Bas-Congo	Bas-Congo
Equateur	Equateur
	Mongala
	Nord-Ubangi
	Sud-Ubangi
	Tshuapa
Kasai Occidental	Kasai Occidental
	Lulua
Kasai Oriental	Sankuru
	Kasai Oriental
	Lomami
Katanga	Haut-Katanga
	Haut-Lomami
	Lualaba
	Tanganika
Maniema	Maniema
Nord-Kivu	Nord-Kivu
Province Orientale	Bas-Uele
	Haut-Uele
	Ituri
	Tshopo
Sud-Kivu	Sud-Kivu

Source: Bha-Avira Mbiya Michel-Casimir, Député, Directeur Général, Démocratie et civisme pour le développement intégral, 'Constitution de la 3ème République en RD Congo: 24 Provinces et non 10 !' 23/11/2004, downloaded 28 May 2005.

Another question that should be debated is whether there are too many layers of administration between the state and the people. At present, a citizen of the Congolese Democratic Republic looks upward, past the village, *groupement*, collectivity, territory, district and province. If this could be simplified, the drain on the budget might be less, and response time might be improved.[40] This question, however, has not been seriously examined.

Basically, one must ask whether dividing the national territory is intended to create more jobs for members of the political class (as was the case, to some extent, in the 1960s) or whether it somehow would serve the interests of the population. Shabunda is 340 kilometres from Bukavu, the capital of the province of South Kivu and the principal transit point for goods coming to or leaving Shabunda. The road is impassable, or so I am told. The people of Shabunda need to have their road repaired so they can get to markets, hospitals and other services. Whether they remain in South Kivu, are transferred to Maniema, or put into a Lega province with Mwenga and Pangi, seems distinctly secondary. The money that would be spent on new provinces could more usefully be spent on transport infrastructure.

Rebirth of nationalism

In recent years, Congolese nationalism has experienced a rebirth. At the same time, sub-national sentiment – especially on the part of some of the most self-conscious ethnic or regional communities – has been resurgent. These two forces, potentially contradictory, both had to be accommodated in the new constitutional order. This is reflected in the language according to which Congo is to be a unitary state, strongly decentralized, and in the replacement of the eleven provinces inherited from Mobutu by twenty-six new provinces.

National feeling is convincingly demonstrated in the survey data summarized by Weiss and Carayannis:

> The data show, first, that the identification of the Congolese with the Congo nation and state over the last 40 years has become stronger, despite predatory leaders, years of war and political fragmentation, devastating poverty, ethnic and linguistic diversity and the virtual collapse of state services. It also suggests that while Congolese identity has become stronger, it has also become exclusionary with regard to one particular ethnic group, the Rwandaphone [sic] peoples. Although these groups constitute a small minority in the Congo, their exclusion from the Congolese nation is significant for any future state-building efforts – not only because they have been an important group historically and politically, but also because that exclusion is tied to two external actors, Rwanda and Burundi, and their actions in the region.[41]

Weiss and Carayannis argue that the 'wars that the Congolese have endured and the humiliation that they have experienced at the hands of foreign armies' have reinforced their sense of identity:

It may also explain the rejection of the Tutsi, all of whom have been linked with the Rwandan invaders. However, this does not explain why the Hutu are also rejected. This is particularly interesting in view of the campaign initiated among Congolese and African elites claiming that a profound division and antagonism exists among Africans of Bantu as against Hamitic or Nilotic backgrounds. This ideological claim, which has dubious scientific basis, places the Hutu among the Bantu and the Tutsi among the Hamitic/Nilotic peoples. Its political purpose has been to mobilize antagonism against the Tutsi and the Tutsi-led Rwandan government, and to legitimate the Kinshasa authorities' alliance with the Rwandan Hutu insurgents in the Congo ... The survey data give almost no support to this ideology. These data suggest that the Hutu are rejected almost as much as the Tutsi and are part of the only group that is excluded from the national community.

I think the ideological cleavage between 'Bantu' and 'Nilotic' continues to function, despite its illogical aspects, i.e. rejection of Hutu. With the benefit of hindsight I would say that the humiliation of invasion was felt more directly in the east than in Kinshasa and the west, and reinforced the Kiswahili–Lingala divide mentioned above in connection with the elections.

BERCI conducted its 2003–04 surveys in four cities in the zone controlled by the central government – Kinshasa, Kikwit, Mbuji-Mayi and Lubumbashi – and in Gemena, then in the hands of the MLC rebels. The RCD refused to allow polling in its zone, perhaps because of fear that the results would reveal its extreme unpopularity.

Respondents in the BERCI polls were asked what they thought when one spoke of unity of the Congo. Gemena was not polled on this question because the question was added later. Respondents in Kinshasa and Kikwit shared similar responses: nearly one-third in each city thought of national unity as the Christian value of brotherly love (29 per cent and 33 per cent respectively), and nearly half of the respondents showed some nostalgia for the days of Mobutu and colonialism by thinking of it as Mobutu's Zaire (23 per cent and 21 per cent respectively) or the Belgian Congo (23 per cent and 20 per cent respectively). In contrast, only 11 per cent of respondents in Lubumbashi thought to equate unity with Mobutu's Zaire and only 14 per cent with the Belgian Congo. Reflecting the secessionist past of Katanga province, 35 per cent of its residents in Lubumbashi equated unity with the territorial integrity of the state, the highest such response rate.[42]

When asked whether the Congo must remain unified, the vast majority of respondents in all five cities said yes, and even advocated the use of force, if necessary, to do so. Earlier BERCI polls conducted in Kinshasa show respondents from all regions (residing in Kinshasa) categorically rejecting the idea of partitioning the country. In an October 1996 survey in Kinshasa, less than one month into the first war, respondents overwhelmingly rejected carving up the country into independent states, with less than 5 per cent in favour. In a November 1998 poll in Kinshasa, an overwhelming 89 per cent were against partitioning the country. The response rates against any threat to the unity of the state have been consistently high every time this type of question has been asked.

As Weiss and Carayannis stress, Congolese national identity is being reinforced at the expense of minorities defined as foreign. When asked about the absolute right of different groups to determine their future, half of the BERCI poll respondents and 79 per cent of those in Gemena said that minority groups should not have the right to determine their own future. The question itself, however, was fairly ambiguous (as Weiss and Carayannis note), and could have included options from the right to self-determination and secession to the right to pursue group self-interest in a centralized political system.

As regards specific ethnic groups, the BERCI survey results strongly suggest a high level of mutual acceptance, at least as regards the recognition that members of 'other' ethnic groups are bona fide Congolese. The Rwandophone populations are a significant exception. Their citizenship rights have been challenged on several occasions in the past. While there are no polling data on popular attitudes towards Rwandophone populations prior to the outbreak of the war in 1996, the Congo wars probably reduced their acceptance sharply.

In order to determine attitudes towards these groups, BERCI tailored a set of questions for each city. Respondents were given a list of ethnic groups and asked which of the ethnic groups on the list living in the Congo were Congolese. The list included prevalent ethnic groups living in their particular city, as well as Hutu, Tutsi and Banyamulenge. All the ethnic groups other than Rwandophone groups were overwhelmingly considered Congolese, except in instances when the respondent was unfamiliar with a particular ethnic group. In those cases, the unfamiliarity was demonstrated by a high rate of non-response for that ethnic group rather than a high rate of objection to that group's nationality status. Of the respondents in the BERCI polls, 54 per cent considered the Banyamulenge not to be Congolese and another 20 per cent were unsure. In other words, only 26 per cent accepted the Banyamulenge as Congolese. This indicates (as Weiss and Carayannis note):

a much greater willingness to consider the Banyamulenge to be Congolese than the Hutu or Tutsi. The two latter groups were categorically rejected as Congolese: 83 percent said the Tutsi were not Congolese and 82 percent said that the Hutu were not. This is consistent with earlier BERCI polls. For example, in a poll taken in Kinshasa four months into the second war, when respondents were asked about the nationality question of the Tutsi an overwhelming majority said that they were not Congolese – only 4 percent said they should be granted citizenship, even as a solution to the war. The exception to this trend is Gemena, where the Tutsi and especially the Hutu fared slightly better than the Banyamulenge. Eighty percent of respondents in Gemena said that the Banyamulenge are not Congolese, 74 percent said that of the Tutsi and 66 percent said that of the Hutu.[43]

One of the more interesting results of these polls is the sharp difference in the acceptance of Tutsi as a general category in contrast to the Banyamulenge Tutsi. Weiss and Carayannis cite two possible explanations of this difference. First, the Banyamulenge 'probably emigrated from Rwanda and Burundi about 200 years ago, and thus probably constitute the longest residing Rwandaphone [sic] community in the Congo'. I doubt that the Banyamulenge came that long ago (see Chapter 4). In any case, the Banyabwisha (Hutu) of North Kivu probably came earlier.

Weiss and Carayannis suggest that the 'inter-Tutsi war' of the Rwandan army and the RCD-Goma against pro-Kinshasa Munyamulenge officer Patrick Masunzu may have modified the attitudes of some members of the Congolese political class. Instead of seeing all Tutsi as a bloc, the Banyamulenge may have gained 'some modest acceptance as genuine Congolese who have paid with blood for their divorce from their fellow Rwandan Tutsi'.[44]

'Merci Kabila'

One of the most difficult aspects of reconstruction of the state will be establishing a relatively correct and transparent management of public finances. This is going against many years of Congolese experience, in particular the thirty-plus years of 'kleptocracy' under Mobutu. Many of the leaders of today's political parties cut their teeth under this system. Laurent Kabila was criticized for re-establishing Mobutism. His son Joseph follows in his father's footsteps.

The shared interest of the president, vice presidents, ministers and parliamentarians was vividly illustrated, late in 2005, by the affair of the vehicles known as 'Merci Kabila' (i.e. Thanks, Kabila).[45] The commission of inquiry set up in 2004 by the Congolese national assembly to review all the contracts signed by the Congolese state during the two wars, 1996–97 and 1998–2003, handed its final report in May 2005 to the national assembly chairman, Olivier Kamitatu. But since then nothing has happened and Kamitatu has been accused of deliberately blocking publication of the report.

Le Phare daily wrote that the 'ultra-sensitivity' of the report's content might be the reason. According to parliamentary sources, the leaders of the transitional government and specifically the president and the vice presidents were accused in the report and any disclosure might be extremely damaging for them in the forthcoming electoral campaign, the paper claimed.

The MPs could request the report from the bureau of the National Assembly, but according to *Le Phare*, members of Kabila's PPRD were clearly not enthusiastic. Other MPs, including those in civil society organizations who were not represented in the club of five who rule the country – the president and the four vice presidents – had their own reasons for seeking to postpone publication.

Le Phare suggests that all MPs were implicated because they owed Kabila a US$9,000 cash advance on the end-of-term bonus that helped them purchase brand-new Nissan 4x4s, nicknamed 'Merci Kabila' on the Kinshasa streets. This purchase was so unpopular that according to another paper, *La Tempête des Tropiques*, crowds damaged a number of these cars in Kinshasa and in Bas-Congo province. The purchase took place in the context of strikes for salary hikes and arrears that started at the beginning of September 2005 in the education sector and in the public administration.

But *Le Phare* suggested there were other reasons for Kamitatu's not releasing the report. Although he was considered the second in command in the MLC after the vice president in charge of economic affairs, Jean-Pierre Bemba, he was seen as moving closer to Kabila, who might appoint him as prime minister if he won the presidential election. In such circumstances Kamitatu had little interest in damaging his potential patron's reputation.

The chairman of the Congolese parliament's commission, Christophe Lutundula Apala, told journalists that he had been intimidated and threatened by members of the presidential entourage and by officials in companies investigated by the commission. The commission is sometimes known as the Commission on Ill-Gotten Gains, after a body of the same name created by the transitional parliament in the early 1990s, to shed light on abuses under Mobutu. The new version investigated the Gécamines copper and mining parastatal, the Kaba-bankola Mining Company (KMC), a joint venture in which the Zim-babwean tycoon John Bredenkamp had an 80 per cent stake through his firm Tremalt Ltd, and Gécamines the remaining 20 per cent. Other contracts with Zimbabwe-linked interests such as Sengamines were also under scrutiny. The Belgian company Forrest, whose CEO was appointed for two years simultaneously with Gécamines' CEO, was also visited by the MPs. The Israeli diamond dealer Dan Gertler, who secured a contract guaranteeing exclusivity for the marketing of the DRC's diamond production and was later involved in another contract which provided a company called Emaxon with the privilege of buying at a fixed price most of the output of the 80 per cent state-owned MIBA diamond mining company, was also investigated.

The findings of the commission of inquiry are partly reflected in the analysis made by Lutundula about the mismanagement of DRC, during a seminar organized by the South African Institute for Global Dialogue, on 30 and 31 May 2005. Lutundula said then that the state property was sold out through 'lion's share' contracts for the personal benefit of relatives of the current rulers, of godfathers and of foreign associates. He also described the current economic environment that perpetuates the looting of his country's riches and the practices of the current rulers.

A sum of US $8m earmarked for the pay of the military and the war budget for the Kivus (over $30m) was reportedly embezzled without any consequence for the perpetrators. Likewise, a minister, a CEO and a presidential adviser shared between themselves a $3 million commission for the reimbursement of a $48 million debt owed to the DRC's electricity company SNEL by its Congo-Brazzaville equivalent which was eventually slashed to only $32 million.

Lutundula also blamed the president and the vice presidents for having exceeded by 300 per cent the expenditure ceiling. Reportedly 57 per cent of public expenditures are not committed through the correct procedures. He also accused the president and the vice presidents of having undertaken many trips abroad with large ministerial delega-tions in search of contracts and support for the forthcoming elections. He blamed the vice presidents for spending at least $200,000 per month each and for failing to pay customs duties on imported goods.

After eight months of delay, the office of the National Assembly headed by Kamitatu decided in February 2006 to distribute the report to all parliamentarians, though no decision was made on when the chamber would examine it. Local sources reported that the delay was due to pressure by senior politicians named in the report and leading figures of some of the main political parties, who wished to bury it before the elections. A coalition of international and Congolese human rights organizations declared that the DR government must act promptly on the recommendations.[46] In the end, Kamitatu emerged as spokesman of the pro-Kabila Alliance for the Presidential Majority and head of a platform called Forces du Renouveau (Forces of Renewal). Lutundula also joined the pro-Kabila alliance. Little more was heard about the problem of plunder, although Olenghankoy and Bemba referred to it during campaign speeches.

Impunity

The struggle to end plunder and corruption, exemplified by the Lutundula report, is central to post-war reconstruction efforts. Another enormous hurdle – arguably even more central and more difficult – faces DR Congo, however, as it attempts to move beyond the decade of warfare. That is the question of impunity for war crimes. On the one hand, it is a question of capacity-building. Congo has university-trained jurists. The judicial system, however, like other subsystems of the Congolese state, is in an advanced state of decay. It will have to be restored if the Congolese people are to have access to justice.

The impunity problem is not simply a question of a system in decay. It is above all a matter of a grossly politicized judicial system.

The trial of the accused assassins of Laurent Kabila exemplifies all that is wrong with Congolese justice.[47] A bodyguard named Rashidi Mizele killed Kabila and in turn was killed by Colonel Eddy Kapend, aide de camp to Kabila. Rashidi was from Kivu. Kapend, a Lunda, was a key member of the 'Katanga clan' that surrounded Kabila. The Congolese authorities announced that the assassination had been carried out by the RCD-Goma, with the backing of Rwanda and Uganda, but they offered no theory of the case, i.e. no coherent explanation of the alleged relationship between the foreign governments, the RCD, Kapend and Rashidi.

Arrests began immediately after the assassination and included other presidential bodyguards, members of the armed forces, members of the security services and at least forty-five civilians. Most of the arrests took place between January and March 2001, with the commission of inquiry (into the murder of Kabila) apparently enjoying unlimited powers to detain suspects without charge or trial. Colonel Kapend was arrested in March 2001. The majority of those brought to trial came from eastern DRC, in particular from the provinces of North Kivu and South Kivu.

Some of the defendants were initially arrested not in connection with the assassination but with an alleged coup plot that the DRC authorities claimed to have uncovered in October 2000. They apparently included nineteen members of the DRC security services who had fled to Brazzaville in neighbouring Republic of Congo and were arrested there in January 2001. Despite the fact that they were registered asylum-seekers with the United Nations refugee agency UNHCR, all nineteen were transferred to the custody of the DRC authorities in Kinshasa on 24 April 2001. A number of female defendants appeared to be on trial purely because they were related to suspects in the assassination.

The trial began with 115 defendants. Bizarrely, the total grew as the trial proceeded. For example, Emile Mota, economics adviser to Laurent Kabila, had been called as a witness, but found himself accused of participation in the plot.

The Military Order Court sentenced twenty-six people to death and acquitted another forty-five accused of involvement in the assassination of Laurent-Désiré Kabila. Those condemned included Colonel Kapend, identified as the ringleader of the killers, but the court acquitted Fono Onokoko, the wife of Rashidi Mizele, Kabila's bodyguard.

The assassination may or may not have been organized by the RCD. Several of its officers were found guilty in absentia. They then took part in resistance to central government control of Bukavu, in 2004. Defence lawyers said they deplored the large number of death sentences from among the 135 accused and said they would strive to have the court's ruling overturned. 'We no longer have the right to appeal and to oppose [the ruling],' Franck Mulenda, Kapend's lawyer, told IRIN. So, he added, the only recourse left to the lawyers was to take 'extraordinary action'. He said that under the circumstances the defence team might have to petition the Supreme Court and even the current president, son of the murdered Laurent Kabila.[48]

The limits to the battle against impunity could be seen in two high-profile cases at the beginning of 2006. A Congolese warlord, Thomas Lubanga Dyilo, appeared before the International Criminal Court in The Hague in March 2006, on charges of conscripting children and using them to participate in hostilities during 2002 and 2003. Lubanga had been the head of the Union des Patriotes congolais (UPC) in Ituri. His men had committed numerous massacres of civilians. They are accused also of killing seven Bangladeshi peacekeepers.

Justice remains politicized, however, in that the predominantly Hema UPC had been allied with Uganda, then with Rwanda. Sending a Rwandan ally to The Hague could not fail to be popular in Kinshasa.

The same could be said of the action of a military tribunal in Bukavu that condemned a leader of a former armed group, called Mudundu 40, to five years' imprisonment for crimes including the illegal detention of children.[49] 'The judgment, which is without precedent, constitutes a significant step forward for Congolese justice in the fight against impunity for these types of crimes against children,' according to MONUC. Previously Human Rights Watch said Mudundu 40 was composed of up to 40 per cent child soldiers. The condemned man, who is reportedly named Kanyanga Biyoyo, was found guilty of illegally detaining children in South Kivu province in April 2004.

As in the case of Lubanga, the recruitment of child soldiers is a serious offence. Singling out and trying Kanyanga for an offence committed by many militia leaders, however, could be seen as partisan. Mudundu 40 was a Maï-Maï-style self-defence organization emanating from the Shi (Bashi) ethnic group. Mudundu 40 was allegedly close to Rwanda at one time. It is widely believed to have aided Laurent Nkunda during his capture of Bukavu in 2004.

Congolese assessments of the struggle against impunity differ in familiar ways. A young university lecturer of Lega origin notes that the transitional government that came to power in the wake of the 'Accord Global et Inclusif' was committed, in principle, to instal a state of law, justice and equity. For several years, however, nothing practical was done to bring about such a state, and crimes remained unpunished, for political reasons.

It is not surprising that the first moves against impunity strike the allies of Rwanda (according to this analyst) who cites several reasons:

1. First, Rwanda made war in DRC behind a screen of Congolese, who felt their powerful backer protected them. Not only had Rwanda defeated Congo on the battlefield, but even on the football pitch, during the African Nations Cup of 2004. The majority of Congolese waited for the moment when they could avenge these humiliations.

2. A second reason might be the fact that these allies of Rwanda have not broken their link to their sponsor. Azarias Ruberwa of the RCD, vice president of DRC, had been denounced as an agent of Rwanda, who defended its interests rather than those of Congo, whose citizen he claimed to be. From this point of view, starting the impunity struggle with allies of Rwanda could be intended

to show them that they are no longer invulnerable and that their sponsor can no longer dominate Congo.

3. In the diplomatic arena, relations with Rwanda's former ally Uganda have improved in some respects. Even if signs of improved relations on the ground are fewer than statements concerning improved relations, the will to improve relations contrasts sharply with the attitude of Rwanda, which continues to complain about the Interahamwe in DR Congo. Bringing Rwanda's allies before the tribunal could be a means of pressurizing one of them to implicate Rwanda, which then might be called to defend itself against the accusation that it had intervened.[50]

This interpretation is not completely convincing. Early in 2006, Uganda was the party threatening to intervene in Congo, to attack the Lord's Resistance Army. The suggestion that Lubanga or some other Rwandan-backed Congolese would implicate Rwanda seems wishful thinking.

A second analyst, a Tutsi from North Kivu, analyses the same behaviour in radically different fashion. Sending Lubanga to The Hague was intended to calm public opinion at Kinshasa and allow Kofi Annan to have a peaceful visit to the Congolese capital, according to this writer. The real question (he continues) is why the international community is willing to take part in this game of manipulating the Congolese population? What is the community afraid of?

The Congolese have already understood the message of this theatrical production, he continues: after the 'Tutsi Hema' of Ituri, it will be the turn of the Tutsi of North Kivu, followed by the Tutsi of South Kivu. Starting the campaign against impunity by punishing Lubanga, Nkunda and Mutebutsi would convey the absurd message that the Banyarwanda Tutsi are the source of Congo's sorrows. Trying to flatter the Congolese, the international community does not see that it is creating another abscess. Behind the Banyarwanda–Tutsi question, there is a more basic problem that will have to be resolved if Congo is to escape from the current crisis. Arresting Lubanga, Nkunda or Mutebutsi solves nothing, because other Lubangas or Nkundas will appear. If there is to be an amnesty for war crimes, then it should be general. If no one wants this amnesty, then let us take all of the presumed authors of war crimes to the International Criminal Tribunal.[51]

Apart from the question of whether Nkunda or some other alleged war criminals will be sent to be judged in The Hague, there is the question of who will go before the country's own tribunals. During

2005–06, journalists and human rights defenders fell victim to violence and threats of violence, from authorities or people acting on their behalf. Few if any of those perpetrators have been punished.

The case of Pascal Kabungulu illustrates the problem of impunity. On 31 July 2005, Kabungulu, Secretary-General of Héritiers de la Justice, a leading Congolese human rights organization, was assassinated at his home in Bukavu. In the early hours of the morning, three armed men in uniform broke into his house, dragged him out of his bedroom and shot him in front of his family. Family members reported that just before his execution the attackers said, 'We were looking for you and today is the day of your death.' The men stole Kabungulu's laptop, a television and a tape recorder.

Héritiers de la Justice is a well-known human rights group that has uncovered grave human rights abuses, including war crimes in eastern DRC. Created in 1991, the organization has been an independent critic of the governments of former Presidents Mobutu Sese Seko, Laurent-Désiré Kabila and the current transitional authorities under Joseph Kabila. The organization has also documented grave abuses by armed groups operating in eastern Congo. Kabungulu joined Héritiers de la Justice in the mid-1990s and became its Secretary-General in 1999.

Since late 2004, a growing number of human rights activists across eastern Congo have received death threats after denouncing serious human rights abuses by provincial authorities. Some activists have had to flee the country fearing for their lives. Several members of Héritiers de la Justice, based in rural areas, have been assassinated in the past.

In a joint statement following Kabungulu's death, Human Rights Watch, Amnesty International and Front Line said, 'Pascal Kabungulu was a highly regarded and courageous defender of human rights who gave hope to ordinary people afflicted by war and misery. Killing a human rights defender means spreading fear across whole communities in Congo.'[52]

Journalists and human rights defenders are crucial to ending the war and establishing a more just and more democratic political system in DR Congo. Powerful figures in the country have an interest in silencing these people.

Holding elections is only a small part of the necessary transformation. The presidential election of 2006 offered the voters a choice among warlords. The legislative election saw the return of many henchmen of the former dictator Mobutu.

As 2007 began, the Congolese state had been reunified, for the most part, but the work of establishing a relatively competent and honest state apparatus had barely begun. The youthful president had fulfilled a campaign promise by naming his ally of the second round, the venerable Antoine Gizenga, as prime minister. The separation of powers between the presidency and the premiership, which had caused so much difficulty in the past, however, remained to be tested.

The regional setting was more hopeful than it had been for years; Rwanda apparently was mediating negotiations between the Congolese government and renegade General Laurent Nkunda. To the north, in Ituri, the integration of warlords into the Congolese army apparently had failed to put an end to insurgency.

Public space in the Great Lakes has been privatized and criminalized, as Filip Reyntjens declares.[53] Many key actors seem to lack the will to transform the situation. As Alison Des Forges of Human Rights Watch puts it, 'A national army staffed by war criminals is unlikely to provide any security to its citizens whether during elections or thereafter.'[54]

The problems of Congo are daunting. It is up to the Congolese themselves to solve them, if they can. I have no illusions that I can play a major part in this effort. If, however, this book can contribute in a small way to helping the Congolese and their neighbours to understand what has happened in the recent past and to heal some of the wounds, then I will be satisfied.

Congo wars chronology

1994

April Plane carrying Hutu presidents of Rwanda and Burundi shot down near Kigali. This action sets off the Rwandan genocide, in which perhaps 800,000 Tutsi were killed. Exodus of 2 million Rwandan Hutu to camps in North and South Kivu, controlled by authorities of the overthrown Hutu regime. From these camps, attacks are launched against Rwanda and against Tutsi in Congo.

1996

October So-called 'Banyamulenge' capture Uvira, Bukavu and Goma. Refugee camps dismantled. Long-time Mobutu opponent Laurent Kabila emerges as head of rebel alliance.

1997

April Kabila and allies control Kasai and Katanga; Angolan troops pour across border.

May Kinshasa falls to Kabila and his allies.

July Paul Kagame says Rwanda planned and directed 'rebellion'.

August UN team begins to investigate fate of Hutu refugees. Investigators leave in March 1998, their work unfinished.

1998

August Anti-Kabila rebels, backed by Rwandan and Uganda, advance to gates of Kinshasa. Intervention of Zimbabwe, Namibia and Angola turns the tide. Ceasefire talks in Zimbabwe fail.

September Rebels face defeat in the west. Addis peace talks fail.

October Rebels capture government stronghold of Kindu as peace talks collapse in Lusaka.

November Rwanda acknowledges its forces are fighting alongside RCD rebels. Uganda-backed MLC advances in the north.

December Efforts to halt war make little progress at the OAU. Rebels accuse Angola and Zimbabwe of launching counter-offensive.

1999

March Government forces and allies seek to halt rebel advance towards diamond-rich city of Mbuji-Mayi.

May Rwanda-backed RCD ousts leader Wamba dia Wamba.

July A ceasefire is agreed and signed in Lusaka by all sides in the conflict except RCD, still locked in a factional dispute. RCD signs up in August.

Troops from Uganda and Rwanda, backing rival rebel factions, clash at Kisangani.

2000

February UN Security Council authorizes 5,500-man force to monitor the ceasefire.

June Tensions between Rwanda and Uganda erupt into the worst fighting yet seen in Kisangani. The adversaries later agree to leave the city in UN-brokered deal. Security Council authorizes Panel of Experts on the Illegal Exploitation of Natural Resources in DRC.

2001

January A bodyguard kills President Laurent Kabila. Joseph Kabila replaces him.

February Joseph Kabila meets Rwandan President Kagame in Washington. Rwanda, Uganda and rebels agree to UN-backed pull-out plan.

April Experts panel says the warring parties are deliberately prolonging the war to plunder gold, diamonds, timber and coltan.

May International Rescue Committee says the war has killed 2.5 million people since 1998.

2002

January New UN Expert Panel to continue inquiry into pillage. Amnesty International accuses DRC security forces of an alarming increase in arbitrary arrests and detentions. Rwanda-backed RCD-Goma forms alliance with UPC of Thomas Lubanga in Ituri.

Catholic bishop of Beni-Butembo accuses Bemba's MLC and Lumbala's RCD-N of cannibalism. Government asks UN Security Council to establish a UN criminal court to try rebels accused of atrocities.

EU parliament calls for measures to punish persons found guilty of pillaging the resources of the DRC, including an investigation by the International Criminal Court into 'acts of genocide and crimes against humanity committed in Africa and elsewhere, where such acts were perpetrated to illegally secure natural resources, such as conflict diamonds and timber'. Ugandan Defence Minister says situation in Bunia is explosive and asks UN to send troops to take control of the area. Human Rights Watch says Uganda should be held responsible for human rights violations taking place in territories it occupies in DRC.

February Some 8,000 Maï-Maï militiamen, accused of cannibalism, are disarmed in Haut Lomami (Katanga).

Kampala and Kinshasa agree on modalities for the implementation of the Ituri Pacification Commission and for the withdrawal of Ugandan troops from DRC.

Belgian Senate commission on exploitation of natural resources in DRC concludes that no illegal acts were committed by the people and companies investigated.

March The UPC signs an accord with the Uganda People's Defence Force (UPDF). The UPDF and allied Lendu and Ngiti militias oust the UPC from Bunia. Parties to the inter-Congolese dialogue in Pretoria agree to a programme for the drafting of a constitution for a period of a national transitional government eventually leading to democratic elections.

Delegates of the Ugandan and DRC governments, different rebel groups and ethnic militias operating in Ituri sign the Ituri Cessation of Hostilities Agreement in Bunia, under which the UPDF is to withdraw from the DRC on 24 April. The UPC does not sign.

Security Council asks Secretary General Annan to increase the presence of MONUC, especially in Ituri, where violence has escalated in the recent past. It also asks Annan to increase the number of personnel in MONUC's human rights component to enhance the capacity of the Congolese parties to investigate all serious violations of international humanitarian law and human rights perpetrated in DRC since 1998.

RCD-Goma appoints to its ranks four former army officers who had been condemned to death for the assassination of President Laurent Kabila.

April In Sun City, South Africa, DRC government and rebel groups unanimously endorse a transitional constitution to govern DRC for two years. President Joseph Kabila to retain his post, supported by four vice presidents from rebel groups and the civilian opposition.

Ituri Pacification Commission is inaugurated in Bunia. The commission includes representatives of the DRC, Uganda and Angola governments, MONUC, civil society bodies, a business people's association, political and military parties to the conflict in Ituri, and ninety grassroots communities.

Kabila sworn in as interim head of state.

International Rescue Committee (IRC) reports that conflict in the DRC has cost more lives than any other since Second World War.

April Government announces abolition of the Military Order Court, which has been criticized by national and international human rights organizations as failing to meet international fair trial standards.

May Azarias Ruberwa, RCD-Goma secretary general, is named as his movement's candidate for the fourth and final vice presidential post for a two-year national transition government, joining the three vice presidential candidates already named: MLC leader Bemba; Kabila ally Yerodia; and Z'ahidi Ngoma from the unarmed opposition.

UPC takes control of Bunia after six days of fighting. Five armed groups that have been fighting around Bunia sign an agreement in Dar es Salaam to cease hostilities and relaunch the Ituri peace process.

Ugandan government vows to take legal action against all individuals identified by the Ugandan Judicial Commission of Inquiry as having been involved in the plunder of DRC's natural resources. However, it will ignore all other allegations made by the UN Expert Panel.

Human Rights Watch and Amnesty International ask UN to authorize the deployment of a rapid reaction force to protect civilians in Ituri, saying MONUC has been unable to protect civilians adequately.

UN Security Council authorizes deployment of an interim emergency multinational force in Bunia, until 1 September. France offers to lead the force, and will contribute 750 troops, with the remainder to come from other EU states.

June Secretary General Annan recommends a one-year extension of MONUC's mandate, and calls for an increase in authorized military strength from 8,700 to 10,800. An advance unit of French soldiers arrives in Bunia to prepare for the arrival of an estimated 1,400 multinational peace enforcement troops. EU agrees to deploy troops as part of the multinational force in Bunia, codenamed 'Artemis'.

RCD-Goma captures Lubero, North Kivu, as a ceasefire deal for the region is signed in Bujumbura among all parties to the conflict: RCD-Goma, the Kinshasa government and the RCD-Kisangani/ Mouvement de libération (RCD-K/ML) to which Kinshasa is allied.

Kabila names his transitional government.

July Amos Namanga Ngongi (Cameroon), Special Representative of Secretary General Annan to DRC, completes two-year mandate, to be replaced by US diplomat William Swing. MONUC announces that a 3,800-strong force will be deployed in Ituri and other locations, to ensure the 1 September handover from the French-led multinational peace enforcement mission.

EU high representative for the common foreign and security policy, Javier Solana, calls on UN Security Council to authorize a stronger mandate for MONUC similar to that of the EU-led multinational peace enforcement mission deployed to Bunia.

First elements of a planned 3,800-strong UN peacekeeping taskforce for Ituri District arrive in Bunia.

The mutilated bodies of twenty-two civilians, primarily women and children, are discovered by a patrol of the EU-led multinational force, north of Bunia. Rival ethnic militias in Ituri agree to disarm and to participate in joint verification exercises.

Eleven Congolese civilians murdered near the town of Baraka in South Kivu, allegedly by fighters belonging to an alliance of the FDD rebel group from neighbouring Burundi; Rwandan former military; and Congolese Maï-Maï.

During its first meeting, the new transitional government resolves to make resolution of the conflict in Ituri a major priority, with a consultative committee to be sent to the area imminently.

UN Security Council unanimously adopts resolution giving MONUC a stronger mandate and increasing its authorized strength from 8,700 to 10,800 troops. The Council also extends the mission's mandate for another year, until 30 July 2004, and institutes a twelve-month arms embargo against foreign and Congolese armed groups in the east.

August Controversy over military leader nominees resolved as RCD-Goma submits a revised list of candidates for top military posts.

Kabila names officers to lead the nation's unified national military, incorporating elements from all former armed rebel groups signatory to a national power-sharing accord, as well as Maï-Maï militias. Human rights activists criticize the appointment of military officials alleged to have been involved in massacres in Kisangani in 2002, including Amisi and Nkunda of the RCD-Goma.

Ituri militias agree to work with transitional government in restoring state authority across the region.

UN Security Council authorizes the EU-led multinational peace enforcement mission in Bunia to provide assistance to MONUC, as the former withdraws and the latter is reinforced and deployed in and around Bunia.

UN special rapporteur on the human rights situation in the DRC, Iulia Motoc, says there are indications that genocide may have occurred in Ituri.

September The French-led multinational force in Bunia hands over security duties to MONUC.

The leadership of a newly unified national military is inaugurated in Kinshasa. DRC military chief of staff Lieutenant General Liwanga Mata Nyamunyobo summons three officers of the RCD-Goma, including Brigadier General Laurent Nkunda, to appear before a military court for having refused to take part in the inauguration of the newly unified national army.

MONUC arrests about 100 people, including two UPC leaders, after fighting erupts during a protest of MONUC's 'Bunia without Arms' campaign.

Two rival militias in Bunia – the primarily Hema UPC and the primarily Lendu FNI – agree to allow the free circulation of people and goods in the region.

The Office of the Prosecutor of the ICC says it will investigate the role of businesses operating in Europe, Asia and North America in fuelling crimes against humanity in the DRC.

2003

Opposition politician Etienne Tshisekedi returns to Kinshasa after a self-imposed two-year exile, but says he will not take part in the transitional government.

October An agreement to cease hostilities between forces of General David Padiri Bulenda's Maï-Maï militia and the RCD-Goma former rebel movement is signed in Shabunda, South Kivu.

Sixteen civilians, primarily women, killed during an attack on the village of Ndunda, 30km north of the town of Uvira, South Kivu. Witnesses tell MONUC that the killings were carried out by a group of twenty who spoke Kirundi, national language of neighbouring Burundi.

Government says it will no longer tolerate the presence on its national territory of Rwandan fighters linked to the genocide (FDLR).

The International Committee to Accompany the Transition (CIAT) chides the national unity government for a wide range of delays that 'risked jeopardizing the holding of nationwide elections within the next twenty-four months'.

UN Panel of Experts on the Illegal Exploitation of Natural Resources and Other Forms of Wealth of the DRC releases its final report, listing names of individuals, companies and governments involved in the plunder of gems and minerals, and recommending measures to be taken. Rwandan Foreign Minister Charles Murigande announces that his government will set up a commission to investigate two cases of alleged illegal exploitation of the DRC's resources by Rwandan companies and individuals.

November MONUC accuses government of blocking an inquiry into the crash landing of a cargo plane believed to have been transporting illegal arms to groups in South Kivu province.

Voluntary return to neighbouring Rwanda of 103 members of the FDLR, including its leader Paul Rwarakabije.

Some 2,000 people associated with Maï-Maï militias are demobilized in Kindu to either return to civilian life or to be integrated into the national army.

DRC and Rwanda recommit themselves to complete the repatriation of Rwandan fighters (Interahamwe ex-FAR in the Congo) within a year.

Ugandan President Museveni's younger brother – Lieutenant General Salim Saleh – resigns amid persistent allegations that he spearheaded his country's plunder of natural resources in DRC during nearly five years of Ugandan occupation.

UN Security Council urges the transitional government to adopt a national disarmament, demobilization, reintegration (DDR) programme, and to accelerate reform of the army and police.

UNICEF and the government launch a national campaign to promote education of all girls.

2004

January South Africa and the Democratic Republic of Congo (DRC) sign a bilateral agreement worth US $10 billion covering defence and security, the economy and finance, agriculture and infrastructure development.

The UN Security Council unanimously adopts a resolution on formation of an integrated army brigade in Kisangani.

The remaining three positions in Congo's unified military high command are filled with the appointment of General Obed Rwibasira (Goma region), colonels Jules Mutebutsi (Bukavu region) and Ciro Nsimba (Bandundu region), all from RCD-Goma.

March MONUC announces it has repatriated 9,775 Rwandan, Ugandan and Burundian combatants and their dependants through its disarmament, demobilization, repatriation, reintegration and resettlement programme.

Combatants, thought to be remnants of Mobutu's Zairian Armed Forces, launch unsuccessful attacks on several military and civilian installations.

May Representatives of seven armed militia groups from Ituri sign an agreement in Kinshasa with the government to disarm and participate in the transitional process towards democracy.

Congolese and Ugandan authorities establish two joint verification teams to monitor and eliminate border violations by rebels between the two countries.

New governors for eleven provinces are sworn in at a ceremony in Kinshasa. Fighting breaks out in Bukavu, between soldiers loyal to the Kinshasa government and renegade soldiers from the former Rwandan-backed RCD (led by Mutebutsi and Nkunda).

The World Bank approves a $100 million grant to help consolidate peace and promote economic stability in the DRC.

July A uranium mine in Shinkolobwe, in Katanga province, collapses, nine miners die. A MONUC team is prevented from accessing the mine collapse site.

The Expert Panel on the Illegal Exploitation of Natural Resources and Other Forms of Wealth in DRC accuses the Rwandan government of supporting Congolese dissidents who seized Bukavu in June, thus breaking UN arms embargo instituted in 2003.

August 150 Banyamulenge Tutsi from DRC are massacred at Gatumba, in Burundi.

Vice President Ruberwa announces in Goma that his RCD-Goma party has suspended its participation in the government, accusing it of failing to establish proper guidelines for integrating former rebels into the new national army.

The DRC, Rwanda and Uganda agree to disarm groups operating in their territories within a year.

September Four days after suspending his participation in the transitional government, Ruberwa returns to Kinshasa. A programme involving the disarmament of some 15,000 ex-combatants in Ituri, and their reintegration into civilian life, is officially launched in Bunia, the main town in the area. At Mahagi, just seven combatants are disarmed on the first day of the programme.

Government troops capture the town of Minova, Nkunda's stronghold in South Kivu province.

Commanders of the military regions in North and South Kivu provinces agree to stop fighting.

October A court condemns a former military prosecutor, Colonel Charles Alamba, and ten other people to death for murder, mutilation and extortion.

The International Criminal Court and the DRC sign an accord allowing the prosecutor to begin investigations into war crimes and crimes against humanity committed in the country.

Some 1,618 Congolese Tutsi refugees, massed at a border crossing between Burundi and the DRC for almost one week, are taken to a site in the centre of Uvira, South Kivu.

Foreign affairs ministers Murigande of Rwanda, Butiime of Uganda and Ramazani Baya of the DRC agree to create a tripartite commission to ensure that existing agreements on peace and security in the region will be implemented.

Some 3,260 Congolese troops and an undisclosed number of UN peacekeepers begin deploying to Walungu Territory, in South Kivu province, to encourage foreign combatants to abide by the disarmament process and return home.

November A declaration of commitment to end conflict in the Great Lakes region is signed in Dar es Salaam by eleven heads of state.

President Kabila suspends six government ministers and ten senior managers of state-owned companies following a report by the National Assembly accusing them of corruption.

Kabila announces he will send 10,000 more troops to the east of the country, in response to a threat by Rwanda to invade.

December MONUC says it has spotted about 100 people suspected of being Rwandan troops, amid persistent reports of their incursion into eastern Congo. The Ugandan army announces it has deployed troops along the border with DRC following reports of renewed activity by Ugandan insurgent groups based in eastern Congo.

With the threat of renewed regional conflict in DRC, the AU Peace and Security Council announces it will seek a greater role in helping to disarm Rwandan combatants based in eastern DRC.

MONUC repels armed men from Rwanda who attempted to enter the town of Bukavu. Fighting resumes in the town of Kanyabayonga in North Kivu province.

The Armed Forces High Command transfers the military commander of the 8th Military Region – North Kivu province – in a move aimed at ending clashes between factions of the army in the province.

The leaders of dissident soldiers in North Kivu province agree to a ceasefire following more than a week of fighting that has displaced tens of thousands of civilians.

2006

June French Ambassador de La Sablière, speaking on behalf of UN Security Council delegation, warns of danger of 'Congolité' idea, drawing parallel with Ivory Coast where 'Ivoirité' led to civil war.

14 June Alleged Interahamwe attack village in South Kivu, kill a baby and kidnap six persons.

17 June President Joseph Kabila marries his long-time companion, Olive Lembe di Sita. Announcement of the marriage revives the polemic concerning the nationality of the president.

30 July First round of presidential voting; voting for national assembly (lower house). Kabila wins 45 per cent of votes, as compared to 20 per cent for Bemba. Octagenarian Antoine Gizenga, Lumumba's vice premier in 1960, finishes third with 13 per cent. The legislative results are similar. Announcement of results leads to three days of fighting in Kinshasa between military units loyal to Kabila and to Bemba.

22 August UN brokers ceasefire after Kinshasa battle between forces of Kabila and Gizenga.

18 September Fire at Bemba headquarters in Kinshasa temporarily disrupts his TV and radio broadcasts.

October Agreement reached between Kabila's AMP alliance and Gizenga's PALU. Gizenga apparently will become prime minister in new government. Mobutu Zanga, son of the late president, supports Kabila. Several deputies elected on CODECO ticket of Pierre Pay-Pay join Kabila's AMP, giving the presidential bloc 300 seats in the assembly.

Violent attack in London on Kabila's chief of staff, Leonard She Okitundu, and two other dignitaries of the regime.

29 October Second round gives Kabila convincing victory over Bemba but confirms east–west split seen in the first round.

Sources: BBC, IRIN, MONUC.

Notes

1 Half a holocaust

1 Philippe Leymarie, 'Fin de règne au Zaire', *Le Monde Diplomatique*, April 1997; Afsane Bassir, 'Zaire: Julius Nyerere – le transfert de pouvoir a été une affaire essentiellement Africaine', *Le Monde*, 21 May 1997.

2 Mwayila Tshiyembe, 'L'ex-Zaïre convoité par ses voisins. Ambitions rivales dans l'Afrique des Grands Lacs', *Le Monde Diplomatique*, January 1999: 10–11. According to journalist Lynne Duke, the expression 'first world war' originated with Susan Rice, US Assistant Secretary of State for Africa (Lynne Duke, *Mandela, Mobutu, and Me*, New York: Doubleday, 2003: 237).

3 Association of Concerned Africanist Scholars (ACAS), *ACAS Bulletin*, 53/54 (Winter 1998), special double issue: *The 1998 Rebellion in the Democratic Republic of the Congo*.

4 I. Bannon and P. Collier (eds), *Natural Resources and Violent Conflict*, Washington, DC: World Bank, 2003; K. Emizet and L. Ndikumana, 'The Economics of Civil War: The Case of the Democratic Republic of Congo', in *Understanding Civil War: Evidence and Analysis*, Washington, DC: World Bank and Oxford University Press, 2005.

5 N. D. Kristoff, 'We're Catching the Refugees and Killing Them', *International Herald Tribune*, 28 April 1997: 1, 9; K. Emizet, 'The Massacre of Refugees in Congo: A Case of UN Peacekeeping Failure and International Law', *Journal of Modern African Studies*, 38 (2) (2000): 163–202.

6 L. Roberts, *Mortality in Eastern DRC. Results from Five Mortality Surveys by the International Rescue Committee May 2000*, Bukavu, DR Congo: International Rescue Committee, 2000; B. Coghlan, R. Brennan et al., *Mortality in the Democratic Republic of Congo: Results from a Nationwide Survey Conducted April–July 2004*, Melbourne and New York: Burnet Institute, International Rescue Committee, 2004: v, 26. Bulletin of Refugees International, 'Eastern Congo: Beyond the Volcano, a Slow Motion Holocaust', 28 January 2002 <www.refugeesinternational.org/content/article/detail/784/>. N. Kristoff, 'What Did You Do During the African Holocaust?', *New York Times*, 27 May 2003, <www.nytimes.com>. Le Soir en ligne, 'Au Congo, deux tsunamis par an', 7 March 2005, <www.lesoir.be>.

7 Roberts, *Mortality in Eastern DRC*.

8 Ibid.

9 C. Braeckman, *Les nouveaux prédateurs*, Paris: Fayard, 2003: 161–5; Corine Lesnes, 'L'ONU dénonce les exactions commises par les rebelles au Congo-Kinshasa', *Le Monde*, 16 January 2003, <http://www.lemonde.fr/imprimer> (article ref/O,5987,3210–305641,00.html).

10 G. Nzongola Ntalaja, *The Congo from Leopold to Kabila. A People's History*, London and New York: Zed Books, 2002: 226.

11 Personal communication from a former RCD militant, October 2005.

12 John Pomfret, 'Rwanda Led Revolt in Congo', *Washington Post*, 2 July 1977. Nzongola, *The Congo from Leopold to Kabila*: 226.

13 'Retrait de la Mission d'enquête de l'ONU', *Info-Congo/Kinshasa* (Montreal), 138, 10 June 1998: 1–2; Karin Davies (Associated Press writer), 'Kabila Asks U.N. to Probe Massacres', *Yahoo News*, 11 November 1998.

14 Nzongola, *The Congo from Leopold to Kabila*: 228.

15 'Political Declaration of the Congolese Rally for Democracy. "The Removal of Kabila and the Alternative Position of the RCD"', *ACAS Bulletin*, 53/54 (Winter 1998).

16 G. Nzongola, 'Position to Professeur Georges Nzongola-Ntalaja sur la Crise en République Démocratique du Congo', *ACAS Bulletin*, 53/54 (Winter 1998).

17 He obviously had learned a lot about Congo geography since 1997 when he did not know whether Kinshasa was on the left bank or right bank of the Congo river. See 'L'Afrique en morceaux … Textes à l'appui. Entretien avec Jihan El Tahri, réalisatrice de L'Afrique en morceaux, la tragédie des Grands Lacs', <www.cndp.fr/tice/teledoc/dossiers/dossier_afrique.htm>.

18 Elsewhere I speculated on Angola's role in the assassination (T. Turner, 'Angola's Role in the Congo War', in J. F. Clark [ed.], *The African Stakes of the Congo War*, New York: Palgrave, 2002). Rwanda, the United States, and other international actors also had an interest in eliminating Kabila. There are too many suspects to make such speculation useful.

19 'Foreign Minister of Democratic Republic Dismissed', Xinhau press agency, posted on MONUC site, 23 July 2004, <www.monuc.org/news. aspx?newsID=3359>. *Congo-Chronicle* 55, 20 December 2004 to 27 February 2005, <www.congonet.dds.n//chroni55.html>.

20 Koen Vlassenroot and Timothy Raeymaekers, *Conflict and Social Transformation in Eastern DR Congo*, Ghent: Academia Press, 2003. For a Congolese view of Uganda's role see A. Maindo Monga Ngonga, '"La Républiquette de l'Ituri" en République Démocratique du Congo: un Far West ougandais', *Politique Africaine* (89) (2003): 181–94.

21 Braeckman, *Les nouveaux prédateurs*: 9, 17; Pierre Baracyetse, 'L'enjeu géopolitique des sociétés minières internationales en République Démocratique du Congo (ex-Zaïre)', *SOS RWANDA-BURUNDI Buzet* (Belgium), December 1999.

22 Kevin C. Dunn, *Imagining the Congo. The International Relations of Identity*, New York and Basingstoke: Palgrave Macmillan, 2003: 172.

23 See the contrasting views of Zimbabwe's motives in Martin R. Rupiya, 'A Political and Military Review of Zimbabwe's Involvement in the Second Congo War', in Clark (ed.), *The African Stakes of the Congo War*: xv, 249; and Global Witness, *Zimbabwe's Resource Colonialism in the DRC*, London: Global Witness, 2001.

24 William Reno, *Warlord Politics and African States*, Boulder, CO: Lynne Rienner, 1998.

25 B. Cosma Wilungula, 'Fizi 1967–1986: Le Maquis Kabila', *Cahiers africains*, 26 (1997); Erik Kennes, 'Footnotes to the Mining Story', *Review of African Political Economy*, 93/94: 601–7.

26 On diamonds, see L. Monnier et al. (eds), 'Chasse au diamant au Congo/Zaire', *Cahiers Africains –Afrika Studies*, 2000 (45/46), Tervuren and Paris: Institut Africain and L'Harmattan, 2001.

27 David Moore, 'Searching for the Iron Fist and Velvet Glove in the Democratic Republic of the Congo', *Canadian Journal of African Studies* (XXXX): 547; for examples see All-Party Parliamentary Group (UK) on the Great Lakes Region and Genocide Prevention, 'Cursed by Riches: Who Benefits from Resource Exploitation in the DCR?', 2002; D. Farah, *Blood from Stones: The Secret Financial Network of Terror*, New York: Broadway Books, 2004; and, to a considerable extent, Braeckman, *Les nouveaux prédateurs*.

28 Stephen Jackson, '"Nos richesses sont pillées!" Economies de guerre et rumeurs de crime au Kivu', *Politique africaine*, 84 (December 2001): 117–35; Jackson, 'Making a Killing: Criminality and Coping in the Kivu War Economy', *Review of African Political Economy*, 93/94 (2002): 517–36; Vlassenroot and Raeymaekers, 'Emerging Complexes in Ituri', in Vlassenroot and Raeymaekers (eds), *Conflict and Social Transformation in Eastern DR Congo*: 177–96.

29 Nzongola, *The Congo from Leopold to Kabila*: 214.

30 Edouard Bustin, 'The Collapse of "Congo/Zaire" and Its Regional Impact', in Daniel C. Bach (ed.), *Regionalization in Africa: Integration and Disintegration*, Oxford and Bloomington, IN: James Currey and Indiana University Press, 1999: 81–90.

31 Reno, *Warlord Politics*.

32 Braeckman, *Les Nouveaux Prédateurs*; Marina Ottaway, Testimony prepared for the Hearings on 'Conflicts in Central Africa', Subcommittee on Africa, US Senate, 8 June 1999, <pages.inifinit.net/glp/documents/docs-039e.htm>.

33 Kennes, 'Footnotes to the Mining Story'.

34 G. Allison, *Essence of Decision: Explaining the Cuban Missile Crisis*, Boston, MA: Little, Brown, 1971; G. Allison and P. Zelikow, *Essence of Decision: Explaining the Cuban Missile Crisis*, Boston, MA: Addison-Wesley, 1999.

35 Reno, *Warlord Politics*: 218.

36 Vlassenroot and Raeymaekers, 'Introduction', in Vlassenroot and Raeymaekers (eds), *Conflict and Social Transformation*: 13.

37 Timothy Longman, 'The Complex Reasons for Rwanda's Engagement in Congo', in Clark (ed.), *The African Stakes of the Congo War*: 129–44.

38 Braeckman, *Les Nouveaux Prédateurs*: 221.

39 Longman, 'Complex Reasons': 137.

40 T. Turner, *Ethnogenèse et nationalisme en Afrique centrale: aux racines de Lumumba*, Paris: L'Harmattan, 2000: 100–1.

41 *L'Afrique en morceaux: la tragedie des Grands Lacs*. French documentary film by Jihan El Tahri and Peter Chappell, 2001. See also El Tahri, 'L'Afrique en morceaux ... ' (note 17).

42 Michael G. Schatzberg, *Political Legitimacy in Middle Africa: Father, Family, Food*, Bloomington, IN: Indiana University Press, 2001.

43 Karl Marx, *The 18th Brumaire of Louis Bonaparte* (electronic resource), London: Electric Book Co., c. 2001.

44 A. Maurel, *La Congo de la colonisation belge à l'indépendance*, Paris: L'Harmattan, 1992; first published as M. Merlier (1963), *Le Congo de la colonisation belge à l'indépendance*, Paris: François Maspero.

45 Yves Person, 'Impérialisme linguistique et colonialisme', *Les temps modernes*, 29 (324/325/326) (1973): 90–118.

46 Ibid.

47 Nzongola, *The Congo from Leopold to Kabila*: 216–18.

48 J. P. Spradley and D. W. McCurdy, *The Cultural Experience: Ethnography in Complex Society*, Chicago, IL: Science Research Associates, 1972: 7–12.

49 Mustafa Rejai, *Comparative Political Ideologies*, New York: St Martin's Press, 1984.

50 Crawford Young, 'The Democratic Republic of the Congo (DROC): Everyone's Problem', in Kent Hughes Butt and Arthur L. Bradshaw, Jr (eds), *Central African Security: Conflict in the Congo*, National Intelligence Council, Carlisle, PA: Collins Center, US Army War College, 2001: 37–46.

51 Murray Edelman, *From Art to Politics. How Artistic Creations Shape Political Conceptions*, Chicago, IL: University of Chicago Press, 1995: 2, 11.

52 J.-P. Chrétien, J.-F. Dupaquier et al., *Rwanda: Les médias du génocide*, Paris: Éditions Karthala, 1995.

53 Thomas Turner, 'Nationalism, Historiography, and the (Re)construction of the Rwandan Past', in C. Norton (ed.) *Nationalism, Historiography and the (Re)construction of the Past*, Washington, DC: New Academia Press, 2006.

54 Paul Tete Wersey, 'Du bon usage des congolismes. Inventivité de la langue. Notre libraire', *Revue des literatures du Sud*, 159: *Langue, langages, inventions* (July–September 2005).

55 On Inakale see B. Jewsiewicki, *Mami Wata: la peinture urbaine au Congo*, Paris: Gallimard, 2003: 45.

56 Thomas Turner, 'Images of Power, Images of Humiliation: Congolese "Colonial" Sculpture for Sale in Rwanda', *African Arts* (Spring 2005).

57 Ibid.: 163.

2 The political economy of pillage

1 See in particular Paul Collier and Anke Hoeffler, 'Greed and Grievance in Civil War', World Bank, 21 October 2001. I agree with Collier and Hoeffler as to the centrality of economics over ethnicity and other motivations, but strongly disagree with their tendency to minimize the international dimension of these so-called civil wars.

2 Central Intelligence Agency, 'The World Factbook – Congo, Democratic Republic of the', <www.cia.gov/cia/publications/factbook/geos/cg.html>, updated 1 November 2005; accessed 18 November 2005.

3 Ibid.

4 On the inadequacy of demography as an explanation of Rwandan political behaviour see David Newbury, 'Ecology and the Politics of Genocide', *Cultural Survival Quarterly*, 22 (4) (Winter 1999). Consulted online 18 November 2005. He is criticizing the over-simplifications of Robert Kaplan, *The Coming Anarchy: Shattering the Dreams of the Post Cold War*, London: Random House, 2000.

5 G. Nzongola Ntalaja, *The Congo from Leopold to Kabila. A People's History*, London and New York: Zed Books, 2002.

6 C. C. Taylor, *Milk, Honey, and Money: Changing Concepts in Rwandan Healing*, Washington, DC: Smithsonian Institution Press, 1992.

7 J. Munyaneza, M. Kakimba et al., '2006 Budget: Gov't to reduce on donor-dependency', *The New Times*, Kigali, 23 October 2005. Consulted online, 18 November 2005.

8 The Free State was not recognized at the Berlin West Africa Conference but at Berlin, alongside the conference (Nzongola, *The Congo from Leopold to Kabila*, ch. 1; S. E. Crowe, *The Berlin West African Conference* [1945], Westport, CT: Greenwood, 1970). The boundaries of the Free State were set much later, in a series of negotiations with the British, the Portuguese, the Germans and the French.

9 On the Royal Museum of Central Africa, built with money from the Congo, see C. Winneker, 'A Perfect Specimen of Colonial Mythmaking', <washingtonpost.com>, 10 August 2003: B04.

10 On the early days in Katanga see R. J. Cornet, *Katanga: Le Katanga avant les Belges et l'expédition Bia-Francqui-Cornet*, Brussels: Éditions L. Cuypers, 1946; R. J. Cornet, *Terre Katangaise. Cinquantième anniversaire du Comité Spécial du Katanga 1900–1950*, Brussels: Comité Spécial du Katanga, 1950.

11 R. Harms, 'The End of Red Rubber: A Reassessment', *Journal of African History*, 16 (1) (1975): 73–88.

12 R. Lemarchand, *Political Awakening in the Belgian Congo*, Berkeley, CA: University of California Press, 1964: 34.

13 P. Joye and R. Levin, *Les Trusts au Congo*, Brussels: Société Populaire d'Editions, 1961; Lemarchand, *Political Awakening*: 114–15.

14 Compulsory cultivation of cotton is discussed in O. Likaka, *Rural Society and Cotton in Colonial Zaire*, Madison, WI: University of Wisconsin Press, 1997; and T. Turner, *Ethnogenèse et nationalisme en Afrique centrale: aux racines de Lumumba*, Paris: L'Harmattan, 2000: ch. V.

15 Nzongola, *The Congo from Leopold to Kabila*: 62–4.

16 J. P. Harroy, *De la féodalité à la démocratie 1955–62*, Brussels: Editions Hayez, 1984.

17 Nzongola, *The Congo from Leopold to Kabila*: 126.

18 J. Gérard-Libois, *The Katanga Secession*, Madison, WI: University of Wisconsin Press, 1966.

19 M. G. Kalb, *Congo Cables: The Cold War in Africa from Eisenhower to Kennedy*, New York: Macmillan, 1982.

20 Nzongola, *The Congo from Leopold to Kabila*: 145; M. C. Young, 'Rebellion and the Congo', in R. I. Rotberg and A. A. Mazrui (eds), *Protest and Power in Black Africa*, New York: Oxford University Press, 1970: 968–1011.

21 AFRODAD, *The Illegitimacy of External Debt: The Case of the Democratic Republic of Congo, Final Report*, 2005: 20.

22 Jean-Claude Willame, *Zaire: l'épopée d'Inga*, Paris: Editions L'Harmattan, 1986.

23 Nzongola, *The Congo from Leopold to Kabila*: 128–31.

24 Peter Uvin, *Aiding Violence: The Development Enterprise in Rwanda*, West Hartford, CT: Kumarian Press, 1998: ix; 273.

25 For a general account of the genocide and the events that led up to it, see Alison Des Forges, *Leave None to Tell the Story: Genocide in Rwanda*, New York: Human Rights Watch and International Federation of Human Rights, 1999.

26 'Addendum to the Report of the Panel of Experts on the Illegal Exploitation of Natural Resources and Other Forms of Wealth of the Democratic Republic of the Congo', New York, 13 November 2001, 1072e. pdf, accessed 8 November 2005.

27 O. Lanotte, *Guerres sans frontières en République Démocratique du Congo*, Brussels: Coédition GRIP-Editions Complexe, 2003: 84–5.

28 J.-C. Willame, *L'odyssée Kabila: Trajectoire pour un Congo nouveau?*, Paris: Karthala, 2000: 46 ; cited by Lanotte, *Guerres sans frontières*: 86.

29 Lanotte, *Guerres sans frontières*: 86–7.

30 M.-F. Cros, 'Le "blues" de Lubumbashi, la Katangaise', *La Libre Belgique*, 19 May 1998; cited by Lanotte, *Guerres sans frontières*: 88.

31 R. Devisch, 'La violence à Kinshasa est l'institution en négatif', *Cahiers d'études africaines*, 2 (1998).

32 K. Vlassenroot, 'Land and Conflict: the Case of Masisi', in K. Vlassenroot and T. Raeymaekers (eds), *Conflict and Social Tranformation in Eastern DR of Congo*, Ghent: Academia Press Scientific Publishers and the Conflict Research Group (Centre for Third World Studies, University of Ghent), in partnership with 11.11.11., NIZA and NOVIB: 81.

33 Ibid.

34 Willame offers the best account of the white elephant projects, in *Zaire: l'épopée d'Inga*. See also W. Reno, *Warlord Politics and African States*, Boulder, CO: Lynne Rienner, 1998.

35 L.-R. Mbala-Bemba, 'Trafic illicite d'uranium dans les mines de Shinkolobwe au Katanga', *L'Observateur*, Kinshasa, 11 March 2005, <Digitalcongo.com>, accessed 12 March 2005; also, 'DRC: UN Mission Denied Access to Collapsed Uranium Mine', *IRIN*, Kinshasa, 21 July 2004.

36 T. Trefon et al., *Reinventing Order in the Congo: How People*

Respond to State Failure in Kinshasa, London: Zed Books, 2004; L. Monnier, B. Jewsiewicki and G. de Villers (eds), *Chasse au diamant au Congo/Zaïre*, Tervuren and Paris: Institut africain and L'Harmattan, 2001.

37 RAID (Rights & Accountability in Development), Response to Anvil Mining's 'Report on the Visit by NGOs to the Dikulushi Mine, DRC', 5 October 2005, <www.raid-uk.org/work/anvil_dikulushi.htm>.

38 Ibid.

39 'World Bank Buries Internal Report on Controversial Congo Mining Project', 31 January 2006, <www.miningwatch.ca>.

40 D. Kosich, 'PD Adamant About Tenke Fungurume Development', 1 February 2006.

41 Global Witness, 'Digging in Corruption', 6 July 2006.

42 BBC News, 'Congo profits "used in campaign"', 5 July 2006, <http://news.bbc.co.uk/go/pr/fr/-/2/hi/africa/5149744.stm>, accessed 5 July 2006.

3 'Congo must be sweet' – image and ideology in the Congo wars

1 D. A. Okee, 'Congo Must be Sweet' (letter), *The Monitor*, Kampala, 13 July 2000: 9.

2 K. Dunn, *Imagining the Congo*, New York: Palgrave Macmillan, 2003.

3 P. Halen (ed.), *Patrice Lumumba entre Dieu et Diable. Un héros africain dans ses images*, Paris: L'Harmattan, 1997.

4 W. MacGaffey, 'Kongo and the King of the Americans', *Journal of Modern African Studies*, 6 (2) (1968): 171–81.

5 C. Young and T. Turner, *The Rise and Decline of the Zairian State*, Madison, WI: University of Wisconsin Press, 1985: 30–1.

6 Roger Anstey, *King Leopold's Legacy: The Congo Under Belgian Rule, 1908–1960*, New York and London: Oxford University Press, 1966.

7 L. De Witte, *The Assassination of Lumumba*, London and New York: Verso, 2001.

8 On Zairianization, see Young and Turner, *Rise and Decline*; on prestige projects as pillage, J.-C. Willame, *Zaire: l'épopée d'Inga*, Paris: Editions L'Harmattan, 1986.

9 C. Braeckman, *Les nouveaux prédateurs*, Paris: Fayard, 2003: 11–48.

10 P. Silverstein, *Trans-Politics: Islam, Berberity, and the French Nation-State*, Chicago, IL: University of Chicago Press, 1998; sources in Alexis de Tocqueville, *Writings on Empire and Slavery* (ed. and trans. Jennifer Pitts), Baltimore and London: Johns Hopkins University Press, 2001.

11 Silverstein, *Trans-Politics*: 80.

12 J. H. Speke, *Journal of the Discovery of the Source of the Nile* [1868], New York: Dover, 1996: ch. IX, 'History of the Wahuma. Content: The Abyssinians and Gallas'.

13 Ludwig Gumplowicz, *Der Rassenkampf* (The Racial Struggle), 1883. On Gumplowicz's contributions to 'race science', see I. Hannaford, *Race: The History of an Idea in the West*, Washington, DC: Woodrow Wilson Center Press, 1996.

14 C. Vidal, 'Situations ethniques au Rwanda', in J. Amselle and E. M'Bokolo (eds), *Au coeur de l'ethnie*, Paris: La Découverte, 1999: 172.

15 J. Vansina, *Le Rwanda ancien: le royaume Nyiginya*, Paris: Karthala, 2001: 178.

16 Kandt, *Kaput Nili*, 1921: 188–95; cited by Vidal, 'Situations ethniques au Rwanda': 172–3.

17 The label Tutsi apparently was the name of one group of pastoralists, otherwise known as Hima, before spreading to most but not all such groups. Twa is the name given to the small-statured, predominantly hunter-gatherer population in Rwanda as in Burundi and eastern Congo. Hutu had three meanings – servant, peasant or rustic, and foreigner – before being transformed into an ethnic label for those Rwandans who are neither Tutsi nor Twa (see Vansina, *Le Rwanda ancien*).

18 On 'fallen from Heaven', see ibid.

19 Jean-Pierre Chrétien, 'La genèse idéologique et politique du génocide. L'histoire d'un ethnisme particulier', in *Mission d'Information*, 7 April 1998, Sénat français: 3.

20 G. Prunier, *The Rwanda Crisis*, New York: Columbia University Press, 1995: 217.

21 Ibid.: 38–9.

22 Some of the northerners seem to think they are Bantu, however. The late President Mobutu was a Ngbandi, that is a speaker of a non-Bantu language of north-western Congo. In the film *Mobutu, roi du Zaïre* he is heard telling a European reporter, 'We are not Cartesians. We are Bantu.' (*Mobutu, roi du Zaïre*, feature-length documentary, directed by Thierry Michel, Paris and Brussels, 1999.)

23 P. Tempels, *La philosophie bantoue*, Elisabethville: Lovania, 1945; Tempels, *Bantu Philosophy*, Paris: Présence Africaine, 1959; A. Kagame, *Philosophie Bantu-rwandaise de l'être*, Brussels: Académie royale coloniale belge, 1956.

24 C. A. Diop, *Antériorité des civilisations nègres – mythe ou vérité historique?*, Paris: Présence Africaine, 1967: 275.

25 K. Arnaut and H. Vanhee, 'History Facing the Present: An Interview with Jan Vansina', *H-Africa*, 2001.

26 For an analysis of one of the first of these fakes, 'Ce que tout Ankutshu doit savoir', see T. Turner, *Ethnogenèse et nationalisme en Afrique centrale: aux racines de Lumumba*, Paris: L'Harmattan, 2000: 267. It probably originated in Catholic Church circles.

27 T. Turner, 'Congo-Kinshasa', in V. A. Olorunsola (ed.), *The Politics of Cultural Sub-Nationalism in Africa*, New York: Doubleday, 1972: 195–279; T. Turner, '"Batetela," "Baluba," "Basonge": Ethnogenesis in Zaire', *Cahiers d'Etudes africaines*, XXXIII (4) (1993): 587–612.

28 C. Young, *Politics in the Congo: Decolonization and Independence*, Princeton, NJ: Princeton University Press, 1960: 281; Turner, 'Congo-Kinshasa' and '"Batetela," "Baluba," "Basonge"'.

29 E. E. Roosens, *Creating Ethnicity: The Process of Ethnogenesis*,

Newbury Park: Sage Publications, 1989.

30 'White Father', *Encyclopedia Britannica*, 2005. Encyclopedia Britannica Premium Service, 26 November 2005, <www.britannica.com/eb/article-9076824>; on Rwanda, Des Forges, 'Kings without Crowns: The White Fathers in Rwanda', in D. McCall, N. Bennett and J. Butler (eds), *Eastern African History*, New York and London: Praeger for the African Studies Center, Boston University, 1969: 176–207; on south-east Congo, A. F. Roberts, 'History, Ethnicity and Change in the "Christian Kingdom" of Southeastern Zaire', in L. Vail (ed.), *The Creation of Tribalism in Southern Africa*, Berkeley, CA: University of California Press, 1989.

31 E. M'Bokolo, *Affonso 1er. Le roi chrétien de l'ancien Congo*, Paris: ABC, 1975.

32 J. K. Thornton, *The Kongolese Saint Anthony: Dona Beatriz Kimpa Vita and the Antonian Movement, 1684–1706*, Cambridge: Cambridge University Press, 1998.

33 'Congo, Democratic Republic of the', in CIA, *The World Factbook*, <https://cia.gov/publications/factbook/geos/cg.html>.

34 Vidal, 'Situations ethniques au Rwanda': 174.

35 J. Semujanga, *Récits fondateurs du drame rwandais. Discours social, idéologies et stéréotypes*, Paris: L'Harmattan, 1998; G. Mbonimana, 'Le Rwanda, Etat-Nation au XIXe siècle', in D. Byanafashe (ed.), *Les Défis de l'Historiographie rwandaise*, Butare: Editions de l'Université Nationale du Rwanda, 2004. Vol. 1: *Les faits controversés*: 132–49.

36 Jean Rumiya, *Le Rwanda sous le régime du mandat belge (1916–1931)*, Paris: L'Harmattan, 1992: 134.

37 Albert Pagès, *Un royaume hamite au centre de l'Afrique*, Brussels: Institut royal colonial belge, 1933.

38 Louis de Lacger, *Ruanda*, Namur: Grands Lacs, 1939.

39 Alexis Kagame, *Le Code des institutions politiques du Rwanda précolonial*, Brussels: Institut royal colonial belge, 1952; C. Vidal, *Sociologie des passions: Rwanda, Côte d'Ivoire*, Paris: Karthala, 1991.

40 David Newbury, 'Trick Cyclists? Recontextualizing Rwandan Dynastic Chronology', *History in Africa*, 21 (1994): 191–217.

41 T. Turner, 'Nationalism, Historiography, and the (Re)construction of the Rwandan Past', in C. Norton (ed.), *Nationalism, Historiography and the (Re)Construction of the Past*, Washington, DC: New Academia Press, 2006.

42 Johan Pottier, *Re-Imagining Rwanda: Conflict, Survival, and Disinformation in the Late Twentieth Century*, Cambridge: Cambridge University Press, 2002: ch. 3.

43 J. J. Maquet, *The Premise of Inequality*, London: Oxford University Press, 1961: 3, cited by Pottier, *Re-Imagining Rwanda*: 111.

44 Pottier, *Re-Imagining Rwanda*: 114.

45 D. Turnbull, *Maps are Territories. Science is an Atlas* [c.1989], Chicago, IL: University of Chicago Press, 1993; M. Sparke, *In the Space of Theory: Post Foundational Geographies of the Nation-State*, Minneapolis, MN: University of Minneapolis Press, 2005.

46 D. Newbury, 'Irredentist Rwanda: Ethnic and Territorial Frontiers in Central Africa', *Africa Today*, 44 (2) (1997): 211–22. This map has a life of its own: Rumiya, *Le Rwanda sous le régime du mandat belge*, reproduced it without crediting it to Kagame, while Byanafashe, *Les Défis de l'Historiographie rwandaise* put it on the cover, crediting it to *Atlas du Rwanda* (1981).

47 Ngongola, *The Congo from Leopold to Kabila*: 19.

48 Ibid.: 20.

49 See the map in Crowe, *The Berlin West Africa Conference* [1945], Westport, CT: Greenwood, 1970.

50 P. van Zuylen, *L'Echiquier congolais, ou le secret du Roi*, Brussels: Charles Dessart, 1959.

51 E. Verhulpen, *Baluba et Balubaïsés du Katanga*, Anvers: Editions de l'Avenir Belge, 1936; G. van der Kerken, *L'Ethnie mongo*, Brussels: Institut royal colonial belge, 1944; A. Moeller de Laddersous, *Les Grandes Lignes des migrations des Bantous de la province orientale du Congo belge*, Brussels: Institut royal colonial belge, 1936.

52 B. Verhaegen, *Rébellions au Congo*, Vol. 2: *Maniema*, Brussels: CRISP, 1969.

53 O. Boone, *Carte ethnique du Congo: quart sud-est*, Tervuren: Musée royal de l'Afrique centrale, 1961; Boone, *Carte ethnique de la République du Zaire. Quart sud-ouest*, Tervuren: Musée royal d'Afrique centrale, 1973.

54 E. M'Bokolo, 'Le séparatisme katangais', in J. Amselle and E. M'Bokolo (eds), *Au coeur de l'ethnie*: 188.

55 Ibid.: 189. M'Bokolo is not much more flattering regarding Vansina's *Introduction à l'ethnographie du Congo* (1966), noting that he like Boone uses various criteria – including political structure, kinship systems, even ethnic labels – to classify the Congolese communities.

56 L. de Saint Moulin, 'Conscience nationale et identités ethniques. Contribution à une culture de paix', *Congo-Afrique*, XXXVIII (330) (December 1998): 587–630.

57 Young, *Politics in the Congo*: 281.

58 Ibid.: 281–2.

59 Ibid.: 282.

60 Turner, '"Batetela," "Baluba," "Basonge"'. For views of the 'mutineers' as proto-nationalist heroes, see G. Nzongola Ntalaja, *The Congo from Leopold to Kabila. A People's History*, London and New York: Zed Books, 2002 and G. De Boeck, *Baoni: Les révoltes de la Force publique sous Léopold II, Congo 1895–1908*, Antwerp: Ed. EPO, 1987.

61 G. Brausch, 'Political Changes in the Upper Lukenyi Area of the Congo', *African Studies*, III (2) (June 1944): 65–74; provincial archives in Kananga cited in Turner, *Ethnogènse et nationalisme*: 209.

62 W. MacGaffey, 'Kibanguism: An African Christianity', *Africa Report*, January–February 1976: 40–3.

63 Nzongola, *The Congo from Leopold to Kabila*: 49.

64 Young, *Politics in the Congo*: 252–3, citing D. Biebuyck, 'La société

kumu face au kitawala', *Zaïre*, XI (1) (1957): 7–40.

65 B. S. Fetter, 'The Luluabourg Revolt at Elisabethville', *African Historical Studies*, II (2) (1969): 269–77.

66 Young, *Politics in the Congo*: 290.

67 H. Weiss, *Political Protest in the Congo: The Parti Solidaire Africain During the Independence Struggle*, Princeton, NJ: Princeton University Press, 1967.

68 J. Fabian and K. M. Tshibumba, *Remembering the Present*, Berkeley, CA: University of California Press, 1996: front cover and 22. On Tshibumba's art as history and politics, see in addition to Fabian's analysis: C. Young, 'Painting the Burden of the Past: History as Tragedy', in B. Jewsiewicki (ed.), *Art pictural zaïrois*, Sillery (Québec): Editions du Septentrion, 1992: 117–38; T. Turner, 'Images of Power, Images of Humiliation: Congolese "Colonial" Sculpture for Sale in Rwanda', *African Arts*, Spring 2005.

69 Fabian and Tshibumba, *Remembering the Present*: 49.

70 On flogging, see M. B. Dembour, 'Whipping as a Symbol of Belgian Colonialism', *Canadian Journal of African Studies*, 26 (1992): 205–25; on the 'Colonie Belge' painting, see Nzongola, *The Congo from Leopold to Kabila*: 37–8; Fabian and Tshibumba, *Remembering the Present*: 68–9; B. Jewsiewicki and F. Mathieu, *Le quotidien, entre la mémoire et l'imaginaire*, Québec: Université Laval, 1985; Jewsiewicki, *Art pictural zaïrois*; 'Painting in Zaire', in S. Vogel, *Africa Explores. 20th Century African Art*, New York: Center for African Art, 1991.

71 C. Newbury, *The Cohesion of Oppression: Clientship and Ethnicity in Rwanda, 1860–1960*, New York: Columbia University Press, 1988, pp. 54–7.

72 F. Nahimana, *Le Rwanda. Emergence d'un Etat*, Paris: L'Harmattan, 1993: 247–67; Alison L. Des Forges, '"The Drum is Greater than the Shout": The 1912 Rebellion in Northern Rwanda', in Donald Crummey (ed.), *Banditry, Rebellion and Social Protest in Africa*, Portsmouth, NH: Heinemann, 1986.

73 Vidal, 'Situations ethniques au Rwanda': 172.

74 Byanafashe, *Les Défis de l'Historiographie rwandaise*: 104, note 17, citing F. Reyntjens, *Pouvoir et Droit au Rwanda: Droit publique et évolution politique, 1916–1973*, Tervuren: Musée royale de l'Afrique centrale, 1985: 250.

75 J.-P. Chrétien, *Rwanda: Les médias du génocide* (rev. edn), Paris: Karthala, 2002: 341–55.

76 Ibid.: 358–60.

77 T. Hodgkin, *Nationalism in Colonial Africa*, London and New York: F. Muller and New York University Press, 1957: 48–55.

78 Professor Charles Gasarasi, 'Modèles politiques fondamentaux', lecture given in training session organized by Forum de concertation des formations politiques, Kigali, 2005; interview with General Frank Rusagara, commandant of the military academy, Ruhengeri, 2005.

4 War in South Kivu

1 According to Müller Ruhibika, 'Les Banyamulenge ont été les premiers à dénoncer l'invasion du Congo et sont des résistants à l'occupation de la RDC', Kinshasa, 5 October 2004, MMC, <Digitalcongo.com>.

2 IRIN (United Nations Department of Humanitarian Affairs, Integrated Regional Information Network), IRIN Update on South Kivu, 26 October 1996, posted on website of University of Pennsylvania African Studies Center, accessed 4 March 2006.

3 Whether or not massacres took place and who directed them has been extensively debated. Congolese political scientist Kisangani Emizet has concluded that hundreds of thousands of Rwandan Hutu were killed in Congo: K. Emizet, 'The Massacre of Refugees in Congo: A Case of UN Peacekeeping Failure and International Law', *Journal of Modern African Studies*, 38 (2) (2000): 163–202. For an attempted refutation, see Great Lakes Centre for Strategic Studies, Fact Finder Bulletin on claims that Rwanda Army and AFDL killed 230,000 refugees in 1996–97: *Fact Finder Bulletin*, 1001 (2006), <*www.glcss.org*>.

4 S. Sebasoni, interview, Kigali, 2005.

5 *L'Afrique en morceaux, la tragédie des Grands Lacs*, French documentary film by Jihan El Tahri and Peter Chappell, 2001.

6 D. L. Schoenbrun, *A Green Place, a Good Place*, Portsmouth, NH: Heinemann, 1998: 23.

7 G. van Bulck, *Carte linguistique du Congo belge*, Brussels: Institut royal colonial belge, Commission Centrale de l'Atlas du Congo, 1954, portion reproduced in J. C. Willame, *Banyarwanda et Banyamulenge. Violences ethniques et gestion de l'identitaire au Kivu*, Brussels and Paris: Institut Africain-CEDAF and L'Harmattan, 1997: 36.

8 J. B. Cuypers in J. Vansina, A. Doutreloux and J. B. Cuypers, *Introduction à l'ethnographie du Congo*, Kinshasa: Editions Universitaires du Congo, 1966.

9 G. Weis, *Le pays d'Uvira. Etude de géographie régionale sur la bordure occidentale du lac Tanganika*, Brussels: Académie royale des Sciences coloniales, 1959: 118.

10 C. Bigirimana Mba, *L'Evolution des violences à caractère ethnique chez les Banyamulenge du Sud-Kivu (1990–1998)*, thesis, Political Science, Butare: National University of Rwanda, 2003: citing E. Bizimana, *Les interdits chez les Banyamulenge, mémoire de licence*, Butare: National University of Rwanda, 2000: 8.

11 Interview with Mwami Ndare, Bukavu, 2005.

12 Weis, *Le pays d'Uvira*: 145–8, 257–70. Another case of a group that was favoured early but then suffered relative neglect is of course that of the Lulua. See A. Mabika-Kalanda, *Baluba et Lulua: Une ethnie à la recherche d'un nouvel équilibre*, Brussels: Editions de Remarques Congolaises, 1959; T. Turner, '"Batetela," "Baluba," "Basonge": Ethnogenesis in Zaire', *Cahiers d'Etudes africaines*, XXXIII (4) (1993): 587–612.

13 Belgique, Ministère des Colonies, 1e Direction, *Recueil à l'usage des*

fonctionnaires et des agents du Service territorial, London, 1918; Belgique, Royaume de Ministère des Colonies, 2e Direction générale, *Recueil à l'usage des fonctionnaires et des agents du Service territorial au Congo belge*, Brussels, 1918.

14 T. Turner, 'Les séquelles d'une politique coloniale incohérente: le cas des Bahina (Maniema)', *Cahiers zaïrois d'Etudes politiques et sociales*, 3 (1975).

15 Weis, *Le pays d'Uvira*: 146. Several Banyamulenge students have reproduced this paragraph in theses. They apparently appreciate it because it shows that their forebears were proto-nationalists, resisting colonialist projects. It can be read in another sense, less favourable to recent Banyamulenge claims. Weis seems to imply that the Banyamulenge were not Congolese but Rwandan, and threatened to establish authority over neighbouring peoples that *were* Congolese. This may have been sufficient reason for the Belgians to refuse to unite them.

16 Kinyalolo vigorously rejects the notion that the Banyamulenge were in Congo prior to colonization. He has eleborated an alternative chronology that has them fleeing the exactions of the Mwami Musinga, under colonial rule: K. Kinyalolo, 'Désinformation, historiographie et paix dans la région des Grands Lacs de l'Afrique centrale', in S. Djungu and L. Kalimbirio (eds), *Grands Lacs d'Afrique: culture de paix vs. culture de violences*, Huy: Pangolin, 2003.

17 Koen Vlassenroot, 'Citizenship, Identity Formation and Conflict in South Kivu: The Case of the Banyamulenge', *Review of African Political Economy*, 29 (93/4) (September/December 2002): 503.

18 Bigirimana Mba, *L'Evolution des violences*: 33, citing Arrêté Départemental No. 0229 of 23 August 1970.

19 J. Depelchin, 'From Pre-Capitalism to Imperialism: A History of Social and Economic Formations in Eastern Zaïre', PhD dissertation in History, Stanford University, 1974. Apart from archival research and extensive interviewing, he cites the following sources on the Rwanda of South Kivu:

a. J. Maquet and Naigisiki, 'Organisation sociale des Rwanda de l'Itombwe', *Foliae Scientificae Africae Centralis*, I (2) (1955);

b. J. Maquet and D. Hiernaux-L'Hoest, 'Les pasteurs de l'Itombwe', *Science et Nature*, 8 (1955): 3–12;

c. J. Hiernaux, 'Note sur les Tutsi de l'Itombwe (République du Congo): La position anthropologique d'une population émigrée', *Bulletins et Mémoires de la Société d'Anthropologie de Paris*, 7 (10) (1965): 361–79.

20 Depelchin, 'From Pre-Capitalism to Imperialism': 64.

21 Ibid.: 65 and note 10.

22 Ibid.: 67. Depelchin notes also that the rigid oral history of the migrations from Rwanda led some of the Rwandophones or Banyamulenge to characterize the Furiiru disdainfully as 'those people who cannot even remember their history'.

23 Ibid.: 70, citing a Furiiru informant.

Notes to chapter 4

24 Ibid.: 74.

25 Ibid.: 75. Depelchin focuses on the conflict between Furiiru and Ban-yamulenge; Vlassenroot gives more importance to the conflict to the south, between Bembe and Banyamulenge.

26 Ibid.: XXX

27 Vlassenroot, 'Citizenship, Identity Formation': 503.

28 Muzuri Basinzira, *Evolution des conflits ethniques dans l'Itombwe (Sud-Kuru): des origines à l'an 1982. Mémoire de Licence en histoire*, Lubumbashi: National University of Zaire, 1983, cited by Vlassenroot: 503.

29 Vlassenroot: 504.

30 Ibid.

31 J.-C. Willame, *Banyamulenge et Banyarwanda*, Paris/Brussels, 1997, citing Muchukiwa Bosco, 'Enjeux des conflits ethniques dans les hauts plateaux d'Itombwe au Sud-Kivu (Zaïre)', handwritten, Tervuren: Archives of Institut Africain/CEDAF, n.d., III-2695: 6–7.

32 J. P. Pabanel, 'La Question de la nationalité au Kiru', *Politique africaine*, 41 (1992): 38.

33 O. Ndeshyo Rurihose, 'La nationalité de la population Congolaise (Zaïroise) d'expression Kinyarwanda au regard de la loi de 29 juin 1981', *Considerations Juridiques*, Kinshasa: CERIA/Edition Electronique ASYST, 1992.

34 Human Rights Watch, '1. Summary. The Rwandan Patriotic Army (RPA) and the Alliance of ...', <www.hrw/org/reports97/congo/Congo1.htm>.

35 Manassé (Müller) Ruhimbika, *Les Banyamulenge (Congo-Zaïre) entre deux guerres* (preface by B. Jewsiewicki), Paris: L'Harmattan, 2001: 30.

36 The Commission did not permit its members to disagree with its find-ings, according to Garretón. A member who criticized it was first prevented from speaking, then dismissed from his post and deprived of his nationality.

37 Human Rights Watch, 'Rwanda/Zaire: Rearming with Impunity', Washington, DC, 1995: 12–13.

38 Ibid.

39 Amnesty International, 'Hidden from Scrutiny: Human Rights Abuses in Eastern Zaire', AI INDEX: AFR 62/29/96, 19 December 1996.

40 IRIN Briefing, 'The Conflict in South Kivu, Zaire and Its Regional Implications', <Africaaction.org.>, 7 October 1996.

41 Ibid.

42 Interview with Fr Didier Dufailly, SJ, Bukavu, 2005.

43 Andrew Maykuth, 'Rebel split poses more peril in Zaire', *Philadelphia Inquirer*, 4 May 1997, <www.maykuth.com/Africa/zaire504.htm>, accessed 1997.

44 Nzongola, *The Congo from Leopold to Kabila*: 227.

45 Ibid.: 230, citing personal communication from Joseph Mutambo and Müller Ruhimbika.

46 DRC: IRIN Interview with Banyamulenge leader on fighting in Minembwe, 3 May 2002 <IRINnews.org>.

47 Human Rights Watch, *Democratic Republic of Congo: Casualties of War*, New York: HRW, 1999. Details of the church killings were obtained by Human Rights Watch through a telephone interview with church officials in Kinshasa. Details were confirmed by several witnesses in Bukavu who had carried out investigations in Kasika. Catholic clergy estimated that over 1,300 people were killed during these incidents.

48 Ibid., citing HRW interviews at Panzi and Bukavu, and the report 'Massacres-Genocides at Kasika-Kilingutwe, territory of Mwenga, South Kivu by Tutsi rebel groups in DRC', by the NGO CADDHOM, 9 September 1998.

49 Depelchin, 'From Pre-Capitalism to Imperialism'.

50 Hans Romkema, *An Analysis of the Civil Society and Peace Building Prospects in the North and South Kivu Provinces, Democratic Republic of Congo*, Bukavu: Life & Peace Institute, November 2001. Shi informants also mentioned the Rwandans pursuing their civil war on Congolese soil and Rwanda's alleged intention of annexing Congolese territory.

51 Aperçu de la situation (guerre du 26 mai au 9 juin 2004), Héritiers de la Justice; Z. Georges Nalenga, Mouvement de la Jeunesse Congolaise, 'L'insécurité qui prévaut à Bukavu est due aux manœuvres du RCD-Goma, à l'incapacité du gouvernement et à la complicité du la MONUC', 26 February 2004.

52 Human Rights Watch, 'War Crimes in Bukavu', June 2004.

53 'RDC Province de Sud Kivu Communiqué Shikama/Banyamulenge', Enock Ruberangabo Sebineza, Member of the National Assembly, e-mail distribution, 2 June 2004.

54 'UN mission says Rwandan troops 'illegally' entered DR Congo', Agence France Presse, 24 April 2004.

55 See Human Rights Watch, short report on DRC, 'War Crimes in Kisangani: The Response of Rwandan-backed Rebels to the May 2002 Mutiny', 14 (6) (August 2002).

56 There is a case to be made for creation of Bunyakiri Territory. Interviewed at Bukavu, a Havu intellectual concedes that it was unfair to make the Tembo travel 150km to Kalehe town to obtain an administrative document that they can now obtain close to home. But he objects to the authorities creating a territory for political reasons.

57 More accurately, the former *groupement* Buzi-Ziralo was divided; Ziralo was attached to the new, Tembo-dominated Bunyakiri Territory (David Newbury, personal communication, December 2005).

58 P. Kanyamachumbi, *Les populations du Nord-Kivu et la loi sur la nationalité. Vraie et fausse problématique*, Kinshasa: Editions Select, 1993.

59 Human Rights Watch, *Burundi: le massacre de Gatumba. Crime de guerre et agendas politiques*, New York: HRW, September 2004.

60 UN Security Council, cited in ibid.

61 Société Civile du Sud-Kivu, 'Analyse des faits sur les tueries des réfugiés ressortissants de la RD-Congo perpétrées à Katumba (au Burundi), 20 août 2004, signé par 36 personnes', cited in ibid.

5 War in North Kivu

1 Irène Safi, personal communication.

2 Y. Musoni, 'La problématique de la cohabitation conflictuelle entre les Banyarwanda et leurs voisins au Congo (RDC): Le cas du Nord-Kivu', thesis, National University of Rwanda, Butare, 2003: 39.

3 'Nord-Kivu. Population au 30 juin 1984 par Collectivités et Zones', Archives de la s/Région du Nord-Kivu, Bureau de Statistiques, in ibid.: annexe VII.

4 Ibid.: 39.

5 J.-C. Willame, *Banyarwanda et Banyamulenge: violences ethniques et gestion de l'identitaire au Kivu*, Paris: L'Harmattan, 1997: 39, citing J. Vansina, 'Sur les sentiers du passé en forêt. Le cheminement de la tradition politique ancienne de l'Afrique equatoriale', *Enquetes et documents d'histoire africaines* (Catholic University of Louvain), 9 (1991): 241.

6 David Newbury, 'Returning Refugees: Four Historical Patterns of "Coming Home" to Rwanda', *Comparative Studies in Society and History*, 47 (2) (2005): 252–85; A. Kraler, 'The State and Population Mobility in the Great Lakes – What is Different about Post-colonial Migrations?' Sussex Migration Working Paper no. 24, University of Sussex, 2004.

7 H. Rukatsi, 'L'intégration des immigrés au Zaïre. Le cas des personnes originaires du Rwanda', thesis, Université Libre, Brussels, 1988: 102, citing A. Kagame, *Inganji Kalinga*, vol. II, Kabgayi: Editions royales, 1947.

8 Ibid., citing M. Pauwels, 'Le Bushiru et son Muhinza', *Annale Lateranensi*, XXXI (1967): 220.

9 R. Kandt, *Kaput Nili*, Vol. 1, Berlin, 1921: 199, cited in C. Vidal, *Sociologie des passions: Rwanda, Côte d'Ivoire*, Paris: Karthala, 1991: 45–61.

10 G. Vervloet, 'Aux sources du Nil. Dans la région des volcans, du Lac Albert-Edouard et du Ruwenzori. Zone de la Rutshuru-Beni, Congo Belge', *Bulletin de la Société Royale Belge de Géographie*, 33–4 (1909–10); 33 (31): 255–98; 34 (4): 107–37; 34 (6): 393–411.

11 Vervloet, 'Aux sources du Nil': 261, citing *Mouvement Géographique*, 21 (22 May 1910): col. 264.

12 Vervloet, 'Aux sources du Nil'; Joseph Maes and Olga Boone, *Les peuplades du Congo belge*, Brussels: Musée du Congo Belge, 1935; Olga Boone, *Carte ethnique du Congo Belge et du Ruanda-Urundi*, Zaire (April 1954): 451–65; Jan Vansina, J. Cuypers, et al., *Introduction à l'ethnographie du Congo*, Kinshasa, Lubumbashi, Kisangani and Brussels: Editions Universitaires du Congo and CRISP, 1966. The various lists may not refer to exactly the same territory; hence some variation as regards the northern and western fringes of North Kivu is normal.

13 Rukatsi, 'L'intégration des immigrés au Zaire': 106–7.

14 On Nyabingi/Nyavingi in North Kivu, see especially Randall M. Packard, 'Chiefship and the History of Nyavingi Possession among the Bashu of Eastern Zaire', *Africa*, 52 (4) (1982): 67–86, 90.

15 Rukatsi, 'L'intégration des immigrés au Zaire': 109.

16 Ibid.: 110.

17 Maurice Lovens, 'La révolte de Masisi-Lubutu (Congo belge, janvier–mai 1944) (première partie)', *Les Cahiers du CEDAF*, 3–4 (1974).

18 Willame, *Banyarwanda et Banyamulenge*: 41, citing Tshibanda Mbwabwe wa Tshibanda, 'Rutshuru, une zone surpeuplée. Présentation d'un dossier des archives de la zone', *Likondoli*, C (1) (1976): 22ff.

19 Willame, *Banyarwanda et Banyamulenge*: 40, citing René Lemarchand, *Political Awakening in the Congo*, Berkeley, CA: University of California Press, 1964: 119.

20 On European stereotypes of 'suitable' African groups see C. Braeckman, *Terreur africaine. Burundi, Rwanda, Zaire: les racines de la violence*, Paris: Fayard, 1996: 25–6; T. Turner, '"Batetela", "Baluba", "Basonge": Ethnogenesis in Zaire', *Cahiers d'Etudes africaines*, 132 (XXXIII-4) (1993): 587–612.

21 Willame, *Banyarwanda et Banyamulenge*: 41, citing Jean-Pierre Pabanel, 'La question de la nationalité au Kivu', *Politique africaine*, 41 (March 1991): 33.

22 Musoni, 'La problématique de la cohabitation conflictuelle': 65–9, citing Rukatsi, 'L'intégration des immigrés au Zaire' and his own interview with Butera, Rwandophone assistant to the Belgian Spitaels, who was in charge of the project of bringing Rwandans to Kivu.

23 For a recent avatar of this version of Rwandan history, see the cover of Vol. 1 of D. Byanafashe (ed.), *Les Défis de l'Historiographie rwandaise*, Butare: Editions de l'Université Nationale du Rwanda, 2004. For an application of these supposed conquests to the analysis of recent conflict in Masisi, see K. Vlassenroot, 'Land and Conflict: The Case of Masisi', in K. Vlassenroot and T. Raeymaekers (eds), *Conflict and Social Transformation in Eastern DR Congo*, Ghent: Academia Press, 2004: 81–102.

24 Kraler, 'The State and Population Mobility in the Great Lakes': 14.

25 Musoni, 'La problématique de la cohabitation conflictuelle': 71, citing P. Mathieu and A. Mafikiri Tsongo, 'Guerres paysannes au Nord-Kivu (République démocratique du Congo), 1937–1994', *Cahiers d'études africaines*, 150–2 (1988).

26 Rukatsi, 'L'intégration des immigrés au Zaire'.

27 Musoni, 'La problématique de la cohabitation conflictuelle': 91.

28 Ibid.: 96.

29 A. Mabika-Kalanda, *Baluba et Lulua: Une ethnie à la recherche d'un nouvel équilibre*, Brussels: Editions de Remarques Congolaises, 1959; J. Gérard-Libois, *The Katanga Secession*, Madison, WI: University of Wisconsin Press, 1966; T. Turner, *Ethnogenèse et nationalisme en Afrique centrale: aux racines de Lumumba*, Paris: L'Harmattan, 2000.

30 Chiefs themselves were integrated into the state's administrative hierarchy, and attempts were made to shift them to posts outside their home areas, as was being done with higher-ranking territorial administrators, from the zone to the provincial level.

31 Vlassenroot, 'Land and Conflict': 86.

32 Ibid.: 87.

33 G. Nzongola Ntalaja, *The Congo from Leopold to Kabila. A People's History*, London and New York: Zed Books, 2002: 196–8.

34 See ibid.; K. Vlassenroot and H. Romkema, 'The Emergence of a New Order?', *Journal of Humanitarian Assistance*, 28 October 2002.

35 Stanislas Bucyalimwe Mararo, 'Le Nord-Kivu au coeur de la crise congolaise', in Filip Reyntjens and Stefaan Marysse (directors), *L'Afrique des Grands Lacs* (Annuaire 2001–02), Antwerp: Centre d'Etude de la Région des Grands Lacs d'Afrique and Paris: L'Harmattan, 2003: 154.

36 Ibid. Not all 'transnationalism' was Tutsi. The Habyarimana government in Rwanda intervened in North Kivu politics via MAGRIVI.

37 Stanislas Bucyalimwe Mararo, 'Pourquoi Mourir au Kivu?', *Canadian Journal of African Studies*, 36 (1) (2002): 48–9.

38 G. Prunier, *The Rwanda Crisis*, New York: Columbia University Press, 1995: 312.

39 African Rights, *Democratic Republic of Congo: The Cycle of Conflict: Which Way Out in the Kivus?* December 2000: 102, citing interview in Byuma (Rwanda), 8 October 1999.

40 Willame, *Banyarwanda et Banyamulenge*: 136.

41 Amnesty International, 'Democratic Republic of Congo: Arming the East', AI Index: AFR 62/006/2005, 5 July 2005.

42 Ibid.

43 Ibid.

44 'Les FARDC auraient environ 100,000 hommes, selon l'EUSEC', interview with Oscar Mercado and Michel Smitall, 16 March 2006, <www.reliefweb.int.>.

45 'Continuing Instability in the Kivus: Testing the DRC transition to the limit', Pretoria: Institute for Security Studies, October 2004.

46 Amnesty International, 'North Kivu: Civilians Pay the Price for Political and Military Rivalry', AI Index: AFR 62/013/2005, 28 September 2005.

47 The reason given publicly by the government for sending these troops was to 'disarm the interahamwe and protect the national borders'. Many of the government troops sent to the fighting were apparently under the impression that they were being sent to camps for military integration. It is doubtful that 10,000 were actually sent: many of the government forces involved in the December fighting were already in the area.

48 MONUC Human Rights Section spokesperson, quoted in IRIN dispatch, 'Army, rebels main suspects of looting, stealing', 3 March 2005.

49 Jackson's militia calls itself Maï-Maï but is not part of the Maï-Maï taking part in the transition process.

50 Letter from Laurent Nkunda Mihigo, Général de Brigade, 25 August 2005, received at Amnesty International by e-mail.

51 MONUC Human Rights Division, 'Human rights situation in January 2006', 7 February 2006, <www.monuc.org>.

52 'Echange de tirs entre soldats dans l'est de la RDC: au moins 1 blessé (Onu)', Agence France-Presse, 5 August 2006; 'Rebel troops clash with army in eastern Congo', Reuters, 5 August 2006, posted on SABC News Online.

53 Amnesty International, 'North Kivu'.

54 'Un universitaire congolais veut supprimer l'appellation rwando-phone', Agence France-Presse, Kinshasa, 22 December 2005.

6 Congo and the 'international community'

1 M. Mikombe, 'Les dessous des cartes dans l'affaire du major Kasongo: révélations sur William Swing et Ruberwa. Le représentant spécial du secrétaire général de l'Onu est un agent de la CIA qui obéit aux ordres du Président rwandais. Swing et Kagame rendent compte à un certain Langley. Ruberwa: une marionnette au service de Bizima et Nyarugabo', Kinshasa, 27 Februry 2004, <www.digitalcongo.com>. Mikombe seems to think that Langley is a person, not a place (CIA headquarters).

2 'Rwanda "shocked" by UN report on DRC', <www.afrol.com/News2002/rwa025_drc_looting.htm>.

3 J. Kurth, 'The American Way of Victory: A Twentieth-Century Trilogy', *The National Interest* (Summer 2000).

4 S. Katzenellenbogen, 'It Didn't Happen at Berlin: Politics, Economics and Ignorance in the Setting of Africa's Colonial Boundaries', in P. Nugent and A. I. Asiwaju (eds), *African Boundaries: Barriers, Conduits and Opportunities*, New York: Pinter-Cassel: 21–34; G. Nzongola Ntalaja, *The Congo from Leopold to Kabila. A People's History*, London and New York: Zed Books, 2002.

5 O. Ndeshyo, 'Les identités transnationales et la construction de la paix dans les pays multiculturels. Le cas de la Communauté rwandophone in RD Congo', in A. Shyaka and F. Rutembesa (eds), *Afrique des Grands Lacs. Sécurité et paix durable*, Butare: Editions de l'Université Nationale du Rwanda, 2004: 184–207.

6 Nzongola, *The Congo from Leopold to Kabila*: ch. 3; P. H. Gendebien, *L'Intervention des Nations Unies au Congo, 1960–1964*, Paris: Mouton et Cie, 1997.

7 K. Nkrumah, *The Challenge of the Congo. A Case Study of Foreign Pressures in an Independent State*, London: Nelson, 1967; Immanuel Wallerstein, *Africa: The Politics of Independence and Unity*, Lincoln, NA: University of Nebraska Press, 2005.

8 L. Duke, *Mandela, Mobutu, and Me*, New York: Doubleday, 2003: 128.

9 D. Newbury, 'Convergent Catastrophes', *H-Africa electronic network*, 1996.

10 M. Barnett, *Eyewitness to a Genocide: The United Nations and Rwanda*, Ithaca, NY and London: Cornell University Press, 2000; Samantha Power, *A Problem from Hell: America and the Age of Genocide*, New York: Basic Books, 2004; Linda Melvern, *A People Betrayed: The Role of the West in Rwanda's Genocide*, New York: Zed Books, 2000.

11 Barnett, *Eyewitness to a Genocide*: 175.

12 Ndiaye, 'Report of the Special Rapporteur on Extrajudicial, Summary, or Arbitrary Executions', Commission on Human Rights, E/CN.4/1994/7/Add. 1, para. 78; Barnett, *Eyewitness to a Genocide*: 69.

13 Barnett, *Eyewitness to a Genocide*: 145, citing United Nations, 'Report of the United Nations High Commissioner for Human Rights on His Mission to Rwanda of 11–12 May 1994', 19 May 1994, E/CN.4/ Ss-3/3.

14 G. Prunier, *The Rwanda Crisis*, New York: Columbia University Press, 1995: 246–7.

15 Human Rights Watch, 'Rwanda : Lessons Learned Ten Years After the Genocide', 29 March 2004, <www.hrw.org/english/docs/2004/03/29/ rwanda8308.htm>.

16 Roméo Dallaire, 'Shake Hands with the Devil: The Failure of Humanity in Rwanda', in Jacques-Roger Booh-Booh (ed.), *Le patron de Dallaire parle. Révélations sur les dérives d'un général de l'ONU au Rwanda*, Paris: Editions Duboiris, 2005.

17 Barnett, *Eyewitness to a Genocide*: 107.

18 Ibid.: 70–2.

19 Ibid.: 102.

20 Duke, *Mandela, Mobutu and Me*: 131–2.

21 O. Lanotte, *Guerres sans frontières en République Démocratique du Congo*, Brussels: Coédition GRIP-Editions Complexe, 2003: 39–66.

22 J. Pottier, *Re-Imagining Rwanda: Conflict, Survival, and Disinformation in the Late Twentieth Century*, Cambridge: Cambridge University Press, 2002: 131.

23 Ibid.: 132.

24 *Le Soir*, 27 July 1995, quoted in Pottier, *Re-Imagining Rwanda*: 133.

25 US General 'Edwyn', i.e. Edwin Smith, in *De Standaard*, cited by Pottier: 148.

26 Emma Bonino, 'Il y a 280.000 disparus dans l'Est de l'ex Zaire', <www.emmabonino.it/press/about_emma.bonino/684>.

27 'Rapport de l'Equipe d'Enquête du Secrétaire général sur les violations graves des droits de l'homme et du droit international humanitaire en République démocratique du Congo', UN, 2 July 1998; Karin Davies, 'Kabila Asks U.N. to Probe Massacres', Agence Presse, Headlines, 11 November 1998, Yahoo! News, accessed 11 November 1998.

28 'Council Calls for Peaceful Solution to Conflict in Democratic Republic of Congo, Including Immediate Ceasefire, Withdrawal of Foreign Forces', Press Release SC/6569, 31 August 1998, <www.un.org/News/Press/ docs/1998/19980836.sc6569.html>.

29 B. Coghlan, R. Brennan, et al., *Mortality in the Democratic Republic of Congo: Results from a Nationwide Survey Conducted April–July 2004*, Melbourne and New York: Burnet Institute, International Rescue Committee, V (26) (2004); L. Roberts, *Mortality in Eastern DRC. Results from Five Mortality Surveys by the International Rescue Committee*, May 2000, Bukavu, DR Congo: International Rescue Committee, 2000.

30 Artemis was the daughter of Leto and Zeus, and the twin of Apollo. Artemis is the goddess of the wilderness, the hunt and wild animals, and fertility, <www.pantheon.org/articles/a/artemis.html>. It is unclear why the

French chose this name for the mission. Were their men going hunting in the wilderness?

31 A. Maindo Monga Ngonga, '"La Républiquette de l'Ituri" en République Démocratique du Congo: un Far West ougandais', *Politique Africaine*, 89 (2003): 181–94; RFI/LP, 'Situation en Ituri: un ancien conseiller de la Monuc pointe du doigt Kinshasa, Kampala et Kigali', *Le Potentiel*, Kinshasa, 4 March 2005.

32 UN News, 'DR of Congo: UN mission in talks to investigate killings in Ituri', 4 March 2003.

33 In its final form, Artemis included personnel from Austria, Belgium, Cyprus, Germany, Greece, Hungary, Ireland, Netherlands, Portugal, Spain, Sweden and the UK, plus three non-members (Brazil, Canada and South Africa).

34 United Nations, Military Division, Peacekeeping Best Practices Unit, 'Operation Artemis: the Lessons of the Interim Emergency Multinational Force', October 2004, <http://pbpu.unlb.org/PBPU/Document. aspx?docid=572>.

35 A. Shyaka, 'La Force multinationale intérimaire d'urgence en Ituri: "Artémis". Quand la géopolitique se sert de l'humanitaire', in A. Shyaka (ed.), *La Résolution des Conflits en Afrique des Grands Lacs*, Butare: Editions de l'Université Nationale du Rwanda, 2004: 27–46.

36 Human Rights Watch, 'D.R. Congo: War Crimes in Bukavu', Human Rights Watch Briefing Paper, June 2004 <http://hrw.org/english/docs/2004/06/11/congo8803.htm>.

37 See Human Rights Watch, short report on DRC, 'War Crimes in Kisangani: The Response of Rwandan-backed Rebels to the May 2002 Mutiny', 14 (6) (August 2002).

38 Among those evacuated by MONUC were the author and his wife.

39 UN Security Council Resolution 1493, 28 July 2003.

40 IRIN, 'DRC: MONUC facilitated dissidents' withdrawal from Bukavu, official says', 10 June 2004.

41 IRIN, 'DRC–Rwanda: Kamanyola back under government control', 22 June 2004, accessed 1 March 2006.

42 B. Ross, D. Scott and R. Schwartz, 'U.N. Sex Crimes in Congo', ABC News, 10 February 2005, accessed 28 February 2006.

43 'Code of Conduct', ABC News, 1 March 2006.

44 A. Van Woudenberg, Human Rights Watch, Statement, Committee on International Relations, US House of Representatives, 1 March 2005, <www.c.house.gov/international_relations/109/vano30105.htm>.

45 Zoe Daniel, 'UN investigates DRC child prostitution', ABC News online, 18 August 2006.

46 Interim report of the United Nations Expert Panel on the Illegal Exploitation of Natural Resources and Other Forms of Wealth of the Democratic Republic of the Congo.

47 Church turned up in London, as director of the Great Lakes Centre for Strategic Studies (<www.glcss.org>). He travels frequently to Rwanda,

where he is interviewed by the pro-government newspaper, *The New Times*, and even writes an occasional guest column. Is he perhaps receiving a subsidy from the Rwandan government? Church also published a report supporting Rwanda's position on the alleged massacre of Hutu refugees in DRC.

48 'La communauté internationale appelle les candidats aux élections à la réconciliation nationale', Xinhua, 10 July 2006.

49 C. Braeckman, 'Des ambassadeurs sous les bombes. Épreuve de force: après des provocations, la garde de Kabila attaque la résidence de Bemba', blog posted at <www.lesoir.be>, 22 August 2006.

50 'Le Comité international des "sages" invite les candidats au respect des résultats', MMC/CL/SL, Kinshasa, 1 August 2006, <www.digitalcongo.net>.

7 After the war

1 Amnesty International, 'Pascal Kabungulu: still no justice for his murder', <http://web.amnesty.org/web/web.nsf/print/B693E8FFBAF256802>, accessed 30 July 2006.

2 'Congo–U.N. operation kills 32 militiamen', <http://edition.cnn.com/2005/WORLD/africa/11/02/congo.reut/index.html>, accessed 2 November 2005.

3 'East Congo ethnic violence threatens poll plans', AlertNet, 25 January 2006.

4 République Démocratique du Congo. Commission Electorale Indépendate, 'Liste definitive des candidates à l'élection présidentielle', <www.rcd-cei.org>, accessed 31 July 2006.

5 C. Braeckman, 'Le carnet de Colette Braeckman. Kisangani n'est pas solidaire de la violence à Kinshasa', <http://blog.lesoir.be/colette-braeckman/?p=63>.

6 See the site of the 'Coordination des forces Lumumbistes Mulelistes Kabilistes', <www.deboutcongolais.info>.

7 'Up to 12 dead as police open fire in Congo town – UN', Reuters, Kinshasa, 30 June 2006, <www.alertnet.org/thenews/L30892803.htm>.

8 'DRC: 32 "mercenaries" arrested in Kinshasa', <IRIN@irinnews.org>, 24 May 2006.

9 'Will Congo's Election for the Rich Change Lives of the Poor?', *The Nation* (Nairobi), 28 July 2006, <allafrica.com/stories/200607280340.html>.

10 'Suspension de l'abbé Rigobert Banyingela, candidat à la Présidence', <www.cenco.cd/secretariageneral/banyingela.htm>.

11 Theodore Trefon, *Reinventing Order in the Congo: How People Respond to State Failure in Kinshasa*, London and New York: Zed Books, 2004; Michael G. Schatzberg, *Political Legitimacy in Middle Africa: Father, Family, Food*, Bloomington, IN: Indiana University Press, 2001.

12 Several parties and candidates associated with the Maï-Maï resistance to Rwanda contested the elections. Most of these supported Kabila and the AMP. Two parties called Mayi Mayi or Maï-Maï and a third called Maï-Maï Patriotic Resistance won seats from Uvira and Fizi territories, in South Kivu, both well known for resistance to the Rwandan occupation and to the Ban-

yamulenge (perceived as allies of Rwanda). Other political parties co-opted Maï-Maï leaders in order to maximize their chances. An example is Baleke Kadudu, well known as a brave Maï-Maï, who was named as a candidate of the Démocratie Chrétienne Fédéraliste-Convention des Fédéralistes. The reputation of the Maï-Maï for patriotism, in contrast to Congolese collaborators, clearly contributed to the victory of these candidates and, indirectly, the victory of Kabila.

13 'MONUC welcomes the successful holding of elections in DR Congo', press release,1 August 2006, <www.monuc.org/News.aspx?newsid=12003>; 'South African observer mission: elections free and fair', BuaNew, 4 August 2006, <www.monuc.org/news.aspx?newID=12043>; 'Congo-Kinshasa: The Carter Center Preliminary Report on its Observations', <allafrica.com/stories/200608010681.html>. For a long list of abuses before and after the polling, see United Nations Mission in the Democratic Republic of Congo (Kinshasa) MONUC, Monthly Human Rights Assessment – July 2006 (dated 15 August 2006) and August 2006 (dated 19 September 2006), <www.monuc.org>, accessed 20 September 2006.

14 'Democratic Republic of Congo (DRC): Fear for Safety: Hubert Tshiswaka (m)', 13 April 2006, <http://web.amnesty.org/library/Index/ENGAFR620112006?open&of=ENG-COD>.

15 'Campagne electorale: un soldat de la garde rapprochée de Ruberwa tué et un autre blessé', RadioOkapi.net, 29 July 2006, <www.radiookapi.net/article.php?id=5103>, accessed 29 July 2006.

16 C. Braeckman, 'La fièvre monte à Kinshasa', <Lesoir.com>, accessed 28 July 2006.

17 'D.R. Congo: Violence Threatens North Kivu Elections', Human Rights Watch, press release, 31 July 2006, posted on Scoop <www.scoop.co.nz>.

18 T. Matotu, 'Le RCD conteste à l'homme d'affaires Ngezayo la qualité de mandataire de Banro', <www.lesoftonline.net/affaire.html>.

19 '32 "mercenaries" arrested in Kinshasa', IRIN, 24 May 2006; 'Congo candidate sees "coup" arrests as intimidation', Reuters, 25 May 2006; 'South African institute discounts "coup plot" theory following arrests', IRIN, Johannesburg, 26 May 2006.

20 'Kinshasa political protest turns violent', <www.mg.co.za/articlePage.aspx?articleid=277072&area=/breaking_news/breaking_news__africa/>.

21 C. Braeckman, 'Le tireur de ficelles', <http://blog.lesoir.be/colette-braeckman/?p=122>.

22 'Alors qu'ils ont tenté de discréditer J. Kabila: Bukavu, Bemba et Pay-Pay humiliés', <www.groupelavenir.net/article.php3?id_article.4616>.

23 Craig Timberg, 'Candidate Alleges "Massive Fraud" in Congo Vote', *Washington Post*, 2 August 2006: A09, <www.washingtonpost.com/wp_dyn/content/article/2006/08/01/AR2006080101370.html>.

24 'Congo ballots go up in flames. Election center responsible for one-quarter of capital's vote', Reuters, Kinshasa, 3 August 2006, <www.cnn.com/2006/WORLD/africa/08/03/congo.ballot.fire.reut/index.html>.

25 'Fire Hits Congolese Candidate's HQ', Associated Press, 18 September 2006.

26 'Echange de tirs entre soldats dans l'est de la RDC: au moins 1 blessé (Onu)', Agence France-Presse, 5 August 2006; 'Rebel troops clash with army in eastern Congo', Reuters, 5 August 2006, posted on SABC News Online.

27 Stanislas Bucyalimwe Mararo, 'Pourquoi Mourir au Kivu?', *Canadian Journal of African Studies*, 36 (1) (2002): 35–67.

28 JRB, 'L'Etat congolais a éclaté en micro-Etats', *Le Phare*, Kinshasa, 15 October 2001, <www.digitalcongo.net>, accessed 1 April 2006.

29 I. W. Zartman, 'Introduction: Posing the Problem of State Collapse', in I. W. Zartman (ed.), *Collapsed States. The Disintegration and Restoration of Legitimate Authority*, Boulder, CO: Lynne Rienner, 1995: 5.

30 Ibid. One could debate this identification of the functions; whether there are three of them or perhaps more. For the purposes of this chapter, Zartman's formulation will suffice.

31 *Le Monde diplomatique*, March 1993, cited by H. Weiss, 'Zaire: Collapsed Society, Surviving State, Future Polity', in Zartman (ed.), *Collapsed States*: 166.

32 John Prendergast and David Smock, 'Putting Humpty Dumpty Together: Reconstructing Peace in the Congo', Special Report, United States Institute of Peace, 31 August 1999, <www.usip.org>.

33 Ibid.

34 United States Department of State, Washington, DC, 'US Applauds Democratic Republic of Congo's New Constitution', press release, 19 May 2005, distributed by AllAfrica Global Media, allAfrica.com.

35 Mukadi Bonyi, 'Avant-Projet de Constitution et règles de technique législative: ignorance ou violation intentionnelle?', *Le Phare*, Kinshasa, 11 May 2005.

36 'D.R. Congo backs new constitution', BBC News, <www.bbc.co.uk/2/hi/Africa/4464438.stm>, accessed 18 March 2006.

37 Front pour la survie de la Démocratie – FSD/DC, <www.fsd.ht.st; frontsurviedemocratiecongo@yahoogroups.com>.

38 Wikipedia (accessed 20 March 2006), citing Congo Online.

39 M. Tshiyembe, 'L'Afrique face au défi de l'Etat multinational', *Le Monde diplomatique*, September 2000: 14–15.

40 Father Léon de Saint-Moulin, SJ, Jesuit demographer, is one of the few to have argued for this.

41 H. F. Weiss and T. Carayannis, 'Reconstructing the Congo', *Journal of International Affairs*, 58 (1) (2004): 115–18. I am not sure what they are trying to say about Burundi, which is not Rwandophone.

42 Ibid.

43 Ibid.

44 Ibid.: 18.

45 'Congo: Unpublished Report on War Contracts May Rock President', SouthScan (London), 1 November 2005, <AllAfrica.Com>, accessed 2 November 2005.

46 Human Rights Watch, 'DR Congo: End Illegal Exploitation of Natural Resources. Government must act on Parliamentary Commission's Recommendations', London, 21 February 2006, <http://hrw.org/english/docs/2006/02/20/congo12692_txt.htm>.

47 Amnesty International, 'Democratic Republic of Congo: from assassination to state murder', <Amnesty.org/library/index/engafr620232002>, accessed 20 March 2006.

48 UN Office for the Coordination of Humanitarian Affairs, IRIN, 'DRC: Court condemns 26 to death, acquits 45 in Kabila murder trial', 7 January 2003, accessed 20 March 2006.

49 'Congo-Kinshasa: Military Tribunal Imprisons Ex-Commander for Abusing Children', IRIN, 20 March 2006.

50 A. Mwilo, personal communication (e-mail), 27 March 2006.

51 Y. Musoni, personal communication (e-mail), 30 March 2006.

52 'DR Congo: Prominent Human Rights Defender Assassinated', <http://hrw.org/english/docs/2005/08/01/congo11549.htm>.

53 Filip Reyntjens, 'The Privatisation and Criminalisation of Public Space in the Geopolitics of the Great Lakes Region', *Journal of Modern African Studies*, 43 (2005): 587–607.

54 'D.R. Congo: As Vote Nears, Abuses Go Unpunished in Katanga', *Human Rights News*, 21 July 2006, <http://hrw.org/english/dodcs/2006/07/21/congo13783.htm>.

Index

Index

235